M000215575

Law Enforcement in the Age of Black Lives Matter

Critical Perspectives on Race, Crime, and Justice

Series Editor

Tony Gaskew, University of Pittsburgh, Bradford

This book series seeks interdisciplinary scholars whose work critically addresses the racialization of criminal justice systems. Grounded within the connective space of history, the nuances of race continue to define the standard of how justice is applied throughout policing, courts, and correctional systems. As such, this series is open to examine monographs and edited volumes that critically analyze race from multiple narratives—sociopolitical, cultural, feminist, psychosocial, ecological, critical theory, philosophical— along criminal justice lines. The *Critical Perspectives on Race, Crime, and Justice* book series speaks to the significant scholarship being produced in an era where race continues to intersect with crime and justice.

Titles in the series

Law Enforcement in the Age of Black Lives Matter

Policing Black and Brown Bodies

Edited by
Sandra E. Weissinger
and Dwayne A. Mack

LEXINGTON BOOKS
Lanham • Boulder • New York • London

Published by Lexington Books
An imprint of The Rowman & Littlefield Publishing Group, Inc.
4501 Forbes Boulevard, Suite 200, Lanham, Maryland 20706
www.rowman.com

Unit A, Whitacre Mews, 26-34 Stannary Street, London SE11 4AB

British Library Cataloguing in Publication Information Available

Library of Congress Cataloging-in-Publication Data Available

ISBN 978-1-4985-5359-9 (cloth : alk. paper)
ISBN 978-1-4985-5360-5 (electronic)

♾™ The paper used in this publication meets the minimum requirements of American National Standard for Information Sciences—Permanence of Paper for Printed Library Materials, ANSI/NISO Z39.48-1992.

Printed in the United States of America

Contents

Acknowledgments

SANDRA E. WEISSINGER

There is a special place in my heart for those within the institution of criminal justice. It is my sincere hope that humanism—above profits, trauma, and socially constructed rules—shapes the way forward. Nothing less will do. Not for officers. Not for those imprisoned. And not for those who are shot down in the streets. Let us not rest on procedure or tradition, but let us—as a nation—be brave and inquisitive.

I give thanks to God who is beyond my understanding, but who gave me strength to put this text into the world and put people in my path so that the work would be done. One piece at a time. I would like to thank Tony Gasgew (Series Editor) and press Acquisitions Editors Carissa Marcelle and Sarah Craig. Thanks for the faith, professionalism, and vision. Lastly, I extend a hearty thank you to my co-editor, Dwayne A. Mack. He is a professional and mentor, through and through, and I am so very fortunate to have crossed his path so many projects ago. May God continue to bless and keep you and yours, D.

DWAYNE A. MACK

First, I want to thank God for allowing me to survive a childhood in a Brooklyn housing project and the ability to process and articulate some of my cultural memory. A sincere thank you goes out to my lead editor, Sandra E. Weissinger. You are a dynamic scholar in the truest sense. Your professionalism and work ethic are unmatched. Thank you for your patience and support.

I would also like to thank the additional leadership of our series editor Tony Gasgew and press Acquisitions Editors Carissa Marcelle, and Sarah Craig. Your solid guidance and expertise have helped to sustain this meaningful project. I also want to thank the contributors for writing such informative and engaging scholarly essays. Without you, the volume would be incomplete. Thank you to friends Gladys Jennings, Herbert Ruffin II, Elwood Watson, Channell Barbour, William Payne, Lamar Patterson, Kevin Lockhart, Joshua Guthman, and Kenneth Morris for their continued support and understanding.

I also thank my dear wife and partner, Felicia W. Mack, for her collaboration and loving support. Finally, to our children, Charity, Liberte, Jelani, and Kosey, who gave up another summer so that their parents could write, I thank you so much. Your sacrifices will not go unrewarded.☺ To our readers: Black and Brown Lives Do Matter!

Introduction

Sandra E. Weissinger
and Dwayne A. Mack

"Thank You Officers."
"Support the Badge."
"Blue Lives Matter."[1]

There is a reason why people claim great respect for officers of the law: the job, by description, is hard—if not deadly. Pay is low.[2] Certainly, the work is not for just anyone. It takes a certain kind of person to accept the consequences of the job—seeing the very worst[3] situations, on a regular basis, and knowing that one's life is on the line every hour of every day. Working in law enforcement is emotionally and psychologically draining (Goldbaum, 2012; Hayasaki, 2014). It effects these public servants both on and off the job. If that were not enough, these officers put the well-being of those who love them on the line too. One wrong move changes not only the life of the officer, but the life of their family (biological and of choice) forever (consider Halpern, 2015; Lecci, 2015). Said plainly, shaking an officer's hand when you see him or her or posting a sign in the front yard that reads "Support the Badge" is lip service. Even going as far as to donate money to a crowdsourcing fundraising site does little to support the long-term professional development needs of officers (Alcindor, Copeland, and Bello, 2014). These are surface level signs of solidarity. They look good at the surface, but do little in terms of showing respect for the job and those who do it. For those who want to do more, and certainly there is much to be done, this text provides reasons and a rationale for doing better by these public servants.

Showing respect does not mean that one agrees with whatever another person or institution claims to be the "right" way. Showing respect and admiration means that we charge individuals to live up to their fullest potentials and integrate innovation wherever possible. In the case of policing in the era of Black Lives Matter, policing as usual simply is not an option any longer. It is disrespectful, to both the officers and those who are being policed, to rest on the laurels of past policing tactics. As we enter a time period in which police interactions are recorded (dash cams or body cams, for example) and new populations are being targeted (Latinx people), there is much to learn about what is working and what is not. One area in need of change is the way in which law enforcement interacts with potential perpetrators, especially people of color. When officers have "street wisdom," they understand (with accuracy) when a person is suspicious and when they are dangerous (Anderson, 1990; Halpern, 2015). The two do not get lumped together and explained away later. Prejudice and adrenaline are less likely to melt together and create a reaction the officer can never take back or unsee—the death of someone, unnecessarily, at his or her own hand.

While some may argue that police[4] need to be able to operate as they see fit, there are psychological ramifications to such carte blanche approvals. Namely, the guilt and complex post-traumatic stress disorder faced by the person wearing the badge and those viewing the pointless violence as well (Marmar et al., 2006; Shucard et al., 2012; van der Kolk, 2015). While those claiming that blue lives matter may say that putting officers in danger (psychologically and physically) is exactly what they do not want, the actions of these supporters encourage the exact opposite. Businesses and institutions change to address the needs of diverse populations in order to avoid failure and redundancy. It is time the institution of policing does the same. Doubling-down on policies and practices that are widely understood to harbor bias does not help officers. Communities do not trust them. And the lives of officers are put at risk because of the lack of trust. Leaning into diversity and inclusion by providing officers' with tools that may very well save their lives is the only sustainable direction left to go.

Staying where we are as a society, with black and brown lives over-policed, clearly does not serve the public effectively. Traditional, status quo, police supporters are calling for unchallenged support of officers' but such a call actually causes harm to police officers. Harms include pigeon-holing and stereotyping officers—making it hard for them to get psychological help when needed. Harms also include harboring and reproducing racism instead of providing greater training so that officers can have an improved street wisdom and greatly improve their safety while on the job. A last harm that this text addresses concerns the degradation of public trust for those on the job.

STEREOTYPING OFFICERS

A common misconception is that the profession of policing has stand-alone characteristics that, automatically, reshape the individual entering the career into something more than he or she is. Firefighters are, chiefly, brave. Teachers are wise. Police officers are noble and full of integrity, always. While these characteristics are subjective, common stereotypes about professions do color our ability to view reality. We hold certain professions in high esteem, as if people who choose these careers are super human—immune to base problems like addiction, greed, or bigotry. But people are people—full of complexities, flaws, and quirks. We, as a society, have a hard time believing that real social ails affect people in particular professions. With regards to the field of policing, our inability to see reality has left us with gaping holes of inequality that, when not addressed, lead to the unnecessary death and incarceration of black and brown bodies. It also leads to the unhealthy coping strategies of officers trying to deal with a complex world, but doing it without the tools that social work, sociology, and psychology can provide.

We are not suggesting that "one bad apple" or "lost soul" is the root of the issues clearly observable in the era of Black Lives Matter. Yes, individual officers of the law struggle with stereotypes, bias, and internalized racism. All people do. Good people participate in racism, as do smart people and others we have put upon a pedestal. Even people of color struggle with race and their placement on the racial hierarchy (Cohen, 1999; Fitzgerald, 2014; Weissinger, 2012). Kindness and dedication to the job does not abdicate anyone from the responsibility of practicing anti-racism and challenging institutions that perpetuate covert and overt racism.

To deny people their humanity due to their profession is both immature and highly problematic—as it makes the issues that emerge from their shortcomings hard to name and certainly harder to address and correct. But more than individual-level interactions, the "bad apple" or "lost soul" effect, these officers are solider-like. What they know and how they know it emerges from their training within the total institution that is law enforcement (Zimbardo, n.d.). Officers act on bias, especially if they are not trained to recognize and address their prejudices. More than this, professionals, like police officers, often participate in systems steeped in racism. As will be addressed by Mack and Mack in this anthology, policing is both an action and an ideology—changing all who interact with the institution. This is not new and has been a standard practice for the vast history of the United States. It is for this reason that those who say they support police need to really lean in and offer support in meaningful ways by supporting career development training (such as de-escalation and implicit bias), which will allow the institution of policing to be honest about race, trauma, and the high-price of unconscious bias (Alexander, 2012).

HARBORING AND REPRODUCING RACISM

It makes sense then that officers act with bias (implicit or otherwise). Not just sometimes, but always. They are people and, especially when in an intense and volatile situation, will fall back on the stereotypes they have been socialized to accept since the day they were born. What makes their participation in racist systems worthy of analysis is the great power these professionals wield. Life and death is held in the power of their hands. And while several professionals shape the life course of a human, few have the power to end a life based on a mistake, misunderstanding, stereotype, policy, or other event. This is why it is important to study and understand how policing is changing in light of global community calls to examine bias in the arrests and deaths of people of color at the hands of law enforcement.

The call that Black Lives Matter may feel new, but (as will be addressed in this anthology by Hurst et al.) it is a reaction to policing in the age of portable technology and recording. The call that Black Lives Matter may feel confusing, but such confusion (or claims of confusion) is a reflection of the person and not the reality. The reality is that violence against black and brown bodies is something people in the United States have participated in, consciously or unconsciously, since people of color were brought on these shores as slaves or driven from their lands in the name of Manifest Destiny (Weissinger, Mack, and Watson, 2017). Such violence is perpetrated by individuals, communities, and institutions and happens with such regularity that a person privileged enough to overlook such effects can easily rationalize the violence as "the way things are." Inability to recognize the symbolic, actual, and perceived violence is a form of denial (and maybe even psychosis) that stems from one's participation in systemic whiteness. Said another way, hegemony (in this case, adhering to the white racial frame) is like a disease, and one is either in recovery or in the disease—there is very little gray to this situation. And because people make up, navigate, and create systems, their disease is imbedded in the social structure. If good people can participate in racism (and we are happy to give folks the benefit of the doubt and believe that people try to be "good"), and smart people can participate in racism, then why do we continue to hold police officers and agents of the state to an unholy and unachievable status? Of course, these individuals harbor racism and act on it (chapters, in this anthology, from Brooms and Reed speak to this). Until they are taught new tools (that effectively employ street wisdom and anti-racist training), they will rely on the old ones. And this is the point of the book: we have the tools and means to do better policing; we, as a society, just have to make the decision to use all of the resources available to us.

SUB-PAR TRAINING

In this book, we outline why a movement toward accountability and de-escalation tactics is both necessary and overdue. While on the job, officers are trained to see and deal with the worst of humanity day in and day out. This is a fact. What is also a fact is that no human being can get away from these tragic events, such as death, murder, and violence, unscathed (consider Hayasaki, 2014). For those who put their lives on the line for us, we, as a society, should be willing to do everything in our power to be of service to these public service workers. The best way to be of service to police officers is to provide resources and supports that help these individuals keep their humanity intact.

Our job, if we say that Blue Lives Matter or that "we support the badge," is to put in place policies and supports so that officers have tools to avoid murder and abuse (and so that we can hold them to not engaging the public in this way). Traumatizing another human being has the tragic effect of harming the perpetrator. No amount of rationalizations, knowledge of policy, or training takes away the grief and loss one must experience should he or she feel compelled to take away the life of another person. Even for officers who participate in racism and elitism, at the end of the day, the energy spent making peace with one's actions (or at least trying to) is a waste. The harm done to the individual becomes a harm done to society, as that officer will live his or her life affected and calloused by the actions of one day on the job.

True support of law enforcement means we give them what they need to keep their humanity and protect ours. Nothing less can possibly do, unless the call for mattering blue lives is nothing more than propaganda—a cover-up for a more menacing issue of controlling black and brown bodies. This book does the job of differentiating the layers of police support. If one's concern is for the officer's long-term psychological well-being and the public good of our republic, then we invite you to keep reading. We offer solutions and provide a rationale for why those solutions need quick implementation.

But if police support is shown as a way to stop social progress, maintain the status quo, and limit true racial integration, then this anthology illuminates how the hard work and health of police are hijacked by thinly veiled racism. Racism, and racist policing policies, do not protect the long-term health of an officer—instead it uses the person and the institution, leaving both broken and bereaved once a new tool of control becomes available.

THE BOOK

In this book, we break down this issue of how policing can change with the information unearthed in the era of Black Lives Matter. We focus on helping and changing the criminal justice system we currently have. Should fundamental supports to officers' training on race, bias, trauma, and stereotypes not occur, a severe and unrepairable fissure will erode community trust in policing. Such break makes law enforcement hard. It also makes the wounds inflicted by the color line that much more traumatic.

Dwayne A. Mack and Felicia W. Mack open up the anthology by laying down the historical policing policies and patterns that have brought us to the era of Black Lives Matter. Long before hashtags and protests, there were slave patrols, Black Codes, and convict lease system. The authors examine how racism against black and brown people emerged and how it came to take center stage in the modern criminal justice system. Wornie Reed's chapter examines a brief history of policing, but sharply focuses on the laws and policies which govern how black and brown bodies are treated by police and within courts. Criminals are created by a biased justice system. This bias dismantles communities of color through racial profiling, criminal profiling, and legal support of police use of force. Like all the chapters in this anthology, Reed argues that individual or micro-level racism is just one aspect that shapes policing. More than individual attitudes and actions, institutional racism, and systems imbued with racism, are where our communal focus should be.

The way the criminal justice system has grown, in addition to the whom and what policing protects, are themes addressed in this text. For many people of color, observing officers at work, there is overwhelming trauma and psychological wounding. While this introduction argues that no one is unscathed, the chapters pay special attention to the people who are targeted for arrest. Derrick Brooms examines the lived experience of black and brown bodies as they attempt to navigate a life in which they are treated as "a problem." His chapter points to the psychological ramifications which shape the oppressed, but it also highlights where and how this psychological reality emerged.

This burden creates psychological disease and this process starts at a young age, as argued in "The Psychological Impact of Policing on African American Students." Ashley Hurst, Marlon Bailey, Nolan Kreuger, Ramya Garba and Kevin Cokley address how media coverage of black lives not mattering has affected students. They address the psychological impact of viewing the deaths and the fear felt when encountering officers. The authors also provide us with hope: the movement, Black Lives Matter, provides a positive coping strategy to youth who would otherwise feel their two-ness, as discussed by Brooms, yet have no way to adequately heal from the trauma of seeing themselves as the next to die at the hands of police.

Racism is embedded in the criminal justice system. Criminals are created. Who we see as criminal is a social construction based on race, gender, and nation of origin. Nayeli Y. Chavez-Dueñas and Hector Y. Adames demonstrate that brown bodies are stigmatized as criminal and this construction is economically profitable. "Criminalizing Hope: Policing Latino/a Immigrant Bodies for Profit" dissects how the detention of undocumented immigrants is normalized and made profitable—driving the implementation of aggressive policing strategies. Corporations and politicians benefit from the incarceration of this vulnerable population. As critical thinkers, the relationship between profits and criminality should be questioned. We should boldly ask "who benefits from making this group criminal?" We should also question who the losers are with this arrangement. Clearly, police and those tasked with carrying out these laws bear the psychological burden. But those who are policed, whole communities of Latinx people, also suffer regular anxiety and physical assault as a result of (federal, state, and local) laws and practices that privilege very few—despite the rhetoric surrounding the practices.

The United States has a history of racialized immigration policing policy, which is resurgent in unprecedented ways under the first year of the Trump administration. As a result, Latino and Latina populations, particularly Deferred Action for Childhood Arrivals (DACA) students on college and university campuses, are under the real threat of hyper-aggressive Immigration and Customs Enforcement (ICE) arrests and detainment (in preparation for deportation). Nevertheless, Dee Hill-Zuganelli and F. Tyler Sergent in "Strengthening the Sanctuary: Institutional Policies to Support DACA Students" stress these institutions have agency—and responsibility—to create policies and implement strategies that can help protect DACA students. Their essay shares dynamic strategies for faculty, staff, and administrators to create a sanctuary for DACA students.

This rhetoric has led many conscientious people to co-sign with very racist policies, ignoring their own family history as immigrants and newcomers to a strange land. As illuminated in the work of Rebecca Martinez's "Sexual Assault (Threat): Policing Brown Women's Bodies on the Mexico–U.S. Border," misleading, harmful, and race-based rhetoric needs to be challenged head on. Donald Trump's call to "build the wall" not only puts policing agencies in harm's way, it transforms these officers by exposing them to socialization in hate—including sexual assault. While many of Trump's supporters claimed to like his support of police and public servants, his rhetoric only goes so far and does more harm than good to those who he proclaims to revere. More than exposing police to dangerous and dehumanizing practices, in the name of border control, Trump's propaganda ignores history while solidifying white privilege. Latinx families flee to the United States for a better life, *esperanza*, like that of the millions of white-skinned immigrants who fled to the United States before them. Surely, immigrants have, historically, made America the country it is today. Forgetting this historical fact for immigrants of color points to conscious or unconscious bias on the part of lay people and those with political power. Those with political power and the charge of doing right by all people should, however, know when their words and actions are civil rights violations. But if they don't, such pandering should come with consequences—as their words put the lives of many in harm's way.

For those who get the message, that words, laws, and systemic racism matter for all people, but especially for cops on the ground (and those targeted by cops on the ground), there is hope for life-preserving reform. Legitimate and practical tools are available. These tools are an extension of the training police already receive. While they will require resources to implement, they are less than the cost we currently pay, as a society. Disparate treatment of human beings is costly in terms of money and long-term well-being. These costs should be impetus enough to move away from the psychologically and socially deformed practices currently engaged in. Shakira A. Kennedy, Folusho Otuyelu, and Warren Graham's "To Protect and Serve: Examining Race, Law Enforcement Culture and Social Work Practice" offers an alternative to force and compliance-based models with tactics for community informed police engagement.

Sandra E. Weissinger's "Leaders are Dealers in Hope: A Look at the Intentional Actions Called for in the Forward through Ferguson Report" also provides alternatives to policing as usual. By highlighting the community informed report, crafted in the aftermath of Michael Brown's untimely death at the hands of former Ferguson police officer Darren Wilson, Weissinger takes seriously the call from the governor-appointed commission of sixteen volunteer civic leaders. This chapter examines the content of the report and the 189 policy recommendations found within the document. Ferguson represents a moment that society can learn and grow from. It is an example for other cities and policing agencies of what to avoid. But if actions are not taken to implement the well-researched policy suggestions, the question must be asked: Are we, as a society, ready to do the work to end racial injustice (especially where it is found within law and order)—to organize differently in the age of Black Lives Matter? Or is it just business as usual?

If it is "business as usual" and policing agencies are unwilling to invest in additional training (for example, cultural competency and de-escalation tactics), the final chapter of this text offers a blueprint for how to move forward: unfriend the police. Tony Gaskew has a long family and career history within law enforcement and uses this lived experience as the backbone for his chapter, "Unfriending the Policing Culture: The Reawakened Black Consciousness." As an invited discussant to the White House, Gaskew is astutely aware of the challenges facing policing today. It is because of this knowledge that he argues policing practices do not serve the interests of black and brown people. They have not served to protect black and brown people for the past 400 years. Moreover, the criminal justice system, specifically the policing culture, has been used to humiliate people of color. The answer, when faced with such imbedded hegemonic inequalities, is to unfriend the police—to search for a system of reform that is not deeply flawed like that which is present. This new way of organizing people celebrates blackness and destroys the shackles of stigma, which have burdened black folks since their arrival in the United States.

In freeing black folks of the debilitating stigma of criminality, we also free officers from the dehumanizing practice of enacting state-supported and -sanctioned violence against black and brown bodies. Police are soldiers in many ways. Supporters of police argue that officers will do what has been asked of them. The time has come to test this assertion and support officers' well-being by changing the organizing principles in which they operate. The system of policing is broken and ensnared in racism. The sooner we enact change, the sooner we will be able to heal from the disastrous disaster that has been US-based racism.

NOTES

1. There are a number of signs in support of police. These statements are simply examples observed in society. For more, see http://bit.ly/2t9nD0z.

2. The Bureau of Labor Statistics (BLS) (2006) has data on the mean salaries of police across the United States and by specific geographic parameters. Examining Missouri, the state which houses Ferguson, the average mean salary for an officer is $47,510. While some may see this as a decent salary, it is important to think about the real risks faced by law enforcement. Even if the officer is physically safe, seeing people addicted to drugs, engaged in domestic violence, or having to lock up individuals is psychically hard. A salary of $48k makes things like psychological visits hard to afford—especially if one has a family to raise. This information can be found by visiting the BLS at https://www.bls.gov/oes/current/oes333051.htm.

3. By "worst," we are simply trying to point out that the things officers see, daily, are situations which are horrifying and trauma inducing; for example, seeing black eyes and blood from a domestic violence situation or seeing abused and neglected children. Car accidents that leave people harmed and mangled are included here, as are situations involving addictions (and the things people engage in to get their next fix). These are examples, however. "Worst" is relative. All that matters here is that police officers are inundated with this regularly.

4. We use the wording "police" or "law enforcement" interchangibly to refer to those working in criminal justice. This includes State Troopers, Sheriffs, ICE, Border Patrol, and SWAT.

REFERENCES

Alexander, M. (2012). *The new Jim Crow: Mass incarceration in the age of color-blindness*. New York: The New Press.

Alcindor, Y., Copeland, L., & Bello, M. (2014, August 22) Crowdfunding for Ferguson officer tops out at $235K *USA Today*. Retrieved from https://www.usatoday.com/story/news/nation/2014/08/22/ferguson-calm-officer-support/14439979/

Anderson, E. (1990). *Streetwise: Race, class, and change in an urban community*. Chicago: University of Chicago Press.

Bureau of Labor Statistics. (2016, May). Occupational employment and wages, May 2016, 33–3051 police and sheriff's patrol officers. Retrieved from https://www.bls.gov/oes/current/oes333051.htm

Cohen, C. J. (1999). *The boundaries of blackness: AIDS and the breakdown of black politics*. Chicago: University of Chicago Press.

Fitzgerald, K. J. (2014). *Recognizing race and ethnicity: Power, privilege, and inequality*. Boulder, CO: Westview Press.

Goldbaum, E. (2012, July 9). Police officer stress creates significant health risks compared to general population, study finds. *University at Buffalo news center*. Retrieved from http://www.buffalo.edu/news/releases/2012/07/13532.html

Halpern, J. (2015, August 10 &17). The man who shot Michael Brown. *The New Yorker*. Retrieved from http://www.newyorker.com/magazine/2015/08/10/the-cop

Hayasaki, E. (2014, March 14). Life of a police officer: Medically and psychologically ruinous. *The Atlantic*. Retrieved from https://www.theatlantic.com/health/archive/2014/03/life-of-a-police-officer-medically-and-psychologically-ruinous/284324/

Lecci, S. (2015, August 8). Ferguson police officer joins force days after Brown's death, aims to build community ties. *St. Louis Public Radio*. Retrieved from http://news.stlpublicradio.org/post/ferguson-police-officer-joins-force-days-after-browns-death-aims-build-community-ties#stream/0

Marmar, C. R., McCaslin, S. E., Metzler, T., Best, S., Weiss, D. S., Fagan, J., Liberman, A., Pole, N., Otte, C., Yehuda, R., Mohr, D., & Neylan, T. (2006). Predictors of posttraumatic stress in police and other first responders. *Annals of the New York Academy of Sciences*, 1071(1), 1–18. doi:10.1196/annals.1364.001

Shucard, J. L., Cox, J., Shucard, D. W, Fetter, H., Chung, C., Ramasamy, D., & Violanti, J. (2012). Symptoms of posttraumatic stress disorder and exposure to traumatic stressors are related to brain structural volumes and behavioral measures of affective stimulus processing in police officers. *Psychiatry Research*, 204(1):25–31. doi: 10.1016/j.pscychresns.2012.04.006

van der Kolk, B. (2015). *The body keeps the score: Brain, mind, and body in the healing of trauma*. New York: Penguin Books.

Weissinger, S. E. (2012). *A sociology of black clergy in the state of Illinois: Activism and acquiescence in the post-civil rights generation*. Lewiston, NY: Edwin Mellen Press.

Weissinger, S. E., Mack, D. A., & Watson, E. (2017). *Violence against black bodies: An intersectional analysis of how black lives continue to matter*. New York: Routledge.

Zimbardo, P. (n.d). Zimbardo Stanford prison experiment. Retrieved from http://www.prisonexp.org/

Chapter One

Policing with Impunity

Racialized Policing in the 21st Century

Dwayne A. Mack and Felicia W. Mack

In his 2008 presidential campaign, Barack Obama rode the wave of optimistic political slogans like "Yes We Can" and "Fired Up? Ready to Go!" Nowhere in his messaging on the political stump did he address the issue of racialized policing. He focused instead on the economy, and his message remained race-neutral, until he was pressed to address his relationship with the activist preacher Jeremiah Wright. On March 18, 2008, in his speech "A More Perfect Union," apparently to appease his white liberal base and conservative detractors, candidate Obama not only denounced and distanced himself from his former pastor, he tactfully articulated the history of the racial baggage of slavery and Jim Crow, and acknowledged the racial divide in the nation (Obama, 2008). However, he avoided discussing police brutality and the policies supporting such abuse. It is problematic to listen to such a narrow historical interpretation of racism and not include a discussion about racialized policing. In this regard, frequent heinous acts of police violence against black and brown bodies are policy driven.[1] This analysis helps us better understand the systemic race-based problem of policing with impunity.

Following Obama's first major political hurdle and his groundbreaking victory over his Republican opponent later that year, some political pundits, the media, and the public advanced the notion that the United States had gloriously evolved into a postracial society because white America had contributed to electing a biracial black man to the highest office in the nation. However, President Obama became the leader of a country with a long history of white supremacy and policing policies aimed at the destruction of black and brown bodies.

In light of federal, state, and local government policies that continued to criminalize black and brown people, numerous high-profile incidents of trigger-happy policing, and white civilians' murder of blacks, Obama's campaign speech on race and his presidency exposed the myth of the postracial or color-blind society. The brutal deaths of blacks at the hands of police and the numerous raids and roundups by Immigration and Customs Enforcement (ICE) agents and Border Patrol agents focused primarily on arresting, detaining, and deporting brown people demonstrate that the United States has a long way to go to improve race relations. For these reasons, Obama's presidency is the best lens through which to view the aggressive policing of black and brown in the 21st century.

ROOTS OF IMPUNITY

To place some patterns of modern policing policy and culture within their proper historical context and the criminality of blackness, it is necessary to explore the racial origins of policing in the United States that Obama inherited. The Slave Codes and Fugitive Slave Acts of 1793 and 1850 permitted the tortures that militia groups, slave catchers and patrols, and bounty hunters inflicted on blacks as they policed plantation and non-plantation communities. To maintain social order, these policing agencies frequently stopped, questioned, and searched slaves and free blacks on the spot (Hadden, 2003).

At the end of the Civil War in 1865, law enforcement played an important role in enforcing racially oppressive and restrictive Black Codes enacted by southern legislatures during Reconstruction (1865–1877). White policymakers designed race-based laws to subordinate blacks and deny them their newly acquired constitutional rights. White landowners forced blacks to sign labor contracts, re-creating the master and servant relationship. Law enforcement also fined, arrested, and/or punished blacks for alleged vagrancy or loitering, using firearms, alcohol consumption, or violating curfew (Higginbotham, 2013). Connected to the Black Codes, under the debt peonage system in the South, with the support of law enforcement, white landowners forced thousands of black sharecroppers and employees to work off debt under conditions similar to slavery (Novak, 2014).

Approximately a century before the modern prison industrial complex, the equally brutal and inhumane convict lease system emerged at the close of the Civil War. Southern sheriffs and their deputies apprehended and arrested blacks whom whites had accused of running afoul of the law. Because of the profitability of black labor, law enforcement even snatched unsuspecting blacks off the streets and tossed them into a county-controlled penal system that leased them out to companies to labor without compensation. Black inmates worked under appalling conditions in construction projects and extractive industries like turpentine, coal, and timber. The convict lease system generated huge revenue for counties, sheriffs, and officers of the peace (Blackmon, 2008). Along with the convict leasing system, white supremacist groups like the Ku Klux Klan, Knights of the White Camellia, and the White Brotherhood emerged to terrorize blacks into subordination; the law enforcement community did not protect black lives and property (Parsons, 2016).

After Reconstruction, law enforcement and the criminal justice system strictly enforced the even more racially repressive codified Jim Crow laws. These laws spread throughout the nation in the later part of the nineteenth century to deny black citizenship and maintain white social order. Local law enforcement was complicit in race riots and the lynching of blacks during the nineteenth and twentieth centuries. For example, during the race riots of the Red Summer of 1919, Tulsa, Oklahoma (1921), and Rosewood, Florida (1923), law enforcement participated and/or stood aside as white mobs destroyed black lives and property. During the modern civil rights movement, episodes such as police officers beating black civil rights activists in Birmingham and Selma, Alabama, also reflected the racist attitude of white local and state law enforcement in the United States.

A LIBERAL APPROACH TO POLICING

The seeds of modern racialized policing were sown through federal policies of the latter part of the twentieth century; the liberal and social reforms of the 1960s were the catalyst for black and brown living under a police state today. After launching his "War on Poverty" in 1964, President Lyndon B. Johnson the following year declared his "War on Crime" to reclaim urban cities ravaged by racial uprisings. Most of the unrest between 1964 and 1967 was black responses to police brutality in New York City, Los Angeles, Philadelphia, Chicago, and Detroit. To examine the causes of urban rebellions, in 1967, Johnson's Executive Order 11365, better known as the Kerner Commission, established the National Advisory Commission on Civil Disorders (Guo, 2016). In January 1968, the Commission's final report urged President Johnson to support progressive reforms like job creation, police accountability, and improved federal funding for schools and housing in black communities. Citing socioeconomic disparities, the Commission warned that the nation was "moving toward two societies, one black, one white—separate and unequal" (National Advisory Commission on Civil Disorders,1968).

Just months following the report, in reaction to the tragic assassination of Dr. Martin Luther King, Jr., poor and segregated black communities erupted in protests. Rather than follow the directives of the Kerner Commission's report, Johnson blamed the uprisings on black lawlessness. The president refused to use that moment to heal racial wounds and move the country forward with a progressive economic and social agenda. He responded to black despair and frustration with raced-based punitive policing policies.[2] Johnson focused on restoring social order to cities ravaged by uprisings and preventing urban rebellions. On June 19, 1968, the president signed the Omnibus Crime Control and Safe Streets Act. The Law Enforcement Assistance Administration (LEAA)[3] created in the new legislation initially allocated $400 million to cities to fund and expand the carceral state. This earmarked money for law enforcement agencies to modernize policing strategies and support the criminal justice system of every state. The federal criminal justice initiative also led to the enormous growth of the criminal justice system, which included adding more sheriffs, police, marshals, judges, prosecutors, defense attorneys, prison staff, and parole and probation officers (Hinton, 2016).

LEAA funded the militarization of police departments. For example, the government dispensed to police departments grants and other streams of funding for the development of the first Special Weapons and Tactics (SWAT) unit in Los Angeles and other paramilitary tactical units to rescue hostages, end hijackings and bank robberies, suppress strikes, and, more importantly, crush groups like the burgeoning Black Panther Party. Through this allocation, SWAT units received automatic and semi-automatic weapons; shoulder radios; protective armor; helicopters; paramilitary training and other tactical, military-grade equipment and "interagency cooperation" (Parenti, 2015).

A CONSERVATIVE APPROACH TO POLICING

In his presidential campaign, Richard Nixon, a Republican who became president in 1969, promised to advance a "law and order" agenda to counter the antiwar and civil rights rebellions. Once in the White House, he focused on race-based policies under the guise of a "war on drugs." According to John Ehrlichman, a former aide, Nixon focused on the criminalization of pot-smoking counterculture hippies and, more importantly, heroin addiction among blacks by creating agencies like the Drug Enforcement Administration in 1973 (Baum, 2016). To complement these efforts, Nixon supported mandatory minimum drug sentencing and law enforcement using no-knock warrants during drug raids (Balko, 2013b). As a result of high arrest rates, black and brown prison populations began to significantly increase during his first term (Taylor, 2016).

During the 1970s and 1980s, Presidents Gerald Ford, Jimmy Carter, Ronald Reagan, and George H.W. Bush also refused to adopt progressive social and economic agendas to improve the declining economic and social status of African Americans. For example, Carter, a Democrat, purposely ignored the high unemployment and inadequate housing, healthcare, and educational opportunities among blacks and other marginalized groups. Carter instead "began to scale back from social welfare programs almost immediately on taking office" in order to revive the slumping economy (Hinton, 2016, 303).

In the 1980s, Carter's Republican successor, Ronald Reagan, continued the carnage, cutting social welfare programs that helped black and brown and refused to develop strategies to rehabilitate black communities devastated by the crack epidemic of the 1980s.[4] His administration punished black and brown drug users as part of his "War on Drugs," signing the bipartisan[5] Anti-Drug Abuse Act in 1986. Under this piece of legislation, anyone convicted of possessing or using 5 grams of crack cocaine (most of whom were black or brown) received a minimum mandatory five-year prison sentence. However, those convicted of possessing 500 grams of powder cocaine (most of whom were white) received the same amount of time in prison even though they possessed 100 times more cocaine (Lassiter, 2015).

The Reagan administration's policy extended into the George Bush presidency. With support of the punitive initiatives and policies of the federal government, Los Angeles Police Department chief Daryl Gates initiated Operation Hammer through its controversial special operations unit, Community Resources Against Street Hoodlums (CRASH). CRASH conducted a number of no-knock drug raids in black and brown communities. On August 1, 1988, the CRASH raid of apartment buildings on 39th Street and Dalton Avenue reflected the inhuman nature of policing. The unit destroyed all the apartments and assaulted their black residents. After the rampage, officers only found six ounces of marijuana and not more than an ounce of cocaine (Balko, 2013a).

BILL WILL RESCUE US

During the presidential candidacy of Democrat William Jefferson Clinton in the early 1990s, social and economic improvement for black America seemed to be on the horizon.[6] However, the federal government's willful neglect of people of color continued. In the summer of 1992, South Central Los Angeles erupted in protest over the acquittal of the four LAPD officers who savagely beat Rodney King. Instead of bringing progressive social and economic reform to black communities, Clinton's neoliberalism embraced an even more aggressive pro-law enforcement agenda. Under Clinton's bipartisan supported Violent Crime Control and Law Enforcement Act (September 1994), the federal government funneled $30 billion into the criminal justice system. The Act gave state and local law enforcement agencies the capacity to hire 100,000 police, build more prisons, and terminate opportunities for the education of incarcerated offenders and mandatory life sentences for certain three time offenders (Alexander, 2012; Alexander, 2016). Besides overfunding and expanding the carceral state, Clinton terminated Aid to Families with Dependent Children. As the leader of the New Democrats[7], his conservative approach to welfare reform failed to curtail the debilitating "cycle of welfare dependency" and intergenerational poverty (Ehrenfreund, 2016), and the number of blacks unemployed and imprisoned continued to increase. In 1996, while these policies took their toll on black America, Nasir Jones (Nas) rapped in "If I Ruled the World," "Cause you could have all the chips, be poor or rich. Still nobody want a nigga having shit. If I ruled the world and everything in it, sky's the limit" (Jones, Oliver, Walker, & Barnes, 1996).

The militarization of police departments continued under Clinton. In the mid-1990s, the president approved the Pentagon's donation of surplus military equipment like rifles, grenade launchers, and armored personnel carriers to local police departments. President George W. Bush, under the guise of providing national security, escalated the militarization of police departments after September 11, 2001. The federal government gave departments military-grade boats, tanks, helicopters, airplanes, and weapons (Taylor, 2016).

THE TRAGEDY OF THE WAR ON CRIME

Through the 1990s, the local and state tactical policing units like CRASH that emerged from federal funding and training contributed to several high-profile acts of police brutality. Nine years before Obama's ascendancy to the presidency, an egregious race-based stop dominated international headlines and enraged the activist community. On February 4, 1999, four white New York Police Department (NYPD) officers from the self-proclaimed elite but controversial Street Crimes Unit, Sean Carroll, Edward McMellon, Kenneth Boss, and Richard Murphy, fired 41 shots at 23-year old Amadou Diallo, hitting him 19 times and instantly killing him in the vestibule of his Bronx apartment building. They alleged the West African immigrant had brandished a gun.[8] Evidence later revealed Diallo had his wallet out to present his identification (Fritsch, 2000; McFadden, 1999).

The Diallo killing was part of a larger problem of race-based policing policies in New York City. In 1999 alone, black and brown who had totaled half the city's population were 84% of the people that the NYPD stopped and frisked (Anderson, 2016). Later that year, along with anti-police brutality protests following the killing, a grand jury indicted the officers on second-degree murder charges. However, in 2000, the trial moved from the majority black and brown borough of the Bronx to the predominantly white city of Albany, where a jury of only four blacks and eight whites acquitted all four officers (Fritsch, 2000).

Although city officials disbanded the Street Crimes Unit in 2002, perhaps as a result of the Diallo killing, race-based stops increased throughout the Obama administration. The NYPD again grabbed international attention with the publicized police killings of Alberta Spruill in 2003, Timothy Stansbury, Jr. in 2004, Sean Bell in 2006, Eric Garner and Akai Gurley in 2014, and many other unnecessary deaths caused by unwarranted and aggressive tactical policing.

INHERITING A SYSTEM OF POLICING WITH IMPUNITY

Less than three weeks before Obama took office, Bay Area Rapid Transit officer Johannes Mehserle shot and killed Oscar Grant on the Fruitvale Station train platform in Oakland. Grant's death sparked protests in the city, a metropolitan space in which the Black Panther Party launched its crusade in the mid-1960s to challenge police brutality. Although the activist community remained hopeful for justice because of Mehserle's conviction, numerous acts of state-sanctioned violence would forever be attached to Obama's legacy, revealing the limits of his authority and the myth of a postracial and color-blind society.

In the first six months of Obama's presidency, the policing of black and brown became even more front and center. Pressured from African Americans to comment on the white police officer Sergeant James Crowley of the Cambridge Police Department's wrongful arrest of black Harvard Professor Henry Louis "Skip" Gates on July 16, 2009, President Obama, six days later, counterframed black and brown concerns over racial profiling and aggressive policing in a press conference (Wingfield & Feagin 2012). He acknowledged the nation's long history of aggressive policing against both groups, and determined that the "Cambridge police acted stupidly" (2012). His comments echoed throughout media outlets, enraging a law enforcement community already sensitive to criticism. Though Obama failed to denounce racialized policing, a significant number of law enforcement labeled the president a racial agitator and demanded an apology. The president tried to defuse the controversy over beer at the White House with Gates and Crowley (Boyd,

2009; Arinde 2009). Predictably, Obama's well intentioned "beer summit" miserably failed to address inherent issues concerning the excessive policing of black and brown.

The criticism that Obama received contributed to his reticence to comment on future confrontations between people of color and law enforcement. The opposition to discussions about race validated Attorney General Eric Holder's comments in 2009 that the United States is a "nation of cowards" when it comes to discourse about racism (Henderson, 2014). Having learned his lesson from the public thrashing over the Wright and Gates controversies, the president better understood the racial optics and social etiquette of white supremacy. Even after video footage exposed black trauma and death at the hands of law enforcement, Obama failed to visit protest hotbeds of Charlotte, Ferguson, St. Louis, Baltimore, Staten Island, Baton Rouge, Chicago, Milwaukee, and Minneapolis. Instead, as a show of solidarity (not reciprocated) with law enforcement, the president spoke in Dallas on July 12, 2016, at a memorial for five Dallas police officers tragically gunned down at an anti-police brutality rally (Silver, 2016).

Because it is easy to ignore policies that contributed to racialized policing, it is easy to criticize Obama's public responses to acts of police brutality. Obama inherited race-based policing policies that contributed to police malfeasance. These long-rooted practices drive law enforcement's use of excessive force. For example, in the early 1980s, criminologists Kelling and Wilson (1982) argued that broken windows reflect neglect of urban and impoverished spaces. A broken window contributed to social disorder, chaos, and the further erosion of a community. They connected minor offenses to the physical deterioration of a neighborhood and warned that, if structures were left unrepaired, more serious crimes were on the horizon (White & Fradella, 2016).

In an effort to reclaim distressed urban spaces decimated by black uprisings and failed government policies, politicians in all levels of government began to seize control of urban America to restore economic and social stability. Politicians and law enforcement collaborated in the 1990s to create a new policing model. An advocate of Kelling and Wilson's criminology policing theories, New York Mayor Rudolph Giuliani and his police chief William Bratton rolled out broken windows policing in black and brown communities. The NYPD's "zero tolerance" method of policing increased the number of arrests and/or summons of misdemeanors such as public urination and intoxication, subway toll-jumping, panhandling, graffiti, disorderly conduct, and loud automobile radios. To support this racialized form of policing, CompStat, a crime management tool, enabled the NYPD to track and map crime, stops, and arrests in black and brown communities.[9] It revealed areas of crime spikes and where the NYPD should focus its crime-fighting efforts (Taylor, 2016; Camp & Heatherton, 2016; Domanick, 2016).

To complement broken windows, the NYPD incorporated stop and frisk. Stop and frisk laws emboldened police officers to stop individuals on suspicion of criminal activity, leading to an increase of excessive force against black and brown bodies. Now unconstitutional in New York City, the stop and frisk program of 2002–2011, failed to curtail gun violence.[10] It did racially target 90% of blacks and Latinos. In 88% (3.8 million) of baseless body searches, officers rarely found weapons (Neidig, 2015; New York Civil Liberties Union, n.d.; Weissinger, Mack & Watson, 2017). According to Domanick (2015), stop and frisk alienated[11] young black and brown men "who had done nothing wrong" (293). Similar unwarranted race-based stops contributed to the fatal chokehold that police officer Daniel Pantaleo applied to Eric Garner on a Staten Island street in the summer of 2014. The overly aggressive policing of blacks became the impetus for "Black Lives Matter," "I Can't Breathe," "Hands Up, Don't Shoot," "Say Her Name" and the emergence of other civil rights organizations during the Obama era.

Racial profiling through broken windows and pedestrian stops was not indigenous to New York City, but the police there perfected its use, and it became a model for other metropolitan spaces. Some other cities adopting these racialized practices included Milwaukee, Los Angeles, Miami, Chicago, Newark, Philadelphia, and Baltimore. For example, following the death of Freddie Gray in the spring of 2015, the U.S. Department of Justice reported that between January 2010 and May 2015 officers in the Baltimore Police Department (BDP) made approximately 300,000 stop and frisks and 200,000 arrests, but because of "underreporting," the actual numbers were perhaps higher. The BPD conducted 44% of its pedestrian stops in two of the city's smallest black neighborhoods that were home to only approximately 11% of the population. Police stopped hundreds of African Americans on at least ten occasions. The Department of Justice concluded that most of the BPD's unconstitutional pedestrian stop and frisk lacked "reasonable suspicion." Frisks, including humiliating public strip searches and pat downs, were common and rarely did officers explain the basis for them (US Department of Justice, 2016).

Though Obama was forced to govern within the margins of a criminal justice system steeped in institutional racism, his Department of Justice initiated more investigations than Clinton's or George W. Bush's, revealing the extent of racialized policing. Led by Attorney Generals Eric Holder and then by Loretta Lynch, the Department of Justice issued detailed reports on the racial disturbances caused by state-sanctioned violence. In many ways, the Department of Justice's findings about poverty and high unemployment in black communities echoes those of the Kerner Commission. In Ferguson, African Americans made up 52% of the population in 2000 and 67% in 2010. Between 2009 and 2013, 25% of the residents lived below the poverty level. Most city officials at the time of Michael Brown's killing in 2014 were white, and only four of the city's 54-member police force were African American (US Department of Justice, 2015).

Compounding the difficulties of living in abject poverty and under a white-controlled criminal justice system, blacks endured "racial disparities in traffic stops, arrests and other actions" (Lowery, Leonnig & Berman, 2014). Police data from a year before Brown's death substantiated the National Association for the Advancement of Colored People's claim of racialized policing in Ferguson. Like the profits whites earned for the peonage and convict leasing systems that followed slavery, in an effort to generate revenue for the municipality through fines and court fees, Ferguson police arrested blacks twice as often as whites during traffic stops (2014).

The year after the uprising in that city and national protests of the killing, the Department of Justice's report on Ferguson revealed, from 2012 to 2014, blacks in Ferguson made up 85% of the traffic stops, 90% of the citations, and 93% of the arrests (US Department of Justice, 2016). "Driving While Black" was a real threat to black lives. Because they are already living in a culture of suspicion, black motorists nationwide also experienced a disproportionate number of fatal traffic stops. For example, in 2015, 1 out of 3 people law enforcement killed during traffic stops were black. In that same year, traffic stops led to the tragic deaths of unarmed black civilian motorists Sam DuBose in Ohio and Walter Scott in South Carolina (Lowery, 2015). Black women are also victims of such traffic stops. Arrested motorist Sandra Bland died in 2015 under a cloud of suspicion while in the custody of the Waller County Jail in Texas. That same year, Kendrick Lamar captured the building despair and frustration of the anti-police brutality movements as he rhymed in "Alright," the police "Wanna kill us dead in the street for sho'" (Duckworth, Spears, and Williams, 2015).

MILITARIZATION OF THE POLICE IN THE 21ST CENTURY

What the Department of Justice reports and most discussions on policing do not mention is the federal government's continued militarization of SWAT teams and other paramilitary units housed within police departments. Since the 1960s, SWAT units have emerged as paramilitary units of law enforcement. According to an American Civil Liberties Union (ACLU) report, the amount of federal support to militarize local and state police agencies has increased significantly since the 1990s. Under the Department of Defense's 1033 Program, the federal government gave local and state police agencies $1 million worth of military equipment to these agencies in 1990, $324 million worth in 1995, and approximately $450 million worth in 2013. A significant amount of this federal funding went to police to keep brown people out of southern Border States like Arizona. Law enforcement there received helicopters, armored vehicles, and military-grade weapons, which have contributed to the militarization and abuse of human rights along the United States–Mexico border (ACLU, 2014). According to a 2011 Department of Justice report, the sheriff of Maricopa County, Arizona, Joe Arpaio directed his heavily militarized department to racially target Latinos. His department conducted unlawful stops, detained, and arrested numbers of brown people (US Department of Justice, 2011).

Though President Obama criticized the transfer of military-grade equipment to local and state law enforcement agencies, the reaction to the 2014 black uprising in Ferguson and other urban spaces reflected the unfettered militarization of police departments. SWAT officers rode in armored vehicles, wearing Kevlar vests, helmets, camouflage, and armed with pistols, shotguns, automatic and semi-automatic rifles, rubber-coated metal pellets, and tear gas. Because these weapons and equipment were designed for battle in Afghanistan and Iraq, not for Missouri, the Obama administration in 2016 notified hundreds of police and sheriff departments to return "unnecessary and misused" military equipment like grenade launchers, bayonets, and armored vehicles (Williams, 2016).

Besides the images of Ferguson, Charlotte, Baltimore, and other areas of police occupation resembling the Palestinian West Bank, the Obama administration had a good reason for the recall. The ACLU reported in 2014 that police and sheriff departments frequently deployed SWAT "unnecessarily and aggressively to execute search warrants in low level drug investigations" (ACLU, 2014, 5). For example, law enforcement agencies deployed SWAT 79% of the time to execute drug warrants and only 7% of the time for hostage or active shooter situations. During SWAT deployments in 2011–2012, 39% of civilians raided were black and 11% were Latino. This hostile form of policing reflected the warrior mindset of SWAT teams and the perception that black and brown were enemies (ACLU, 2014).

Many of these SWAT sweeps ended with black and brown deaths. On May 16, 2010, while executing a high risk warrant, a member of the Detroit police department's Special Response Team shot and killed 7-year old Aiyana Stanley-Jones as she slept (Warikoo, Sally, & Smith, 2010). The following year, on May 5, a SWAT unit from the Pima County Sheriff's department in Tucson, Arizona, raided the home of a suspected drug dealer. After bursting into the house, the paramilitary clad officers fired off 71 rounds, hitting Marine and Iraq war veteran Jose Guerena Ortiz 22 times. After Ortiz was dead, law officials determined they had killed a hardworking husband and parent, not a criminal (Myers, 2011).

PLAYING THE FEAR CARD

Police operate with impunity because of the discretionary authority the legal system bestows upon law enforcement. Rarely does the criminal justice system indict and convict police officers for acts of malfeasance. The implicit biases of law enforcement also contribute to policing with impunity. As a common form of prejudicial and rush-to-judgment policing, implicit bias is related to the "attitudes or stereotypes that affect our understanding, actions, and decisions in an unconscious manner" (Staats, Capatosto, Wright & Contractor, 2015, 62). The historical patterns of racially preconceived judgments by officers and the militarization of policing make African Americans into enemy combatants that must be treated with deadly force.

Racial population data from the United States 2010 census estimated, in 2016, 76.9% of people self-identified as white; black, 13.3%; Hispanic/Latino, 17.8%; American Indian/Alaska Native, 1.3%; Asian, 5.7% (United States Census Bureau, 2016). However, although blacks comprise 13% of the population they are 24% of those killed by police. Two-thirds of those fatally wounded in 2015 by police were unarmed black or Latino (Kindy, 2015). Reporter Charles Blow's "Officers' Race Matters Less Than You Think" (2015) cites a 2015 report by the Department of Justice regarding the Philadelphia Police Department's use of force from 2007 through 2013. The study determined an officer's discharge of a weapon was attributed to threat perception failures (TPF) where police mistook harmless objects for deadly weapons and shot the suspect. Blacks had a TPF rating of 8.8% compared to white suspects (3.1%). The Department of Justice's report concluded that blacks " . . . during this time were disproportionately impacted by extreme violence involving the police" (Blow, 2015). Today in America when adjusted for the population demographics, blacks are more likely to be shot and killed by law enforcement officials than those who identify as white Americans (Lowery, 2016; Nix, Campbell, Byers, & Alpert, 2017).

One of the common historical threads in these fatal encounters is the police claiming fear as an excuse to gun down blacks. On September 16, 2016, while on their way to a domestic violence call, white Tulsa, Oklahoma, police officers Betty Jo Shelby and Tyler Turnbough encountered 40-year-old Terence Crutcher, an African American, standing away from his SUV as the vehicle blocked the middle of a busy roadway. A police helicopter circling the scene captured the officers directing Crutcher back to his vehicle. Though video footage appeared to show Crutcher complying with the officers, walking slowly with his hands up toward his vehicle, the officers in the helicopter commented over the radio dispatch that Crutcher had refused to follow the commands of Shelby and Turnbough to stop. An officer in the helicopter said, "Time for a taser, I think. I got a feeling that's about to happen. That looks like a bad dude, too. Must be on something" (Grace, Cabrera, & Zarrell, 2016). Seconds later, Turnbough tased Crutcher, and Shelby, without provocation, shot him in his chest (Barker, 2016, 1, 33). As blood saturated Crutcher's white t-shirt, Shelby checked his pockets for weapons. He was unarmed. Shelby refused to administer first aid, and Crutcher died. Without having administered a field narcotics test, Shelby had assumed that Crutcher was on PCP and was reaching for a weapon through the closed window of his vehicle. For this reason, the officer claimed that she feared for her life (Walinchus & Pérez-Peña, 2017). Because Shelby, like Darren Wilson's perception of Brown in Ferguson, saw Crutcher as an imminent threat, her rush to use lethal force characterizes the culture of policing that Crutcher and other unarmed black and brown people frequently encounter in 21st century America.[12]

POLICING WHILE BLACK AND BROWN

In the United States, though breakthroughs in racial equality have been achieved since the 1960s and Obama served two terms as President of the United States, we are all shaped by institutional racism, and we reproduce discriminatory interactions—sometimes unknowingly. In 2013, a Department of Justice survey revealed 12,000 police departments employed 477,000 officers, of whom approximately 130,000 (27%) were people of color compared to only 52,000 in 1987. Out of the numbers in 2013, there were 58,000 black officers and 55,000 brown officers (Reaves, 2015; Kesling & McWhirter, 2015). Despite the hiring diversity initiatives of some police departments and the moderate increase in the number of black and brown officers, civilians from the same racial cohorts throughout the nation disproportionately continued to be traumatized by racially biased policing.

An officer's race was not a determinant of the outcome of interactions with people of color. Data from the Department of Justice's findings from their study of Philadelphia's police department revealed that black police officers (11.4%) are more likely than white officers (6.8%) to perceive black suspects as threatening and thus respond with deadly force. Blow insisted that although racialized policing tactics have less to do with the race of the officer, the race of the suspect can determine the outcome of an encounter with that officer (Blow, 2015).

On July 6, 2016, dash cam footage captured Latino officer Jeronimo Yanez in Falcon Heights, Minnesota, inexplicably pull his gun during a routine traffic stop. Within only seconds of informing African American motorist Philando Castile of a broken break light and learning from Castile that he had a licensed concealed weapon, Yanez drew his gun. Despite Castile's girlfriend, Diamond Reynolds, sitting in the front passenger seat and her four-year-old daughter in the backseat, Yanez fired seven shots into the vehicle, hitting Castile five times. Jackson's cell phone video camera captured an emotionally unhinged Yanez swearing and waving his gun at a blood soaked, dying man (Smith, 2017). Later that same year, African American officer Brentley Vinson killed black motorist Keith Lamont Scott in Charlotte, North Carolina, under similar circumstances. For years, hip-hop has captured how black and brown officers operated through a racialized lens. Chuck D rhymed in 1990 in Public Enemy's "Welcome to the Terrordome," "Every brother ain't a brother cause a color" (Ridenhour & Boxley, 1990), and three years later, KRS-One rapped in "Black Cop," "Recently police trained black cop to stand on the corner, and take gunshot. This type of warfare isn't new or a shock" (Parker, 1993). Both timeless tracks also reflect the racial attitude of black and brown police officers in the 21st century; they bleed blue.

POLICING CHILDREN

Policing with impunity is not limited to adults. Children of color are not immune to such violence. Some police interactions with children result in death. In 2014, a police officer in Cleveland, Ohio, determined that 12-year old Tamir Rice was an imminent threat before shooting him within seconds of their encounter at a city park. Black children also experience other forms of police aggression. In the summer of 2015, a white McKinney, Texas, police officer drew his gun on black teenagers at a pool party, slammed a 14-year-old black girl in a bikini to the ground and sat on her. Later that same year, a white male school resource officer in Columbia, South Carolina, brutally arrested a 16-year-old African American female student for using a cell phone in her high school classroom. The arrest of the student and her black female classmate for video recording the incident on a cell phone reflected the aggressive nature of resource officers and the reality of the school-to-prison pipeline for black and brown children.

These episodes garnered international attention. Acts of white brutality against African American schoolchildren compelled the Working Group of Experts on People of African Descent of the United Nations in January 2016 to visit primary and secondary schools in the United States to investigate and report on "structural barriers" facing black children. Their findings reconfirmed that black children, like adults, experienced the problem of police brutality and incarceration (Klein, 2016; Weissinger et al., 2017).

ICE poses a serious threat to Latino children who have already been traumatized. In January 2016, ICE agents in Charlotte, North Carolina arrested a Central American immigrant teenager, Yefri Sorto-Hernandez, along with five other high school students who were waiting for their school bus. Sorto-Hernandez and the other students remained in a detention center for months. They were part of a wave of unaccompanied Central American children who came to the United States between 2009 and 2014 to flee high crime rates in countries like Guatemala, El Salvador, and Honduras (Price, 2016). Though federal officials claim that bus stops and school campuses were off limits for deportation arrests, Latino and other Deferred Action for Childhood Arrivals (DACA) students attend school under the threat deportation.

COLLATERAL DAMAGE OF POLICING

Another layer to racialized policing in the 21st century is the double standard in reports of acts of violent death. Graphic violence against black people is broadcast to play into white fears about black unruliness. Simultaneously, the media reminds blacks of the tragic consequences for perceived challenges to white law and order. Curry (2015) found that television media avoided broadcasting the uncut footage of the murder of white reporter Alison Parker and her cameraman. Nonetheless, the same stations air uncensored footage of black agony and death at the hands of police. This inequitable and disturbing standard in reporting traumatized black viewers and the families of the victims (Weissinger, et al., 2017). Like in the graphic police killings of Laquan McDonald in Chicago, Alton Sterling in Baton Rouge, and John Crawford III in Beavercreek, Ohio, viewers become numb to black deaths each time media outlets and law enforcement release these graphic videos.

Racialized policing also emboldens civilians to use deadly force against blacks. In February 2012, an overzealous member of a neighborhood watch, George Zimmerman, killed 17-year-old African American Trayvon Martin. The following November, a white male, Michael Dunn, fired ten bullets into a parked car containing four African American teenagers. Eighteen-year-old Jordan Davis was killed. Both shootings occurred in the Stand-Your-Ground state of Florida. Defendants used the legal argument that they had the right to use force to defend themselves against a real or perceived threat.

POLICING REFORM THROUGH CONSENT DECREES

With the increased number of law enforcement killings of unarmed black and brown people, Obama initiated consent decrees for approximately a dozen police departments across the country (Johnson, 2017). Consent decrees legally force policing agencies to reform their policies and practices after an exhaustive investigation by the Justice Department, state and local law officials, and community partners conclude there was official police misconduct and civil rights violations (US Department of Justice Civil Rights Division, 2017).

Unfortunately, the policing of African Americans and Latinos living at the mercy of discretionary policing are why Justice Department investigations are warranted. However, the validation of police misconduct does not lead to change. Consent decrees are designed to reform policing and restore community trust through non-bias, equitable policing, and federal judicial oversight. Furthermore, consent decrees monitor police department activity through disparate impact analysis and implicit bias training to make sure their actions are not discriminatory due to the race, gender, sexual orientation, origin, or religion of a suspect (2017).

Following the Justice Department's findings that the city of Baltimore Police Department violated the civil rights of residents and federal laws, a consent decree was issued. Baltimore Mayor Stephanie Rawlings-Blake admitted that although policing reforms were very costly, they were needed to reform the department (Bacon & Eversley, 2016). Some of the federal oversight required the BPD to address:

- Trainings on proper protocol to engage with suspects and avoid needless low-level offenses that escalate to arrests
- Establish community review boards
- Responding to individuals who exhibit mental health disorders
- Encouraging positive police and youth relationships
- Safe transportation of suspects in custody
- Use of technology such as body and dash cameras to increase transparency and establish confidence in policing

- Reviewing and implementing hiring and retention strategies to diversify the police force
- Investigating and punishing police misconduct (US Department of Justice, 2017).

Like the recent Baltimore consent decree, other cities agreed to such similar actions. Unfortunately, with the election of Donald Trump and the confirmation of Jeff Sessions as attorney general, there is uncertainty if the Justice Department is committed to the use of judicial oversight to enforce commitment to police reform. Turning a blind eye to police brutality, Sessions suggested that Obama's criminal justice reform measures had "somehow, someway, . . . undermined respect for police and made—oftentimes—their job more difficult." He claimed, "We need to help police officers get better rather than reduce their effectiveness, and I'm afraid we've done some of that. So, we're going to pull back a little on this. I don't think that it's wrong or mean or insensitive to civil rights or human rights" (Johnson, 2017).

CONCLUSION

It is *insensitive* because the policing of black and brown is a topic that must be taken serious by policymakers. It is not acceptable for police to act with impunity. It is also unacceptable to normalize black and brown suffering. As the presidency of Donald Trump unfolds, it is difficult to remain optimistic and hopeful for policy reform. During his presidential campaign, he branded Mexicans entering the United States as "rapists," "criminals," and "bad hombres." If the former reality television host and his attorney general follow through with their racialized immigration and policing agendas, black and brown will continue to experience trauma.

The federal government should require all police departments to participate in implicit bias training. This is one way to possibly reduce the number of fatal encounters between police and suspects of color. Simply stated, the old adage of placing oneself in another person's shoes still rings true. According to Spencer, Charbonneau, and Glaser (2016), diversity training to address officer bias, which ranges from personal assessment of bias and stereotypes to increasing interracial interactions with people outside of the norm has shown to reduce officer bias when compared to officers who do not receive such trainings. However, Spencer et al. (2016) are quick to note that although these types of individualized trainings offer some hope, they are short-lived and thus not a cure-all for long term changes in police attitudes regarding race. Again, this is why judicial oversight in the form of multifaceted and collaborative consent decrees are needed. They hold police departments accountable for their actions. They offer reformation along with the punitive weight of the Justice Department to compel police departments to address, monitor, and reevaluate how they police. In the first year of the Trump administration, there has already been an acceleration of ICE arrests, detainments, deportations of brown, and a presidential pardoning of former sheriff Joe Arpaio. Consent decrees seem to be the only way to reverse acts of police misconduct. Without federal oversight, it is impossible to change the racialized culture of police departments. Since policies allow police to act with impunity, a top-down approach is needed to reform the policing of black and brown. Arresting, indicting, and convicting police officers who kill unjustifiably and other acts of misconduct will also force them to think twice about policing with impunity.

NOTES

1. Ibram X. Kendi in *Stamped from the beginning: The definitive history of racist ideas in America* (New York: Nation Books, 2016) makes the broader argument that racist policies drive racist attitudes and ideas.

2. The criminal justice reform measures of the late 1960s reveal that no one party has ever been pro-black. Racism was and is policy driven from the top down.

3. When the program ended in 1981, the Act had allocated a total of $10 billion to policing.

4. The president and other policymakers empathized with white suburban addicts. They referred to drug abuse in these communities as an epidemic and that drug cartels and drug dealers from urban communities were destroying American society.

5. Black policymakers were complicit in the criminalization of other black people. African American Harlem Congressman Charles Rangel served as one of the architects of the bill and his African American colleagues supported its passage.

6. On the campaign trail Clinton had ingratiated himself with the black community. He appeared on the popular late-night "The Arsenio Hall Show," playing the saxophone, and professing his love of fast food. Candidate Clinton became so popular with black America that some referred to him as the nation's "first black president."

7. These democrats emerged during the presidency of George H.W. Bush. To maintain and gain political power, they supported get-tough-on-crime and anti-welfare policies.

8. A similar incident happened during the summer of 1999. A Chicago police officer fatally shot LaTanya Haggerty, an African American woman after mistaking her cell phone for a gun.

9. Funding from President Clinton's anti-crime legislation in 1994 allowed cities like New York to hire thousands of police officers and implement high-tech policing methods.

10. The ACLU report revealed that in 2002, 1,892 people were shot, and police made 97,296 race-based stops. In 2011, 1,821 people fell victim to gun violence, but police made 685,724 race-based stops.

11. Alienation is related to the fact that law enforcement prejudges black and brown men. They are always viewed as being suspects. As a result of being treated like second-class citizens, black and brown suffer from a lack of self-worth. Stop and frisk eroded an already fragile relationship between black men and police.

12. In April 2015, Robert Bates, a white volunteer deputy at the Tulsa County Sheriff's Office, shot and killed unarmed 44-year-old Eric Harris during a failed drug sting operation. In 2016, a jury convicted Harris of second-degree manslaughter.

REFERENCES

Alexander, M. (2012). *The new Jim Crow: Mass incarceration in the age of color-blindness*. New York: The New Press.

Alexander, M. (2016, February 10).Why Hillary Clinton doesn't deserve the black vote. *The Nation*. Retrieved from https://www.thenation.com/article/hillary-clinton-does-not-deserve-black-peoples-votes/

American Civil Liberties Union. (2014, June). War comes home: The excessive militarization of American policing. Retrieved from https://www.aclu.org/report/war-comes-home-excessive-militarization-american-police.

Anderson, C. (2016). *White rage: The unspoken truth of our racial divide*. New York: Bloomsbury Publishing.

Arinde, N. (2009, July 20-August 5). Gates and Obama: A sorry state of affairs. *The New York Amsterdam News*, 6.

Bacon, J., & Eversley, M. (2016, August 11). Baltimore cops vow reform after DOJ report. *USA Today*. Retrieved from https://berea.idm.oclc.org/login?url=http://search.ebscohost.com/login.aspx?direct=true&db=a9h&AN=J0E096422461716&site=ehost-live

Balko, R. (2013a, February 5). Raid of the day: The 39th and dalton edition. *Huffington Post*. Retrieved from http://www.huffingtonpost.com/2013/02/05/raid-of-the-day-the-39th-_n_2621763.html

Balko, R. (2013b). *Rise of the warrior cop: The militarization of America's police forces*. New York: Public Affairs.

Barker, C. J. (2016, September 22). Cops kill again: Two fatal police shootings spark nationwide outrage. *New York Amsterdam News*, 1, 33.

Baum, D. (2016, April). Legalize it all: How to win the war on drugs. *Harper's Magazine*.

Blackmon, D. A. (2008). *Slavery by another name: The re-enslavement of black Americans from the Civil War to World War II*. New York: Double Day.

Blow, C. M. (2015, March 26). Officers' race matters less than you think. *The New York Times* Retrieved from http://www.nytimes.com/2015/03/26/opinion/charles-blow-officer-race-matters-less-than-you-think.html?partner=bloomberg

Boyd, H. (2009, July 30). Gates, Crowley, Obama and a beer. *New York Amsterdam News*, 4, 31.

Camp, J. T., & Heatherton, C. (2016). *Policing the planet: Why the policing crisis led to black lives matter.* London: Verso.

Curry, G. E. (2015, September 7). Double standard when covering violent tragedies. *New York Beacon.* Retrieved from http://search.proquest.com/docview/171830337 4?accountid=8578

Domanick, J. (2015). *Blue: The LAPD and the battle to redeem American policing.* New York: Simon & Schuster.

Duckworth, K, Spears, M., & Williams, P. (2015). Alright (Duckworth & Williams). On to pimp a butterfly. [Digital]. Santa Monica, California: Aftermath Records.

Ehrenfreund, M. (2016, August 30). The major flaw in president Clinton's welfare reform that almost no one noticed. *The Washington Post.* Retrieved from https:// search-proquest-com.berea.idm.oclc.org/docview/1815256000?accountid=8578

Fritsch, J. (2000, February 26). The Diallo verdict: The overview; four officers in Diallo shooting are acquitted of all charges. *The New York Times.* Retrieved from https:// searchproquest-com.berea.idm.oclc.org/docview/91754847?accountid=8578

Grace, N., Cabrera, A., & Zarrell, M. (2016). *Unarmed man shot dead by Tulsa police.* Atlanta: CQ Roll Call. Retrieved from https://search-proquest-com.berea.idm .oclc.org/docview/1822541781?accountid=8578

Guo, J. (2016, May 2). America's tough approach to policing black communities began as a liberal idea: A surprising new history of policing in America. *The Washington Post.* Retrieved from https://search-proquest-com.berea.idm.oclc.org/docvie w/1785895549?accountid=8578

Hadden, S. E. (2003). *Slave patrols: Law and violence in Virginia and Carolinas.* Cambridge: Harvard University Press.

Henderson, N. M. (2015, September 26). Eric Holder was the black leader Obama could never be. *The Washington Post.* Retrieved from https://search-proquest-com .berea.idm.oclc.org/docview/1566072032?accountid=8578

Higginbotham, F. M. (2013). *Ghosts of Jim Crow: Ending racism in post-racial America.* New York; London: NYU Press. Retrieved from http://www.jstor.org .berea.idm.oclc.org/stable/j.ctt9qfd17.7

Hinton, E. (2016). *From the war on poverty to the war on crime: The making of mass incarceration in America.* Cambridge: Harvard University Press.

Johnson, K. (2017, March 1). Sessions says rising violence is a 'danger': AG warns of uptick despite downward trend in crime rate. *USA Today.* Retrieved from https:// berea.idm.oclc.org/login?url=http://search.ebscohost.com/login.aspx?direct=true& db=a9h&AN=J0E183258335917&site=ehost-live

Jones, N., Oliver, J-C, Walker, K., & Barnes, S. (1996). If I ruled the world (Recorded by Nas and Lauren Hill). On it was written. [Digital]. New York: Columbia Records.

Kelling, G. L., & Wilson, J. Q. (1982, March). Broken windows: The police and neighborhood safety. *Atlantic Monthly, 249*(3), 29–38.

Kendi, I. X. (2016). *Stamped from the beginning: The definitive history of racist ideas in America.* New York: Nation Books.

Kesling, B., & McWhirter, C. (2015, May 14). Percentage of African-Americans in U.S. police departments remains flat since 2007; but police hiring of other minorities has increased, report shows. *Wall Street Journal* (Online). Retrieved from https://search-proquest-com.berea.idm.oclc.org/docview/1680773375?accou ntid=8578

Kindy, K. (2015, May 31). Fatal police shootings in 2015 approaching 400 nation-wide.*The Washington Post.* Retrieved from http://libproxy.eku.edu/login?url=http: //search.proquest.com/docview/1684977460?accountid=10628

Klein, R. (2016, February 2). U.N. experts seem horrified by how American schools treat black children. *Huffington Post.* Retrieved from http://www.huffingtonpost .com/entry/school-discrimination-united-nations_us_56b141e1e4b01d80b24474d3

Lassiter, M. D. (2015, June). Impossible criminals: The suburban imperatives of America's war on drugs. *The Journal of American History*, 102(1), 126–140.

Lowery, W. (2015, December 24). A disproportionate number of black victims in fa-tal traffic stops. *The Washington Post.* Retrieved from https://search-proquest-com .berea.idm.oclc.org/docview/1751657195?accountid=8578

Lowery, W. (2016, April 7). Study finds police fatally shoot unarmed black men at disproportionate rates. *The Washington Post.* Retrieved from washing tonpost.com/national/study-finds-police-fatally-shoot-unarmed-Black-men-at -disproportionate-rates/2016/04/06/e494563e-fa74–11e5–80e4-c381214de1a3_ story.html?tid=sm_tw.

Lowery, W., Leonnig, C. D., & Berman, M. (2014, August 14). Even before Michael Brown's slaying in Ferguson, racial questions hung over police. *The Washington Post.* Retrieved from https://search-proquest-com.berea.idm.oclc.org/docview/155 3031465?accountid=8578

McFadden, R. D. (1999, March 26). Four officers indicted for murder in killing of Diallo, lawyer says. *The New York Times.* Retrieved from http://libproxy.eku.edu/ login?url=http://search.proquest.com /docview/1646065039?accountid=10628

Myers, A. L. (2011, November 27). SWAT team shatters family's life; Jose Guerena Ortiz, brandishing a gun, was shot to death at home by a Pima county squad execut-ing a search warrant. *Los Angeles Times.* Retrieved from https://search-proquest-com.berea.idm.oclc.org/docview/906094041?accountid=8578

National Advisory Commission on Civil Disorders. (1968). *Supplemental studies for the national advisory commission on civil disorders.* Washington, DC: U.S. Gov-ernment Printing Office.

Neidig, H. (2015, January 15). NYPD slowdown a show of irony. *University Wire.* Retrieved from http://libproxy.eku.edu/login?url=http://search.proquest.com/docvi ew/1646065039?accountid=10628

New York Civil Liberties Union. (n.d.). *Stop and frisk facts.* New York: New York Civil Liberties Union. Retrieved from https://www.nyclu.org/en/stop-and-frisk -facts

Nix, J., Campbell, B. A., Byers, E. H., & Alpert, G. P. (2017). A bird's eye view of civilians killed by police in 2015. *Criminology & Public Policy*, *16*(1), 309–340. doi:10.1111/1745–9133. Retrieved from http://libproxy.eku.edu/login?url=http:// search.ebscohost.com/login.aspx?direct=true&db=a9h&AN=121388679&site=eh ost-live&scope=site

Novak, D. A. (2014). *The wheel of servitude: Black forced labor after slavery.* Lex-ington: The University Press of Kentucky.

Obama, B. (2008, March 19). "Barack Obama gives speech on race in U.S." [speech transcript]. *Chicago Defender*. Retrieved from https://search proquestcom.berea .idm.oclc.org/docview/246898780?accountid=8578

Parenti, C. (2015, July 29). The making of the American police state. *Jacobin Magazine*. Retrieved from https://www.jacobinmag.com/2015/07/incarceration -capitalism-black-lives-matter/

Parker, L. K. (1993). Black cop. On return of the boom bap. [Digital]. New York: Jive Records.

Parsons, E. F. (2016). *Ku-klux: The birth of the klan during reconstruction*. The University of North Carolina Press.

Price, M. (2016, July 1). West Meck high student says ICE agents arrested him at school bus stop. *The Charlotte Observer*. Retrieved from http://www.charlotteob server.com/news/local/article87169637.html

Reaves, B. A. (2013). Local police departments, 2015: Personnel, policies, and practices. Washington, D.C.: United States Department of Justice, Office of Justice Programs, Bureau of Justice Statistics. Retrieved from https://www.bjs.gov/index .cfm?ty=pbdetail&iid=5279

Ridenhour, C., & Boxley, K. M. (1990). Welcome to the terrordome (Recorded by Public Enemy). On fear of a black planet. [Digital]. New York: Def Jam Recordings.

Silver, J. (2016, July 12). Obama, Bush call for unity at Dallas memorial. *The Texas Tribune*. Retrieved from https://search-proquest-com.berea.idm.oclc.org/docview/ 1803281007?accountid=8578

Smith, M. (2017, June 21). Video of police killing of Philando Castile is publicly released. *The New York Times*. Retrieved from https://search-proquest-com.berea .idm.oclc.org/docview/1911477052?accountid=8578

Spencer, K. B., Charbonneau, A. K., & Glaser, J. (2016). Implicit bias and policing. *Social & Personality Psychology Compass*, 10(1), 50–63. doi:10.1111/spc3.12210

Staats, C., Capatosto, K., Wright, R., & Contractor, D. (2015). *State of the science: Implicit bias review, 2015*. Columbus, OH: Kirwan Institute, The Ohio State University.

Taylor, K-Y. (2016). *From #blacklivesmatter to black liberation*. Chicago: Haymarket Books.

United States Census Bureau. (2016). U.S. census bureau quick facts: Population estimates, July 1, 2016. Retrieved from https://www.census.gov/quickfacts/

United States Department of Justice (2017). Fact sheet: Justice department consent decree with Baltimore police department and the city of Baltimore. Retrieved from https://www.justice.gov/opa/file/925026/download

United States Department of Justice Civil Rights Division. (2017, January). The civil rights division's pattern and practice police reform work: 1994-present. Washington: Government Printing Office.

United States Department of Justice Civil Rights Division. (2016, August 10). Investigation of the Baltimore city police department. Washington: Government Printing Office.

United States Department of Justice Civil Rights Division. (2015, March 4). United States investigation of the Ferguson police department. Washington: Government Printing Office.

United States Department of Justice Civil Rights Division. (2011, December 15). United States' investigation of the Maricopa County sheriff's department. Washington: Government Printing Office.

Walinchus, L., & Pérez-Peña, R. (2017, May 17). White Tulsa officer is acquitted in killing of black driver. *The New York Times.* Retrieved from https://search -proquest-com.berea.idm.oclc.org/docview/1899680602?accountid=8578

Warikoo, N., Sally, T. S., & Smith, M. W. (2010, May 16). Sleeping on couch, Detroit girl, 7, fatally shot by cop. *McClatchy-Tribune News Service.* Retrieved from https://search-proquest-com.berea.idm.oclc.org/docview/288163160?accoun tid=8578

Weissinger, S., Mack, D. A., & Watson, E. (Eds.). (2017). *Violence against black bodies: How black lives continue to matter.* New York: Routledge.

White, M. D., &, Fradella, H. F. (2016). *Stop and frisk: The use and abuse of a controversial policing tactic.* New York: New York University Press.

Williams, T. (2016, January 27). U.S. taking back military gear from local law enforcement. *The New York Times.* Retrieved from https://search-proquest-com. berea.idm.oclc.org/docview/1760231075?accountid=8578

Wingfield, A. H., & Feagin, J. (2012). The racial dialectic: President Barack Obama and the white racial frame. *Qualitative Sociology, 35*(2), 143–162. Retrieved from doi:http://dx.doi.org/10.1007/s11133–012–9223–7

Chapter Two

Police Use of Force

Practices, Policies, and the Law

Wornie Reed

The use of deadly force by police officers against black Americans is an old problem, which in recent years has become a more prominent issue as the number of black[1] men and women killed increases. Whether increasing or not these homicides are drawing more public attention than they did in past decades.

According to one source (*The Guardian*, 2016), unarmed blacks were killed at five times the rate of unarmed whites in 2015. Police killed at least 102 unarmed black people in 2015 and in only 10 of the 102 cases were officers charged with a crime, and in only two of the deaths were officers convicted. These rates are much lower than when one civilian kills another. From federal data we know that the overall percentage of murders that are successfully prosecuted and someone is convicted is just under 40 percent of total murders (Murder Accountability Project, 2016). If we eliminate the un-solved murders—over 35 percent—for direct comparison, as almost all police homicides are known, the rate of civilian convictions with known offenders is over 60 percent (Extrano's Alley, 2014).

What is it about the law and the practice of policing that produce this few number of convictions? One answer points to the close relationship between prosecutors and law enforcement officials, which may tilt prosecutors for police officers. While that close relationship sometimes appears to be at play, it may be only one of the factors, along with existing policies and practices in policing.

TRENDS

In response to the upsurge in public interest in police killings, the *Washington Post* and *The Guardian* newspapers have stepped in to perform a task not being done by the government: the recording of every police killing and data on the circumstances of each homicide. Though the newspapers use slightly different methods, both draw on two citizen-initiated sources, "Killed by Police" and "Fatal Encounters," which collect news reports of people killed by law enforcement officers, and both include data on whether the person was armed. In addition to the time and place of the killings, both databases include basic demographic information, including race, gender, and age. Neither attempts to determine whether the killings should be deemed "justified."

According to *The Guardian*:

- 1,136 Americans were killed by police in 2015. Of these, 300 were black—25 percent of the police homicides.
- Police killed blacks at more than twice the rate of white people: The rate, per million in population, was 7.13 for blacks, 3.48 for Hispanics/Latinos, 3.4 for Native Americans, and 2.91 for whites.
- About 25 percent of blacks killed were unarmed, compared with 17 percent of whites.

Krieger et al. (2015) took a public health approach to the development of data on police homicides. They examined long-term trends in deaths due to law enforcement actions by analyzing US national mortality data for the period 1960–2010, using individual-level mortality records and Census data. Between 1960 and 2010, 15,699 US deaths occurred from legal intervention. Of these, nearly two-thirds, 9,934, were of men 15–34 years of age. Blacks were 42.3 percent, comprising over three times the proportion of blacks in the population. The rates for black men in this age group rose sharply in the 1960s and 1970s to more than 3 per 100,000 in the population and then declined and plateaued beginning in the 1980s when it started being around one per 100,000 (Kreiger et al., 2015).

RACIAL PROFILING

Racial profiling is often a factor in cases of police use of force. As Zack (2015) reveals, police racial profiling sets the stage for both the arbitrary violence and its impunity. In most of the well-publicized cases of police killings of unarmed black men, there was the usual sequence of events. First is the racial profiling, then there is the stop, or attempted stop, following by the application of lethal force, which is then followed by public protests. After a passage of time, the officer is often acquitted or not indicted, which is followed by more protests. Racial profiling sets these activities in motion.

There is a difference between criminal profiling and racial profiling. Criminal profiling, or offender profiling, is a technique used by law enforcement to identify likely suspects for a specific crime. In this instance, of course, they can use race as one of the factors in profiling the offender. That process is distinguished from racial profiling where the race is the only or primary criterion. The Fourth Amendment to the US Constitution, which provides protection against unreasonable search and seizure and the equal protection provisions of the Fourteenth Amendment, make racial profiling illegal (Harris, 2002).

One of the first major cases of racial profiling occurred in New Jersey during the 1990s. Former New Jersey Governor Christine Todd Whitman fired the State Police superintendent for admitting and defending the practice of racial profiling. Racial profiling by the State Police was demonstrated by John Lamberth, who found that whites were 75 percent of the motorists and traffic violators along a stretch of I-95 in New Jersey, yet 80 percent of the vehicles stopped and searched belonged to minorities (Harris, 2002).

The Maryland section of Interstate Highway 95 was notorious for racial profiling. The Maryland State Police held that the corridor was infested with drug runners, and since drug runners were defined as being black or Hispanic, there was a need to stop more of those motorists. Blacks accounted for nearly 30 percent of drivers who were stopped, which was substantially greater than their percentage of all vehicles, and they were 73 percent of drivers searched, an even larger disparity (Mathis, 2002; Blank et al. 2004).

There are several well-known cases of blacks being stopped and searched seemingly indiscriminately. In one notable case, a Harvard law graduate and attorney with the District of Columbia Public Defender Service Robert Wilkins was pulled over by Maryland State Troopers, forced out of the car along with his other black male relatives, and forced to submit to a search of the automobile by police dogs. Wilkins, joined by the American Civil Liberties Union, filed suit against the Maryland State Police. He and his relatives received a settlement, amounting to $50,000 in damages plus $46,000 in attorney fees. As a part of the agreement, the state agreed to stop using race-based drug courier profiles as law enforcement tools and to track the reason for traffic stops and the race of the person stopped. Maryland State Police reports indicated that between 70 and 75 percent of the people searched on I-95 were black, even though they represented only 17 percent of those driving on the highway and only 17 percent of traffic violators (Dunn and Reed, 2011).

Examples of racial profiling are plentiful. It is not new, as for years it was known as DWB, "driving while black." In his book, *The Presumption of Guilt*, Charles Olgletree (2010) analyzed 100 cases of racial profiling against professional black men. This "driving while black" list includes stories about such prominent black American professionals as Justice Thurgood Marshall, John Hope Franklin, Johnnie Cochran, Jr., Julian Bond, Roger Wilkins, Eric Holder, and William Julius Wilson, who discussed being racially profiled. The list included judges, several prominent law school graduates, law professors, university professors, engineers, and movie stars.

Many states, because of lawsuits like the Wilkins case in Maryland or because of legislation, collect demographic, outcome, and other data on all traffic stops. Dunn and Reed (2011) analyzed data from 13 of these states and found that in comparison to their proportions of the populations, black motorists were stopped and searched excessively. The critical issue is the yield rate. Do blacks tend to have contraband in their vehicles at higher rates than whites? The answer is no. Of the nine states providing search results data, in six states blacks had lower yields than whites. Whites who were stopped less often and searched less often tended to have more contraband than blacks. Thus, criminal profiling was obviated in these states as there was no criminal justice reason for blacks to be stopped and searched more often (Dunn and Reed, 2011).

Dunn and Reed (2011) conducted a study of traffic ticketing in a northern city where blacks were ticketed at higher rates than whites. They found that the disparate ticketing was not the result of "rogue," or racist, police officers, but rather from the pattern of patrol car deployment. They compared ticketing and speeds of two different thoroughfares, one used predominantly by whites and the other predominantly by blacks. Four to five times more patrol cars were deployed on the "black" route than the "white" route. Thus, more tickets were written on the black route even though there were more traffic and more speeding on the white route. The disproportionate distribution of patrol cars was an admitted longtime policy and practice of the police department. Consequently, this racial discrimination (of ticketing) was institutional—institutional racism. This chapter, similarly, takes an institutional—or systemic—approach to the police use of force.

PRACTICES, POLICIES, AND THE LAW

Police Use of Force: Practices

The excess black versus white mortality rate from police homicides is longstanding and documented, especially among men 15–34 years of age (Sikora and Mulvihill, 2002; Walker, Spohn, and Delone, 2012; Krieger et al., 2015). In the 1960s and 1970s, the black to white ratio was nearly 8. In 1965, it was 7.65. In 1975, it was 7.56. (See Table 2.1.) Excess black mortality may be the result of police brutality against blacks during the civil rights era (Gabbidon and Greene, 2013). The ratio declined to 4.48 in 1985 and then plateaued to around 3.0.

Table 2.1. Trends in US Deaths Due to Legal Intervention Among Black and White Men, Age 15–34 Years, by Year: 1965–2002.

| | *Death Due to Legal Intervention* | | |
| | *Race* | | |
Year	*Black*	*White*	*B/W Ratio*
1965	3.33	0.44	7.65
1975	2.96	0.39	7.56
1985	1.25	0.28	4.48
1995	1.21	0.36	3.37
2005	0.94	0.37	2.57

What Table 2.1 indicates is that deaths by legal intervention among young black men were much higher 40 to 50 years ago than in recent years. However, more recent data suggest the ratio between black and white men in this age group is growing (Mapping Police Violence, 2016).

One reason for this downtrend in the 1990s was the Supreme Court decision in *Tennessee v. Garner*, the result of one of the most significant police shootings in US history. In October of 1974, Memphis police officers shot and killed Edward Garner, a 15-year-old, slightly built African American boy in the back of the head while he was fleeing with a stolen purse containing $10. The officers were acting under the *fleeing felon* rule, which allowed a police officer—or victim or bystander—to use force, including deadly force, against an individual suspected of a felony and in "clear flight." Garner's father sued the police officer and city departments and officials in Federal Court. The case went to the US Supreme Court, which ruled that the fleeing felon rule was unconstitutional in that it violated the Fourth Amendment protection against unreasonable searches and seizures, holding that shooting a person was in effect a seizure (Walker et al, 2012).

The *Garner* decision is considered a major factor in the reduction in the use of deadly force, but changes in police practices played a part also. Many police departments began to use the "defense of life" rule, permitting shootings in situations that posed a threat to the life of the officer or some other person. In comparison, the fleeing felon rule undoubtedly played a large role in the much higher rates of police homicides in the 1960s and 1970s.

Police Use of Force: Policies

One of the most important policy changes to the use of force rules came from the *Garner* decision in 1985, which abolished the fleeing felon rule.

This rule had allowed a police officer to use all necessary means to arrest the defendant who was resisting arrest by fleeing. The Supreme Court ruled that all claims of excessive force occurring during an arrest or investigatory stop—deadly or otherwise—are governed by the Fourth Amendment's prohibition against unreasonable seizures. The Court asserted that killing a person did not further the goals of the criminal justice process. Apparently, some police departments changed their policies to adhere to this stricter guideline, as one comprehensive study found that overall police homicides decreased in the years immediately following the *Garner* decision (Tennenbaum, 1994).

In more recent years, some policing policies condition officers to be very aggressive with suspects, especially minorities. For example, in 2013, the New York State Senate heard testimony that the former NYPD Commissioner Kelly told the New York State governor, Andrew Cuomo, that his aim was to instill fear in young black and Latino men every time they left home. A recording made at a Brooklyn Police Station revealed that Kelly's views permeated the NYPD: "If you get too big of a crowd there, you know, they're going to get out of control, and they're going to think that they own the block. They don't own the block, alright? They might live there, but we own the block, alright? We own the streets here" (Eisen, A. [2016, March 6]).

Police Use of Force: The Law

One of the most significant Supreme Court rulings on the use of force was the *Garner* ruling in 1985, which in a 6–3 decision held that the use of deadly force against a fleeing felon is unconstitutional. The decision asserted that killing a person did not further the goals of the criminal justice process since it circumvents bringing the person to justice. The decision rejected the application of deadly force against a person for merely committing a felony and went on to describe when such force was permissible.

Where the officer has probable cause to believe that the suspect poses a threat of serious physical harm, either to the officer or others, it is not constitutionally unreasonable to prevent escape by using deadly force. Thus, if the suspect threatens the officer with a weapon or there is probable cause to believe that he has committed a crime involving the infliction or threatened infliction of serious physical harm, deadly force may be used if necessary to prevent escape, and if, where feasible, some warning has been given (*Tennessee v. Garner*, 1985).

Beginning with *Garner*, the Supreme Court has ruled that all claims of excessive force occurring during an arrest or investigatory stop—deadly or otherwise—are governed by the Fourth Amendment's prohibition against unreasonable seizures. This judicial precedent holds that all uses of force must be "objectively reasonable" based on the totality of the circumstances viewed through the lens of the officer in the field. However, the courts have been deferential to officers in the field, holding that officers are disadvantaged as they are required to make split-second decisions in dangerous situations. Also, these rulings hold that officers need not use the least intrusive means to effectuate a seizure so long as their actions are reasonable (Thompson, 2015).

What about the use of non-deadly force? Four years after *Garner* the Supreme Court considered this issue in *Graham v. Connor* (1989). In this case, police officers pulled over an individual suspected of shoplifting. In response to the suspect's erratic behavior, the officers forcefully slammed him into the police cruiser and then into the car, with the suspect sustaining significant injuries. The suspect sued the police for using excessive force.

The case made its way to the Supreme Court, which held that all claims that law enforcement officers have used excessive force—deadly or not—in the course of an arrest, investigatory stop, or other seizure should be analyzed under the Fourth Amendment and its reasonable standard, which depends upon the facts and circumstances of each particular case, including the severity of the crime at issue, whether the suspect poses an immediate threat to the safety of the officers or others, and whether the suspect is resisting or attempting to evade arrest. Further, the reasonableness of a particular use of force is judged from the perspective of the officer on the scene (Thompson, 2015).

The Supreme Court directed the lower courts to consider three questions to measure the lawfulness of a particular use of force. First, what was the severity of the crime that the officer believed the suspect to have committed or to be committing? Second, did the suspect present an immediate threat to the safety of officers or the public? Third, was the suspect actively resisting arrest or attempting to escape (Thompson, 2015)?

Based on *Garner* and *Graham*, lower courts began to apply the following tests. For deadly force cases, the court would assess whether the suspect posed a threat to the safety of the officers or others; for non-deadly cases, they would use the three factors from *Graham*. However, in the case, *Scott v. Harris* (2007), the Court considered the question, does a police officer who stops a high-speed chase by ramming a fleeing suspect's car violate the Fourth Amendment's protection against unreasonable seizure? The Court, in an 8–1 decision, ruled that the officer's actions were reasonable under the Fourth Amendment, since the plaintiff, the suspect, posed an imminent threat to bystanders (Thompson, 2015).

DEADLY FORCE AGAINST UNARMED SUSPECTS

A critical issue that has played out in high-profile cases of police use of deadly force has been the killings of unarmed suspects. Police are permitted to use deadly force when the suspect is carrying a deadly weapon, but two other considerations obtain for unarmed suspects. One is that even when a suspect turns out to not have a firearm, the courts have held that officers are still justified in using deadly force if they reasonably believed the suspect was carrying a gun. Another is that the courts tend not to second-guess officers in the field and approve the use of force in a wide variety of situations.

Thompson (2015) cited several cases relevant to this use of force policy. One federal court noted that "[t]his standard contains a built-in measure of deference to the officer's on-the-spot judgment about the level of force necessary in light of the circumstances of the particular case" (*Edwards v. City of Martins Ferry*, 2008). This deference results in rules such as the one that officers are not required to use less intrusive force if the use of force in question was reasonable under the Fourth Amendment (*Plakas v. Drinski*, 1994; *Scott v. Heinrich*, 1994). In upholding this rule, the Ninth Circuit argued, "[r]equiring officers to find and choose the least intrusive alternative would require them to exercise superhuman judgment" and could "induce tentativeness" in officers that might deter them from protecting the public and themselves (*Scott v. Heinrich*, 1994, 7–8).

There is a built-in deference to officers' on-the-spot judgment about the level of force necessary. This position of some courts results from the rule that officers are not required to use less intrusive force if the use of force in question was reasonable under the Fourth Amendment. However, some courts have held that the availability of alternative means is relevant to a Fourth Amendment analysis (Thompson, 2015). Thus, it would appear that the legal issue is not necessarily settled in the situation of unarmed individuals.

In the *Garner* decision, the Supreme Court provided a remedy to the terrible fleeing felony rule, which evidently caused a decline in extrajudicial killings (Thompson, 2015, Walker et al., 2012). However, these extrajudicial killings did not disappear. They declined and then plateaued, perhaps because of later decisions of the Court. In *Garner,* the Court held that since the use of force was a seizure and subject to Fourth Amendment protections, the courts must balance the intrusion of the individual's Fourth Amendment interests against the importance of the governmental interests alleged to justify the intrusion. Thus, police officer actions were seen as actions of the state—the government.

The *Graham* decision changed the focus. It in effect changed the view of the police use of force from that of an individual encountering a state action that could potentially be a violation of the person's constitutional rights under the Fourth Amendment to that of the police officer's right, the right to act if they have reasonable fear (Zack, 2015). In other words, this shifts the focus from the citizens' rights to the rights of individual workers in a profession. In practice, the emphasis moved from legal or moral criteria toward the normative behavior of the law enforcement profession. The current question is whether that policy comports with individual rights under the Constitution.

REMEDIES FOR THE USE OF FORCE

Past efforts to address the issue of police use of force can be characterized into either of three approaches: (1) providing legal remedies for the unconstitutional use of force by law enforcement officers, (2) reforming the police use of force, and (3) legislation.

Legal remedies for the unconstitutional use of force by law enforcement officers rely on three federal statutes: (1) a criminal offense for violations of constitutional rights, including excessive force; (2) a civil cause of action for deprivation of such rights; and (3) a statute authorizing the Attorney General to bring civil suits for injunctive relief against police departments engaged in a "pattern or practice" of such unconstitutional use of force (Thompson, 2015). The first two rely on statutes enacted during the Reconstruction era. They have not been used to much effect in recent cases (Harmon, 2009).

The "pattern or practice" suits brought by the Attorney General seem to be an appropriate approach for systemic problems in police departments. However, recent results have been mixed under Attorney General Eric Holder. With opportunities to establish case law in cases before the Supreme Court, limited progress is being made (Thompson, 2015; Apuzzo and Liptak, 2015). Moreover, as this is being written, the Attorney General appointed by President Trump, Jeff Sessions, announced that he will reduce the use of this authority, in effect closing down any "policing" of police departments (Raasch, 2017).

REFORMING THE POLICE USE OF FORCE

In response to the police killing of 18-year-old Michael Brown in Ferguson, Missouri, and other police homicides elsewhere, several proposals were suggested by officials as well as advocates to remedy the police use of force issue. Congressional legislators offered bills that would clarify some excessive force practices (the Excessive Use of Force Prevention Act of 2015—H.R. 2052), create a new federal crime for certain homicides committed by law enforcement officers (the Police Accountability Act of 2015—H.R. 1102), and require state or local governments to report data concerning police use of excessive force, and the collection of such data (the National Statistics on Deadly Force Transparency Act of 2015—H.R. 306). However, none of these bills passed into law.

As a result of the protest demonstrations and calls for police reforms, in December 2014, President Barack Obama issued an executive order establishing the Task Force on 21st Century Policing. The Task Force was charged with identifying the best police practices, including the use of force. In May 2015 this Task Force issued its final report (Final Report of the President's Task Force on 21st Century Policing, 2015), a comprehensive set of suggestions, including the following:

- Develop comprehensive policies on the use of force that include training, investigations, prosecutions, data collection, and information sharing.
- Mandate external and independent criminal investigations in cases of police use of force resulting in death, officer-involved shootings resulting in injury or death, or in-custody deaths.
- Mandate the use of external and independent prosecutors in cases of police use of force resulting in death, officer-involved shootings resulting in injury or death, or in-custody deaths.
- Require agencies to collect, maintain, and report data to the federal government on all officer-involved shootings, whether fatal or nonfatal, as well as any in-custody death.

The steps recommended by the Task Force are the kind criminal justice reformers have advocated. However, there has been no movement to implement these types of policies.

DISCUSSION

Some of the key remedies for extrajudicial killings by police officers are (1) legislation to prohibit racial profiling, (2) requirements for law enforcement to collect and report the data on police homicides of civilians, and (3) require independent prosecution of police officers involved in excessive use of force. Every Congressional Session since 2001 Representative John Conyers and colleagues in the House of Representatives have introduced the End Racial Profiling Act legislation. Among other provisions, this Act would ban profiling by race, religion, ethnicity, or national origin by police and other law enforcement at all levels of government. Racial profiling would become a crime. That is a first step in addressing police encounters with blacks that sometimes end in the use of excessive force. However, it has yet to pass Congress (Conyers, 2015).

Knowledge about circumstances of deaths due to the use of lethal force can inform the development of prevention strategies and perhaps modify law enforcement responses and prevent fatalities associated with law enforcement intervention (DeGue, Fowler, and Calkins, 2016). Consequentially, there is a need to establish legal requirements for law enforcement agencies to collect and report data on the occurrence and circumstances of each extrajudicial killing.

There is a natural conflict of interest when district attorneys are called upon to prosecute police officers. Typically they work with officers to bring cases against suspected criminals, and they count on officers' testimony to support their cases. Consequently, they may be hesitant to bring such cases, and further, they may be reluctant to initiate a request for a special prosecutor because of how that might also affect relations with officers. A requirement to always have a special prosecutor in cases of questionable use of force would solve all—or at least most—of these issues.

In addressing remedies for social problems, it is vital to start with an accurate definition of the problem. Often concerns about the excessive use of force by law enforcement devolve into a discussion of the willfulness and the character of the individual officer. Even some police departments point to some officers as "bad apples." However, as Dunn and Reed (2011) demonstrated, in many instances, it may be the racially discriminatory policies and practices of police departments and not the bigotry of individual policers. Thus, a systemic approach is desirable.

If we follow a systemic approach, we may have heightened interest in the "pattern or practice" statute that is already on the books. To the remedies mentioned above, we would add the more regular use of the "pattern or practice" federal statute which prohibits government authorities or agents acting on their behalf from engaging in a pattern or practice of conduct by law enforcement officers that deprives persons of their Constitutional rights. It authorizes the Attorney General to sue law enforcement agencies if he or she has reasonable cause to believe that a pattern of such violations has occurred. Under President Obama, the Department of Justice opened 25 pattern or practice investigations of police departments across the country, including Baltimore, Chicago, and Ferguson, Missouri. A more regular use or threat of use of this procedure could have some level of preventive effect. At a minimum, it would define illegal practices and provide examples of what can happen when they occur. This enhanced use of the pattern or practice statute is seen as a viable approach irrespective of who serves as Attorney General.

Police Accountability

Of at least 4,024 people killed by police between January 2013 and June 2016, only 85 of these cases led to an officer being charged with a crime, and only six of these resulted in convictions (Mapping Police Violence, 2016). A committee of Black Lives Matter investigated police union contracts and statewide Law Enforcement Officer's Bill of Rights laws and found them problematic for police accountability. Working with legal experts, advocates, and academics with expertise in this subject, they identified six major areas where these contracts and bills of rights contribute to making it harder to hold police accountable for misconduct:

1. Disqualifying misconduct complaints that are submitted too many days after an incident occurs or if an investigation takes too long to complete
2. Preventing police officers from being interrogated immediately after being involved in an incident or otherwise restricting how, when, or where they can be interrogated
3. Giving officers access to information that civilians do not get before being interrogated
4. Limiting disciplinary consequences for officers or limiting the capacity of civilian oversight structures and the media to hold police accountable
5. Requiring cities to pay costs related to police misconduct including by giving officers paid leave while under investigation, paying legal fees, and the cost of settlements
6. Preventing information on past misconduct investigations from being recorded or retained in an officer's personnel file (Campaign Zero, 2016).

The team reviewed contracts in 81 cities and found that deals in 72 cities included at least one of these barriers to police accountability. Of 14 states with police bills of right, 13 included one of these types of policy provisions. Collective bargaining agreements (these contracts) are meant to ensure that workers are treated fairly; however, it appears that these have crossed the line and disadvantaged citizens (Campaign Zero, 2016).

Where Do We Go From Here?

Fran Healy, a Philadelphia Police Department spokesperson (as cited in Balko, 2013, 333) said: "Officers' safety comes first, and not infringing on people's rights comes second."

As the above quote indicates quite clearly, the result of extending the rights and privileges of police officers is manifesting itself in the police-civilian encounter. The practice of interpreting the appropriate use of force permits the officer to shoot and kill a civilian if the officer believes the civilian has a gun. That practice seems to step beyond the law. For example, the Fourth Circuit Court in *Cooper v. Sheehan* held that it is the *threat* posed by the possession of a firearm that justifies the use of force, not the mere possession of a firearm. The court stated that Cooper, in this case, posed no threat, even though he held a gun. The gun was pointed toward the ground, he made no sudden moves, made no threats, and did not ignore the officer's commands (Lambert, 2013). It would seem that having a gun might pose a greater threat than reaching for something unseen and unannounced.

In some cases, a police officer has avoided prosecution for an extrajudicial killing because he feared that the person was reaching for an imaginary gun. This assumption is a privilege not usually granted in a civilian-to-civilian encounter. It is extremely unlikely that citizen A would be excused for shooting and killing citizen B if he offered the excuse that he feared that citizen B was reaching for a gun—when there was no gun. It would appear that by providing the officer that privilege he or she is given more rights than a civilian, meaning that an officer's life is more important than a civilian's. The very opposite should be true. Police officers, like soldiers, lay their life on the line for citizens. That is a principal reason they are revered.

If the intended situation is to place the police officer's life equal to that of the civilian, we need to make these rules clear and have police practices conform. If the intent is to value the police officer's life as greater, we need to debate this issue in public and the courts. A large proportion of the citizenry might object to that orientation as a cultural practice.

NOTE

1. The term "black" is used to include other blacks as well as African Americans as much of the data does not make a distinction.

REFERENCES

Apuzzo, M., and Liptak, A. (2015, April 21). *At Supreme Court, Eric Holder's Justice Department Routinely Backs Officers' Use of Force.* Retrieved from New York Times: https://www.nytimes.com/2015/04/22/us/at-supreme-court-holders-justice-dept-routinely-backs-officers-use-of-force.html?_r=0

Balko, R. (2013). *Rise of the Warrior Cop: The Militarization of America's Police Forces.* New York, NY: PublicAffairs.

Blank, R. M., M. Dabady, and C. F. Citro (eds). (2004). *Measuring Racial Discrimination*. Washington, DC: National Academies Press.

Campaign Zero. (2016). *Police Union Contracts and Police Bill of Rights Analysis.* Retrieved from Check the Police: http://checkthepolice.org/#project

Conyers Jr., J. (2015, April 22). *Congressman Conyers and Senator Ben Cardin Reintroduce The End Racial Profiling Act of 2015*. Retrieved from Congressman John Conyers, Jr.: https://conyers.house.gov/media-center/press-releases/congressman -conyers-and-senator-ben-cardin-reintroduce-end-racial

DeGue, S., Fowler, K.A., and Calkins, C. (2016, February). Deaths Due to Use of Lethal Forse by Law Enforcement. *American Journal of Preventive Medicine, 51*(5), S173-s187.

Dunn, R. A., and Reed, W. (2011). *Racial Profiling: Causes and Consequences.* Dubuque, IA: Kendall Hunt Publishing.

Eisen, A. (2016, March 6). *Update on 'Operation Ghetto Storm.'* Retrieved from Racial Justice Allies: http://www.racialjusticeallies.org/update-on-operation-ghetto -storm/

Extrano's Alley. (2014). *US Murder Conviction Rate*. Retrieved from http://extrano salley.com/us-murder-conviction-rate/

Final Report of the President's Task Force on 21st Century Policing. (2015). Retrieved from Community Oriented Policing Services, US Department of Justice: https://cops.usdoj.gov/pdf/taskforce/TaskForce_FinalReport.pdf

Gabbidon, S. L., and Greene, H. T. (2013). *Race and Crime.* Thousand Oaks, CA: Sage Publishing.

Graham v. Connor, 87–6571 (US Supreme Court 1989).

The Guardian. (2016). *The Counted*. Retrieved from https://www.theguardian.com/ us-news/2015/de/31/the-counted-police-killings-2015-young-black-men.

Hanzlick, R., Combs, D., Parrish, R., and Ing, R. (1993). Death Investigation in the United States, 1990: A Survey of Statutes, Systems, and Educational Requirements. *Journal Forensic Science, 38(3)*, 628–632.

Harmon, R. A. (2009, December). Promoting Civil Rights Through Proactive Policing Reform. *Stanford Law Review, 62*(1), 1–68. Retrieved from http://www.jstor .org/stable/40379719?seq=1#page_scan_tab_contents

Harris, D. (2002). *Profiles in Injustice: Why Racial Profiling Cannot Work.* New York, NY: The New Press.

Krieger, N., Kiang, M., Chen, J., and Waterman, P. (2015). Trends in US Deaths Due to Legal Intervention among Black and White Men, Age 15–34 Years, by County Income Level: 1960–2010. *Harvard Public Health Review, 3.*

Lambert, W.B. (2013). *Cooper v. Sheehan*, No. 13–1071 (2013). Retrieved from http://sclawreview.org/cooper-v-sheehan-13–1071/

Loftin, C., Wiersema, B., McDowell, D., and Dorbin, A. (2003, July). Underreporting of Justifiable Homicides Committed by Police Officers in the United States, 1976–1998. *American Journal of Public Health, 93*(7), 1117–1121.

Mapping Police Violence. (2016). Retrieved from https://mappingpoliceviolence.org.

Mathis, D. (2002). *Yet a Stranger: Why Black Americans Still Don't Feel at Home.* New York, NY: Grand Central Publishing.

Murder Accountability Project. (2016). *Homicides Reports for 2015 Now Available.* Retrieved from http://www.murderdata.org/

National Research Council. (2004). *Measuring Racial Discrimination* (R. M. Blank, M. Dabady, & C. F. Citro, Eds.). Washington, DC: The National Academies Press.

Ogletree, C. (2010). *The Presumption of Guilt: The Arrest of Henry Louis Gates, Jr. and Race.* New York, NY: Palgrave-MacMillan.

Raasch, C. (2017, March 1). *Sessions Signals Justice Deparmtent Will 'Pull Back' on Civil Rights Suits against Police Departments.* Retrieved from RawStory: http://www.rawstory.com/2017/03/sessions-signals-justice-department-will-pull-back-on-civil-rights-suits-against-police-departments/

Scott v. Harris, 05–1631 (U.S. Supreme Court 2007).

Sikora, A. G., & Mulvihill, M. (2002, May). Trends in Mortality Due to Legal Intervention in the United States. *American Journal of Public Health, 92*(5), 841–843.

Tennenbaum, A. N. (1994). The Influence of the Garner Decision on Police Use of Deadly Forse. *Journal of Criminal Law and Criminology, 85*(1), 241–260.

Tennessee v. Garner, 471 U.S. 1 (US Supreme Court 1985).

Thompson, R. M. (2015) *Police Use of Force: Rules, Remedies, and Reforms.* Washington, DC: Congressional Research Service.

Walker, S., Spohn, C., & Delone, M. (2012). *The Color of Justice: Race, Ethnicity, and Crime in America* (5th ed.). Belmont, CA: Wadsworth, Cengage Learning.

Zack, N. (2015). *White Privilege and Black Rights: The Injustice of U.S. Police Racial Profiling and Homicide.* Lanham, MD: Rowman and Littlefield.

Chapter Three

The Psychological Impact of Policing on African American Students

Ashley N. Hurst, Marlon L. Bailey,
Nolan T. Krueger, Ramya Garba,
and Kevin Cokley

For years, there has been an uneven and often contentious relationship between the police and black communities. Police brutality and murder of black people is not a recent phenomenon. The beating of Rodney King, brutalization of Abner Louima, and shooting death of Amadou Diallo during the 1990s were symbols of racial tensions and police brutality in the black community. Especially in the case of Rodney King, the evidence captured on video confirmed what many in the black community had known all along about the harsh and often deadly treatment black people experienced at the hands of the police (Lopez, 2016). Social media, the use of advanced technology (e.g., cell phones and dash cameras), and news outlets now provide constant exposure to instances of police brutality against black people. The death of Trayvon Martin in 2012 and the acquittal of his murderer prompted three black women to create #BlackLivesMatter, which has grown into the Black Lives Matter (BLM) movement that focuses on, among other things, the racial inequality of policing. Subsequent high-profile deaths of black individuals at the hands of police have sparked a new era of black student activism.[1] These experiences of state-sanctioned police violence against black people represent manifestations of institutional racism, where policies and practices by a social institution (e.g., law enforcement) disproportionately target and harm black people. While resistance to institutional racism is a normal, adaptive, and healthy response, little is known about the psychological impact that discriminatory policing has on African American students.[2] Surprisingly, very little research has been conducted on this topic.

To address this issue, police shootings of black people must be placed in context. The current number of black people killed by police in 2017 is 62 ("National Police Shootings," n.d.). In 2016 the total number of black people killed by police was 233 ("National Police Shootings," n.d.). These incidents are not only devastating because of the lives lost, but also because of how common the nature of this phenomenon is. Among the barrage of social and political issues that assault people of color, state-sanctioned violence against black people continues to take a harmful psychological toll on the black community. This chapter will facilitate a more nuanced understanding of the impact of this violence on black students by first tracing the roots of policing as one of the many tools used to perpetuate systemic oppression and control. Additionally, we explore the impact of policing on mental health for black people as well as the ways in which black people respond to these experiences, with a focus on black students.

HISTORY AND CURRENT
MANIFESTATION OF POLICING

While the beating of Rodney King captured national attention and sparked a national conversation on race and police brutality, in reality a contentious relationship between black citizens and law enforcement has festered throughout much of American history. Slavery saw the repression of black potential using overseers, the surveillance of slaves to prevent escape, and the return of escaped slaves. In the decades following slavery, authorities adapted and translated their brutal protocol for controlling slaves into the oppressive law enforcement practices known as Jim Crow. These practices maintained both social stratification and segregation, all the while reinforcing African American's status as inferior citizens. Terrorist tactics such as lynching and cross-burnings were common practice, both for police officers as well as white citizens emboldened by law enforcement's laissez-faire policy on protecting black Americans (Jeffries, 2001). White citizens were even deputized for the sole purpose of monitoring black people (McVeigh & Cunningham, 2012).

Between 1865 and the mid-1900s, the Ku Klux Klan contributed to thousands of murders and assaults of black people (Equal Justice Initiative, 2015). One estimate totals the number to over 4,000 lynchings of black people by the KKK between 1877 and 1950 (Equal Justice Initiative, 2015). Despite the illegality of the Klan's actions, these incidents were mostly ignored by law enforcement at the time (Sewell, Horsford, Coleman, & Watkins, 2016). Lynchings provided white supremacists a tool to inflict psychological wounds[3] and traumatize the black community.

When the civil rights era began in the mid-1950s, the relationship between black citizens and law enforcement remained volatile. In 1968 and 1969, violent encounters between black students and police occurred during a four-and-a-half-month-long student strike at San Francisco State University

(Thompson, 2004). Police in southern states had begun engaging in brutal suppression efforts targeting peaceful black protesters and actively encroaching on their 1st, 14th, and 15th amendment rights to assemble, protest, speak freely, and vote. Law enforcement's methods included dog attacks, firehosing, and intimidation, to name but a few of the savage tactics employed. Similarly, law enforcement employed hyper-surveillance[4] of prominent black figures and organizations (Sewell et al., 2016).

After the civil rights movement, law enforcement priorities, guided by federal policy, increased vigilance against drug offenses. This resulted in mass arrests and incarceration of black people. Black men, especially, were targeted creating dire situations for black families and communities (Goode, 2002). Historically and to the present, the relationship between black people and law enforcement has been marked by racialized or disproportionate policing, arrests, surveillance, injury, and fatal actions by law enforcement (Alexander, 2011). For example, there is a 21 times greater chance that a black male will be fatally shot by police than his white counterpart (Gabrielson, Jones, & Sagara, 2014). In 1991, Rodney King was brutally beaten by several white officers. The beating was captured on video, and all the officers involved were acquitted, sparking the LA Riots (Medina, 2012). In 2010, after the acquittal of George Zimmerman on charges of murder for killing Trayvon Martin, race again became very salient and the emergence of social media and prevalence of cameras made the ability to record police brutality easier. Since then, a number of incidences of police killing unarmed African Americans have been filmed and shared via media (CNN, 2017). In many of the cases, reminiscent to the injustice of the acquittals of the officers in the Rodney King beating, officers filmed killing unarmed black men were acquitted or never charged with a crime. This sense of injustice exacerbates the anxiety experienced when African Americans encounter the police.

FEAR

George Zimmerman's murder of 17-year-old Trayvon Martin in February of 2012 and his subsequent acquittal of murder charges in July of 2013 ignited strong protest throughout the country. Many felt that, considering the details and circumstances of Trayvon's death, Zimmerman's acquittal was unfathomable and, when it occurred, a significant amount of people were pained with sadness at what was (and is still) considered by many a miscarriage of justice. Zimmerman was not an official law enforcement agent, but claimed to be acting as the neighborhood watch. The case primed the country to consider how race contributed to the hardships and danger that black citizens and especially young black men feel. Shortly after the murder of Trayvon, as racialized tension was at a high level for the country, a string of stories, some with video footage, about police killing unarmed black men pervaded the airways (Bonilla & Rosa, 2015).

As news of the unarmed killings of African Americans by police officers intermittently dominated the news cycle, black people and especially students, who see themselves in the young black victims, attempted to reconcile the idea of the police as peacekeepers with the fear that was provoked by videos and stories that could be seen on media outlets. Parents feared for their children, and family members were especially fearful that black sons, brothers, and fathers could become victims of police violence. Historical mistrust and fear toward police became deeper for many and more pervasive. What may have previously been an innocuous encounter with police, such as walking past an officer on the street, became more likely to engender fear and paranoia. What would have previously just been an uncomfortable or unpleasant experience of being pulled over by an officer became a situation that begets questions of profiling and survival (Brooms & Perry, 2016).

Black students began to struggle with how to survive police encounters because of the variety of circumstances in which police claimed black lives. These circumstances ranged from when individuals were already cuffed and sitting on the ground,[5] to when individuals were seemingly obeying police orders,[6] or were not given a chance to comply with police orders[7] before they were shot. As a result, the chant "hands up don't shoot" became a rallying cry symbolically referring to the injustice of violent acts against black individuals in even the most innocuous positions. Increasing the painful encounter and sense of injustice, often the officers are acquitted of charges, given short sentences, or charges are never filed (Brooms & Perry, 2016; Okafor, 2015).

While fatalities at the hands of the police garnered the most attention, it is important to note that the justice system's interactions with African Americans include: disproportionate targeting, excessive sentencing, and mistreatment during incarceration. These patterns contribute to the discomfort and fear experienced by African American students. Indeed, state-sanctioned police violence and the resulting fear and vulnerability have a significant negative psychological impact among this population.

MENTAL HEALTH CONSEQUENCES

As the previous sections have explored, the presence and implementation of policing constitutes a significant stressor on African American students. One area of research has focused on the frequency and the mental health impact of police interactions. While African American college students do not, on average, represent those that are most targeted by police, they report the highest frequency of physical contact and fear of coming into contact with police (Landers, Rollock, Rolfes, & Moore, 2011). This fear is substantiated by statistics showing that the highest arrest rate is accounted for by those between the ages of 15 and 24. Besides the commonality of age within this population, black college students are very diverse in terms of their backgrounds, geographic locations, and socioeconomic statuses (US Department of Justice, Office of Justice Programs, Bureau of Justice Statistics, 1999, 2002a, 2002b). Police violence exacts a tremendous toll on the psychological well-being of black students through both direct (e.g., police contact, presence, and arrest) and indirect channels (e.g., perpetuation of stereotypes and witnessing of police violence shared on social media).

A review of the literature indicates that just having contact with the police has significant negative mental health impacts (Sewell et al., 2016). For example, in a study conducted by Landers and colleagues (2011), findings revealed that African American men reported greater degrees of stress from contact with police. Other studies have found that individuals who report having a negative experience with the police endorse higher levels of psychological distress and physical illnesses (e.g., Langan, Greenfield, Smith, Durose, & Levin, 2001; Durose, Schmitt, & Langan, 2005). This could be caused by the effects of stress that have been found to have prolonged and cumulative mental health consequences for African Americans from all socioeconomic statuses (Carter, 2007; Smedley, Stith, & Nelson, 2003; as cited in Sewell et al., 2016). One of these consequences includes depressive symptoms; African Americans have been found to experience depressive symptoms at the highest rate, 12.8 percent, out of whites, Latinx, and other ethnic groups (DHHS, 2010; as cited in Sewell et al., 2016). Another consequence is the experience of post-traumatic symptoms, which occur at higher rates for people of color compared to other ethnic groups in reaction to traumatic events (Carter, 2007; as cited in Sewell et al., 2016).

Soldiers at war face chronic exposure to indirect and explicit danger. They often witness others being hurt or killed, while facing the ubiquitous threat of being hurt or killed as well. They often find themselves in a perpetual state of hypervigilance. Over time, the cumulative effects of such conditions often lead to psychological trauma in the form of post-traumatic stress disorder, or PTSD. PTSD is a psychological disorder characterized by extended hypervigilance, emotional distress, and intrusive traumatic memories, to name a few (Solomon, Mikulincer, & Waysman, 1991). Research has found that after exposure to traumatic events, 20–40 percent of people of color experience more symptoms of PTSD in comparison to 5–10 percent of the rest of the population (Carter, 2007; as cited by Sewell et al., 2016). While the literature has documented the detrimental impacts of trauma on children and adolescents (Reviere, 1996; Terr, 1990; as cited in Jernigan & Daniel, 2011), there is a gap in the literature exploring racial discrimination as traumatic experiences.

In the past, clinicians utilizing the DSM-IV-TR[8] were not able to adequately account for symptoms of PTSD within clients due to the narrow criteria included in the diagnostic manual, particularly because racial discrimination may not be primarily physical. Previous literature has identified how schools are major sources of racial discrimination which could be traumatic, including teacher-student interactions, punishment practices, and prevalence of racist incidents (e.g., Irvine, 1986; Hurtado & Carter, 1997; Mattison & Aber, 2007; as cited in Jernigan & Daniel, 2011). Therefore, more research on black student's experiences of PTSD is needed, especially more implicit forms including being in the presence of police. Currently, diagnoses of PTSD do not account for the particular accumulation of experiences of trauma that occur as the result of racism (Jernigan & Daniel, 2011). This limitation must be addressed because, for people of color, contact with the police can be a potentially traumatic experience if they attribute the aversive encounters to race. This type of interaction can be classified as a type of racial harassment that involves feelings, thoughts, actions, strategies, behaviors, or policies that reinforce the subordinate position of people of color in a white supremacist system in our country (Carter, 2007; as cited in Sewell et al., 2016). This type of harassment perpetuates institutional racist practices and forces targets to "fall into line" as a condition of continued social participation; individuals may fear repercussions of reporting acts of racism (Carter, 2007; as cited in Sewell et al., 2016). Similarly, chronic exposure to racialized threats vis à vis racial profiling, police brutality, and the mass criminalization of African Americans results in what some scholars refer to as racial battle fatigue.

Racial battle fatigue (RBF) is an interdisciplinary theoretical framework for examining the cumulative effects of racism on racially marginalized groups. According to William Smith (2004, 2008a, 2008b, 2010), RBF is the psychological-physiological response to the constant, front-line racial battles that people of color face in a historically racist society. On the psychological level, RBF is characterized by, but not limited to, anxiety, irritability, shock, helplessness (Seligman, 1975), and fear; on the physiological level, it is characterized by insomnia, high blood pressure, gastric distress, and muscle aches, to name a few physiological symptoms (Smith, Yosso, & Solórzano, 2006). In a qualitative study on misandric microaggressions and RBF (Smith, Mustaffa, Jones, Curry, & Allen, 2016), black males attending predominantly white institutions reported experiencing RBF as a result of constantly being treated as illegitimate members of their campus communities. For example, many black males reported several run-ins with law enforcement. One Harvard University student shared the following anecdote:

> At one point, my friend and I were coming back from Wayne Paterson University, the school in New Jersey. We were coming back on the highway about 11:00 at night from a party. We were pulled over for allegedly speeding. The state trooper said we were going at least 70 and he had to go all the way up to 65 in order to catch us. So, we immediately were like 'What?' And he then went back to his car, ran my friend's plates and the next thing there were six patrol cars there. They took us out of the car, patted us down, searched the car, and found nothing. *There was nothing to find* . . . (Smith et al., 2016, 9).

In each account, the students reported similar psychological responses such as frustration, shock, avoidance/withdrawal, disbelief, anger, defensiveness, uncertainty/confusion, resentment, anxiety, helplessness, hopelessness, and fear. Moreover, they unanimously perceived the college environment as much more hostile and unwelcoming toward black males than any other group. However, the results of multiethnic empirical studies suggest that both black males and females struggle to survive academically while battling against racism (Allen & Solórzano, 2001; Swim, Hyers, Cohen, Fitzgerald, & Bylsma, 2003). Thus, in addition to the aforementioned psychological effects of racism, black students are also indirectly affected by police through the maintenance of stereotypes and consistent exposure to police violence.

According to Smith's model, "stereotype threat" is one of several cognitive-behavioral manifestations of racial battle fatigue (Smith et al., 2006). Originally coined by prominent black psychologist, Claude Steele, stereotype threat is defined as being at risk of confirming a negative stereotype about one's group, such as the widely held belief that blacks are intellectually inferior to whites (Steele & Aronson, 1995). In this study, Steele helped explain historically disparate levels of academic performance between blacks and their white counterparts. Through a controlled experiment, they found that exposure to negative racial stereotypes (i.e., that blacks are better suited as criminal suspects than scholars) undermines their academic performance through disruptive cognitive-behavioral processes (i.e., anxious thought streams and/or reduced working memory) (Steele & Aronson, 1995). They also found that one need not believe or internalize the negative stereotype in order to experience stereotype threat; rather, the individual just has to believe that his or her performance may be judged through the lens of a negative in-group stereotype. For instance, when high-achieving black students believed their exam performance (27 items from the verbal section of the Graduate Record Examination) was not diagnostic, they performed comparably to their white counterparts. However, when they believed their performance was diagnostic of their (negatively stereotyped) intelligence, their scores were lower than their white peers (after the experimenters controlled for prior SAT scores) (Steele & Aronson, 1995).

In essence, Steele and other scholars found that when made salient, mere membership of a heavily stereotyped racial group may result in higher levels of anxiety, reduced working memory, and, ultimately, lower academic performance among black students (Steele & Aronson, 1995; Hutchison, Smith, & Ferris, 2013), and it may also result in more pronounced feelings of isolation and inferiority among black students in primarily white institutions (Walton & Cohen, 2007; Purdie-Vaughns, Steele, Davies, Ditlmann, & Crosby, 2008). Thus, the racial battle fatigue framework, including the "stereotype threat effect," asserts that African American college students, in comparison to their white counterparts, are unjustly placed under increased surveillance by community and local policing tactics on and off campus. Moreover, black male students, in particular, are often viewed and treated as "out of place" and "fitting the description" of illegitimate members of primarily white campus communities (Smith, Allen, & Danley, 2007, 1). In addition to the perpetuation of these harmful perceptions, black students have to also contend with consistent exposure to police violence distributed through social media platforms.

While increased coverage and connectedness create conditions for powerful healing to take place within and across black communities, it is also important to acknowledge the psychological risk factors at play when coverage of police brutality is widespread and pervasive. Continuous exposure to images of black and brown bodies lying lifeless in the street can have detrimental effects on the mental health of black Americans, particularly those who have not experienced the violence directly, but are nonetheless influenced by the publicized content. Black students fall into this category. The compound effect of continuous exposure to both video footage and ongoing social media posts discussing police violence can affect how young black students process fear and discrimination. In other words, young black students look to social media as a barometer of racism in the United States (Nellis & Savage, 2012), which can trigger a sense of shared vulnerability that "many African Americans have some level of psychological consciousness about the potential physical and psychic danger of living in a society that has a history of racial animus toward them" (Aymer, 2013, 134). Considering the context of these mental health consequences, the pervasiveness of social justice activism can be understood through the lens of both healthy and unhealthy coping strategies adopted in response to this continued state-sanctioned violence by the police.

ACTIVISM AS A HEALTHY COPING STRATEGY

As previously reviewed, state-sanctioned violence at the hands of law enforcement has threatened black Americans since slavery (Hawkins & Thomas, 1991) and continues to inform African American identity and feature prominently in the black lived experience. One of the most important responses to these injustices has been social justice activism. The mention of black activism often draws audiences to the civil rights movement where notable activists like Dorothy Height, Martin Luther King Jr., Rosa Parks, and John Lewis often surrendered themselves to the justice system stating "we shall overcome" in order to bring attention to unjust laws and unjust law enforcement. Subsequent activism often focused on the self-determination of black people through the Black Power movement and the Black Panthers. Similarly, the movement saw government vilification by the Nixon administration and police departments around the country. Black activism was recently reinvigorated after the publicity surrounding the murder of Trayvon Martin by George Zimmerman and a number of murders of unarmed black individuals by police officers. Furthermore, there's a long history of student activism. Among prominent examples are the Woolworth's sit-ins in 1960 completed by college-age activists, the Kent State protest in 1970, and the protest by the 2015–2016 University of Missouri football team. Activism creates an opportunity for students to involve themselves in a societal change process and to seek solidarity with people who share their passion for change. Perpetuating the injustice, neither Zimmerman, nor many of the police responsible for killing unarmed black men, was dealt any punishment for their actions. Participating in activism can lead to societal changes, but also has the potential to affect the individual.

Sociopolitical control, or the belief that social and political actions can lead to desirable outcomes, was found to limit negative consequences of helplessness on mental health for young African Americans (Zimmerman, Ramirez-Valez, & Maton, 1999). Similarly, according to Klar and Kasser (2009), conventional activism is associated with higher psychological well-being. Self-identifying as an activist and participating in or intending to participate in activist behavior led participants to report increased well-being and greater likelihood to experience satisfaction of basic psychological needs and human flourishing (Klar & Kasser, 2009; Keyes, 2002).

Social media platforms have become a place to share not only details of your individual and social life, but also details of your personal, political, and social ideologies. These platforms have become a place to state opinions on social issues and politicians. These comments relay the alliances, grievances, or humor that may or may not reflect one's endorsement or begin discourse.

Social media could also be considered a means to promote traditional forms of protest by helping to connect people online and notify them of offline demonstrations (Valenzuela, 2013). Social media can and is often the way students prefer to engage politically (Smith, 2013). Social media activism can also be primarily online; for example, some use platforms to voice dissent directly to the companies, politicians, or source of the issue. These comments sections are sometimes a place to find like-minded individuals or sources with differing opinions creating cognitive dissonance for formerly one-sided participators (Ciszek, 2016). Similarly, social media activism can be a way of voicing dissent or correcting or emphasizing the bias of other media (Bonilla & Rosa, 2015). One other important factor is that social media platforms are also a place that people with the same passion form a collective identity. It is on these social media platforms that, for example, people angered by police violence toward black individuals voiced their grievances as a part of the larger collective identity "Black Lives Matter" (Gerbaudo & Trere, 2015).

Activism is an outlet for black students to give voice to their feelings and combat racial trauma associated with exposure to police brutality. Sociopolitical awareness and activism builds critical consciousness and may decrease internalized oppression (Watts, Griffith, & Abdul-Adil, 1999). Thus, activism in itself is a way of coping with the deleterious effects described earlier in this chapter. Utilizing social media as a means of activism has become a novel, yet common, method for participating in activism. Social media's prominence within activism was created by the emergence of technology that allowed people to witness the unjustified violence against unarmed African Americans.

EMERGENCE OF TECHNOLOGY

The contemporary sociopolitical and cultural atmosphere surrounding police brutality has been transforming. Fatal shootings and violent attacks on black Americans are being recorded by civilians using handheld devices, police officers wearing body cameras, and law enforcement vehicles equipped with dashboard cameras. Despite the ACLU's recommendations that law enforcement release footage to any individuals they capture on video, there is no clear-cut legal precedent requiring police to make these recordings public (BBC News, 2016; Stanley, 2013). Nevertheless, public pressure can lead law enforcement to release footage, as in the case of Keith Lamont Scott.[9] In other cases, a judge can order the release of video footage, as in the case of Laquan McDonald.[10] Even more commonly, civilians are recording and disseminating incidents of police brutality on major social media platforms such as Facebook, Twitter, and YouTube. These new trends in police account-ability, civilian journalism, and social media constitute a departure from the traditional standards of practice that limited documentation to police officers' written and verbal accounts, and limited coverage and broadcasting to main-stream media news outlets.

The late 2000s brought dynamic, user-generated content to the internet and inspired the growth of bottom-up, grassroots news circulation through social media platforms like Twitter and Facebook. In previous decades, top-down news media outlets enjoyed monopolized power over how news was publicized and presented. This follows from "guard dog theory," which suggests that mass media determines the news and how it should be covered based on an agenda that protects the status quo (McCombs & Shaw, 1972). In the United States, that status quo is white supremacy. Not surprisingly, mass media's widespread and powerful influence has had direct bearing on the public's conceptualization of race, crime, and law enforcement. When an incident involves African Americans and the police, African Americans are more likely than whites to be portrayed as criminals (Dixon & Linz, 2000).

The 2009 murder of Oscar Grant sparked a massive sea change in the complex relationship between police brutality in black communities and how these violent, often fatal, acts are publicized. Oscar Grant, an unarmed 22-year-old black man, was shot to death on New Year's Eve by Bay Area Rapid Transit police officer Johannes Mehserle. Several individuals in a crowd of bystanders captured the murder using phones equipped with video-recording capabilities. Despite officers' attempts to confiscate onlookers' cell phones, raw footage of the shooting was uploaded to video-sharing websites such as YouTube within hours. These unstable, lo-fi recordings were eventu-ally used to convict Mehserle of manslaughter. In the aftermath of Grant's death, user-driven social media platforms and video-sharing websites circu-lating footage of Grant's murder became intense mediums and outlets for expression, communication, and organization (Antony & Thomas, 2010). This outcry was the first in a line of increasingly fervent, widespread social media responses to state-sanctioned violence in black communities across the United States.

Despite clear benefits for communities of color and victims of police bru-tality, civilian journalism is not without risk. The Supreme Court has yet to set definitive legal precedent protecting the right to record law enforcement (Potere, 2012). The US Court of Appeals for the First Circuit wrote that "rea-sonable restrictions on the exercise of the right to film may be imposed when the circumstances justify them." The key word in this excerpt, *reasonable*, bestows the power of interpretation upon law enforcement, leaving civilians vulnerable (Volokh, 2014). Even if civilians are not penalized directly, they may be targeted for retaliation. Some might suggest this was the case with Ramsey Orta, the man who filmed the death of Eric Garner.[11] Orta was arrested and charged with gun possession only two weeks after Garner's death.

The rise of civilian journalism in response to the murder of Oscar Grant played a critical role not only in black communities, but the public at large by reawakening the nation en masse to law enforcement's unchecked and excessive use of force against unarmed black individuals. Raw footage of police brutality spread through the powerful conduit of social media and began to force the mass media needle away from biased underreporting that vilified black Americans, toward a more watch-dog approach representing the interests of the populace (Antony & Thomas, 2010).

Social media platforms, with YouTube and Facebook at the fore, have begun to emerge in black communities as powerful forums for collectively processing and expressing solidarity in response to acts of police violence across the country (Bonilla & Rosa, 2015). Chronic profiling, harassment, police violence, and underreporting all create learned helplessness[12] in black communities (Burke, Clavesilla, D'Eloia, & Hinckley, n.d.). Social media, however, mitigates learned helplessness by facilitating a level of intercommunal connectedness for black Americans that, in past decades, simply was not possible. In response to Trayvon Martin's slaying, for instance, the hashtag #HoodiesUp became a widely circulated symbol protesting the pervasive and discriminatory practice of racial profiling that played a major role in Martin's death (Bonilla & Rosa, 2015). At the same time, thousands of black Facebook users began changing their profile pictures to depict themselves wearing hooded sweatshirts accompanied by the hashtag #WeAreTrayvonMartin, which caught fire as a powerful symbol of solidarity. Mass showings such as these counteract learned helplessness and feelings of powerlessness by allowing geographically distant groups to share their pains, fears, and enthusiasms in the fight for social justice (Paik, 2014). Social media has fostered a connectedness capable of empowering movements.

In addition to major psychological ramifications for black Americans, both positive and negative, advanced technology and the emergence of social media have also stimulated large-scale protest and activism. The rise in citizen journalism (and subsequent introduction of dash cams in police cars and body cams on police officers) has not only transformed how police violence is documented, but has focused the national microscope on the discrepancy between excessive use of force in black communities, and the chronic, predictable lack of repercussions for those officers involved (Aymer, 2016; Wheeler, 2016). Contemporary authorized police brutality in black communities mirrors the state-sanctioned lynchings of the 19th and 20th centuries (Petersen & Ward, 2015) and bears eerie resemblance to cases such as the brutalization and murder of Emmett Till[13] in which both his killers were acquitted. Civilian journalism holds a spotlight on the US criminal justice system's continual failure to hold law enforcement accountable for the excessive use of force against unarmed black individuals. For example, bystander footage was clearly instrumental in Johannes Mehserle's manslaughter conviction, but he ultimately served only 146 days behind bars for what many in the black community and beyond viewed as a cold-blooded public execution. Fast-forward three years to February 2012, George Zimmerman shoots and kills Trayvon Martin, a 17-year-old unarmed black boy walking home from a nearby convenience store. Similarly, Zimmerman was eventually acquitted of all charges. In the interim between the Grant and Martin shooting, however, social media had become firmly cemented as a powerfully influential, impactful, and dynamic forum for exposing and protesting state-sanctioned violence in communities of color. Social media has provided the platform for a deeply frustrated, outraged, and fearful black public to organize collectively and begin demanding accountability for the violence that law enforcement has perpetrated on black and brown bodies for centuries.

In response to the Trayvon Martin slaying, black activists Alicia Garza, Patrisse Cullors, and Opal Tometi managed to tap into and utilize social media's potency by channeling the platform's potential political energy into kinetic political energy under the twitter hashtag #BlackLivesMatter. The #BlackLivesMatter movement called on black Americans to organize, resist, and fight back against the "systematic and intentional" targeting of black lives for demise (Garza, Tometi, & Cullors, 2014). Again in 2014, two independent police killings of unarmed black men took place, both within 30 days of one another. Eric Garner, 43, was choked to death by NYPD. Michael Brown, 18, was fatally shot by a police officer in Ferguson, Missouri. In both cases, the officers responsible were acquitted. These highly publicized incidents of police brutality inspired the viral hashtag #ferguson and contributed significantly to the heightened fervor of the #BlackLivesMatter movement. In fact, preliminary evidence suggests that the interplay of advanced technology and activist efforts may be inspiring substantive changes to longstanding precedents in the American criminal justice system.

On October 20, 2014, Chicago police officer Jason Van Dyke fired 16 rounds into LaQuan McDonald, an African American high-school student. The shooting was captured by Van Dyke's dashboard camera and, following its release, sparked impassioned protests from Chicago's black community. The protests continued for over four months and, ultimately, Van Dyke was charged with first-degree murder. The case marked the first time in nearly 35 years that a Chicago police officer had been charged with first-degree murder for an on-duty fatality (Gorner, Sweeney, & Meisner, 2015). In the summer of

2016, officer Jeronimo Yanez shot and killed Philando Castile, a black Minnesota native. Though armed, Castile was legally permitted to own and carry a firearm. Before reaching for his identification, Castile notified the officer but suffered seven deadly shots from Yanez. Castile's girlfriend, Diamond Reynolds, bore witness to the tragic incident. In Castile's final moments, she began recording and live streaming a video to the social media platform Facebook. Almost immediately, Castile's death sparked massive protests across the nation. Officer Yanez was ultimately charged with second-degree manslaughter, the first Minnesotan officer charged for a fatal shooting in more than 200 cases spanning over 30 years (Collins, Feshir, & Nelson, 2016). However, hope that there would finally be justice in an unjustified extrajudicial police killing was lost in June 2017 when a jury acquitted Yanez of all charges in the shooting. In spite of this disappointing outcome, witnessing new judicial precedents that champion black lives and hold officers accountable for their actions may imbue black students with a sense of control and help combat the powerlessness and helplessness that so many experience daily. It is important to recognize that while there are several ways people demonstrate their resilience through healthy coping strategies, the harm caused by these events can also potentially lead to more aversive responses.

UNHEALTHY COPING STRATEGIES

Alternatively, there are ways that people cope with the stressors of injustice that could be considered unhealthy for the individuals themselves and what some envision as the movement's purpose. For example, after Darren Wilson, a Ferguson, Missouri, police officer, shot teenager Michael Brown, Missouri's peaceful protest was accompanied by destruction of property and a dangerous scene of inflamed businesses and police cars. While a relatively small number of protesters took part in the destruction of property, the destruction diverted some attention from the cause of a portion of protestors. That said, the intensity of the protest may have inspired a deeper investigation into Ferguson by journalists resulting in the highlighting of a pattern of racial police enforcement discrepancies in the city (Opotow, 2016). Similarly, a generalized disdain for police that exemplifies itself at its worse in violence against police could potentially be an unhealthy way of coping and possibly counterproductive to the more popular activist causes. For example, in 2016 at a Black Lives Matter march in Dallas, Texas, Micah Johnson, a military veteran, targeted police officers, specifically killing five (Karimi, Shoichet, & Ellis, 2016).

Another method of unhealthy coping is substance use and abuse. Being subjected to news about police violence toward young black individuals including seeing videos of their deaths or their dead bodies can engender painful emotions or create what seems like an absence of emotion (Nellis & Savage, 2012). Substances can help individuals alleviate painful effects or cope with overwhelming or seemingly absent emotions (Khantzian, 1997). These unhealthy coping methods could be considered as behavioral representations of the negative mental health impacts elaborated on earlier in the chapter.

CONCLUSION

The need to understand the mental health impact of policing on black people cannot be emphasized more. While there is some debate regarding the intentions of individual police officers to cause unnecessary harm, research and scholarly analyses have revealed systemic policies and actions that result in disproportionate violence against black people. This chapter explored some of the ways this violence affects the mental health of black people, particularly of black students. Adopting the perspective in which social justice activism can be a coping strategy, the chapter investigated how various manifestations of activism, including increased awareness through the utilization of technology and protests, promote healing through individual actions and community building. However, this sense of awareness and activism can also exact a psychological toll that should be comprehensively addressed within these targeted communities. This chapter hopes to encourage more research on the mental health impacts of policing on black students. This objective would re-emphasize the need for a higher focus on the mental health needs of black students on university campuses, especially regarding the presence and utilization of police. Additionally, this information could help students decide, to the degree that they can, how they will consume and process news about police violence, including the degree of involvement in activism they will engage in. This chapter also calls on the agencies of law enforcement to thoroughly consider their role in providing support to black people. While proposing more training and awareness for police officers is a positive recommendation, dissecting the ways in which the historical origins of policing are being perpetuated is a necessary action that must be taken.

NOTES

1. Examples include increased awareness and discussion through social media platforms, Black Lives Matter movement, and other student-led marches, etc.
2. Research has found that the largest number of arrests are accounted by adolescents/young adults between the ages of 15 to 24; additionally, the greatest amount of fear of arrest is reported by those between the ages of 18 and 24 (US Department of Justice, Office of Justice Programs, Bureau of Justice Statistics, 1999, 2002a, 2002b).

In alignment with these statistics, our general reference to students will include the age range from 15 to 24 years old and those that are specifically within the higher education context are those from 18 to 24 year olds.

3. By psychological wounds the authors refer to the fear and anxiety experienced by the constant possibility of being a victim of public white violence.

4. Example, in 1963 the FBI (led by J. Edgar Hoover) was granted permission by Attorney General Robert Kennedy to break into Martin Luther King's and his associates phones and bug their homes and offices (Christensen, 2008).

5. For example, Oscar Grant (in Oakland, California) was shot while handcuffed on the ground (Kambon, 2015).

6. For example, Philando Castile (in St. Paul, Minnesota) was shot while attempting to produce an officer requested item (Capecchi & Smith, 2016).

7. For example, Tamir Rice (in Cleveland, Ohio) was shot within two seconds of an officer's arrival (Byrne, 2016).

8. The DSM-IV-TR refers to the *Diagnostic and Statistical Manual of Mental Disorders*, Fourth Edition (Text Revision) published by the American Psychological Association in 2000. This manual lists and classifies the criteria for mental disorders by mental health professionals.

9. Keith Lamont Scott (in Charlotte, North Carolina) was shot upon exiting his vehicle because he was allegedly armed. It was later found out that law enforcement had been searching for an unrelated man with an outstanding warrant (Shoichet, 2016).

10. Laquan McDonald (in Chicago, Illinois) was shot by law enforcement while carrying a knife and walking away from officers (Sanburn, 2015).

11. Eric Garner (in New York City, New York), an unarmed black man, was murdered after being put in a sustained chokehold by Officer Daniel Pantaleo despite repeated exclamations of "I can't breathe" (Okafor, 2015).

12. The theory of learned helplessness was formulated by Martin Seligman (1975), who proposed that if people are repeatedly exposed to situations in which they have no control, they will develop a sense that their ability to change a situation will be ineffective.

13. Emmett Till was a 14-year-old black boy lynched in Mississippi in 1955 for allegedly flirting with a white woman (Whitfield, 1991).

REFERENCES

Alexander, M. (2011). *The New Jim Crow*. New York, NY: New Press.

Allen, W., & Solórzano, D. (2001). Affirmative action, educational equity and campus racial climate: A case study of the university of Michigan Law School. *La Raza Law Journal, 12*, 237–363.

Antony, M. G., & Thomas, R. J. (2010). "This is citizen journalism at its finest": YouTube and the public sphere in the Oscar Grant shooting incident. *New Media & Society, 12*(8), 1280–1296.

Aymer, S. R. (2013). An Afrocentric approach to working with African American families. In E.P. Congress & M. J. González (Eds.), *Multicultural perspectives in social work practice with families* (3rd ed., 129–138). New York, NY: Springer Publishing Company.

Aymer, S. R. (2016). "I can't breathe": A case study—Helping black men cope with race-related trauma stemming from police killing and brutality. *Journal of Human Behavior in the Social Environment, 26*(3–4), 367–376.

BBC News. (2016, September 25). Police accountability: Why body cam footage is not always released. Retrieved 2017, from http://www.bbc.com/news/world-us-canada-37440114.

Bonilla, Y., and Rosa, J. (2015). #Ferguson: Digital protest, hashtag ethnography, and the racial politics of social media in the United States. *American Ethnologist, 42*, 4–17. doi:10.1111/amet.12112.

Brooms, D. R., & Perry, A. R. (2016). "It's simply because we're black men." *Journal Of Men's Studies, 24*(2), 166–184. doi:10.1177/1060826516641105.

Burke, M., Clavesilla, B., D'Eloia, G., Hinckley, M. (n.d.). Police violence and misuse of power [PowerPoint Slides]. Retrieved from https://web.csulb.edu/colleges/chhs/departments/social-work/documents/PoliceViolenceProject.pdf.

Byrne, M. (2016). The shooting of Tamir Rice. *Arena Magazine (Fitzroy, Vic), (140)*, 10–11.

Capecchi, C., & Smith, M. (2016). Officer who shot Philando Castile is charged with manslaughter. *The New York Times*. Retrieved from https://www.nytimes.com/2016/11/17/us/philando-castile-shooting-minnesota.html?_r=0.

Christensen, J. (2008, December 29). FBI tracked King's every move. CNN. Retrieved from http://www.cnn.com/2008/US/03/31/mlk.fbi.conspiracy/.

Ciszek, E. L. (2016). Digital activism: How social media and dissensus inform theory and practice. *Public Relations Review, 42*(2), 314–321. doi:10.1016/j.pubrev.2016.02.002.

CNN Library (2017, February, 14). Trayvon Martin shooting fast facts. *CNN Library.* Retrieved from http://www.cnn.com/2013/06/05/us/trayvon-martin-shooting-fast-facts/.

Collins, J., Feshir, R., Nelson, T. (2016, November 16). Officer charged in Castile shooting. NPR News. Retrieved from http://www.mprnews.org/story/2016/11/16/officer-charged-in-castile-shooting.

Dixon, T. L., & Linz, D. (2000). Overrepresentation and underrepresentation of African Americans and Latinos as lawbreakers on television news. *Journal of Communication, 50*(2), 131–154.

Durose, M. R., Schmitt, E. L., & Langan, P. A., Ph.D. (2005, April). Contacts between Police and the Public: Findings from the 2002 National Survey. Retrieved 2017, from https://www.bjs.gov/content/pub/pdf/cpp02.pdf.

Equal Justice Initiative. (2015). Retrieved from http://eji.org/reports/lynching-in-america.

Gabrielson, R., Jones, R. G., & Sagara, E. (2014, October 10). Deadly force, in black and white. *Propublica*. Retrieved from http://www.propublica.org/article/deadly-force-in-black-and-white.

Garza, A., Cullors, P., & Tometi, O. (2014). A herstory of the #BlackLivesMatter movement. *The Feminist Wire.* Retrieved from http://www.thefeministwire.com/2014/10/blacklivesmatter-2/.

Gerbaudo, P., & Trere, E. (2015). In search of the "we" of social media activism: Introduction to the special issue on social media and protest identities. *Information, Communication & Society, 18*(8), 865–871. doi:10.1080/1369118X.2015.1043319.

Goode, E. (2002). Drug arrests at the millennium. *Society, 39*(5), 41–45. doi:10.1007/BF02717543.

Gorner, J., Sweeney, A., & Meisner, J. (2015, November 23). Cop in dash-cam video to face murder charge. *The Chicago Tribune.* Retrieved from http://www.chicagotribune.com/news/ct-chicago-cop-shooting-video-laquan-mcdonald-charges-20151123-story.html.

Hawkins, H., & Thomas, R. (1991). White policing of black populations: A history of race and social control in America. In Cashmore and McLaughlin (Eds.), *Out of Order: Policing Black People* (65–86). London: Routledge.

Hutchison, K. A., Smith, J. L., & Ferris, A. (2013). Goals can be threatened to extinction: Using the stroop task to clarify working memory depletion under stereotype threat. *Social Psychological and Personality Science, 4*(1), 74–81.

Jeffries, J. L. (2001). Police brutality of black men and the destruction of the African-American community. *Negro Educational Review, 52*(4), 115–130.

Jernigan, M. M., & Daniel, J. H. (2011). Racial trauma in the lives of black children and adolescents: Challenges and implications. *Journal of Child & Adolescent Trauma, 4,* 123–141.

Kambon, M. (2015, February 25). Centuries of rage: The murder of Oscar Grant III. *San Francisco Bay View: National Black Newspaper.* Retrieved from http://sfbayview.com/2015/02/centuries-of-rage-the-murder-of-oscar-grant-iii/.

Karimi, F., Shoichet, C., Ellis, R., (2016). Dallas sniper attack, 5 officers killed, suspect identified, CNN. Retrieved from http://www.cnn.com/2016/07/08/us/philando-castile-alton-sterling-protests/.

Keyes, C. L. M. (2002). The mental health continuum: From languishing to flourishing in life. *Journal of Health and Social Behavior, 43,* 207–222.

Khantzian, E. J. (1997). The self-medication hypothesis of substance use disorders: A reconsideration and recent applications. *Harvard Review of Psychiatry, 4*(5), 231–244.

Klar, M., & Kasser, T. (2009). Some benefits of being an activist: Measuring activism and its role in psychological well-being. *Political Psychology, 30*(5), 755–777. doi:10.1111/j.1467–9221.2009.00724.x.

Landers, A. J., Rollock, D., Rolfes, C. D., & Moore, D. L. (2011). Police contacts and stress among African American college students. *American Journal of Orthopsychiatry, 81*(1), 72–81.

Langan, P. A., Ph.D., Greenfield, L. A., Smith, S. K., Ph.D., Durose, M. R., & Levin, D. J. (2001, February). Contacts between Police and the Public: Findings from the 1999 National Survey. Retrieved 2017, from https://www.bjs.gov/content/pub/pdf/cpp99.pdf.

Lopez, G. (2016). How video changed Americans' views toward the police, from Rodney King to Alton Sterling. *Justice Policy Institute.* Retrieved from http://www.justicepolicy.org/ news/10557.

McCombs, M. E., & Shaw, D. L. (1972). The agenda-setting function of mass media. *The Public Opinion Quarterly*, 36(2), 176–187. Retrieved 2017, from http://www.jstor.org/stable/2747787.

Medina, J. (2012, June, 17). Rodney King dies at 47; Police beating victim who asked "Can't We All Just Get Along?" *The New York Times.* Retrieved from http://www.nytimes.com/2012/06/18/us/rodney-king-whose-beating-led-to-la-riots-dead-at-47.html.

McVeigh, R., & Cunningham, D. (2012). Enduring consequences of right-wing extremism: Klan mobilization and homicides in southern counties. *Social Forces, 90*(3), 843–862. doi:10.1093/sf/sor007

National Police Shootings. (n.d.). *The Washington Post.* Retrieved from https://www.washingtonpost.com/graphics/national/police-shootings-2017/.

Nellis, A. M., & Savage, J. (2012). Does watching the news affect fear of terrorism? The importance of media exposure on terrorism fear. *Crime & Delinquency, 58*(5), 748–768.

Okafor, V. O. (2015). Trayvon Martin, Michael Brown, Eric Garner, et al.: A survey of emergent grassroots protests & public perceptions of justice. *The Journal of Pan African Studies* (Online), 7(8), 43–63.

Opotow, S. (2016). Protest and Policing: Conflict, Justice, and History in Ferguson, Missouri. In *Leading through Conflict: Into the fray* (pp. 155–178). New York: Palgrave McMillan. doi: https://doi.org/10.1007/978-1-137-56677-5_8.

Paik, S. (2014). Building bridges: Articulating Dalit and African American women's solidarity. *WSQ: Women's Studies Quarterly, 42*(3), 74–96.

Petersen, N., & Ward, G. (2015). The transmission of historical racial violence: Lynching, civil rights–era terror, and contemporary interracial homicide. *Race and Justice, 5*(2), 114–143.

Potere, M. (2012). Who will watch the watchers?: Citizens recording police conduct. *Northwestern University Law Review, 106*(1), 273–316.

Purdie-Vaughns, V., Steele, C., Davies, P. G., Ditlmann, R., & Crosby, J. R. (2008). Social identity contingencies: How diversity cues signal threat or safety for African Americans in mainstream institutions. *Journal of Personality and Social Psychology, 94*(4), 615–630.

Sanburn, J. (2015). Chicago releases video of Laquan McDonald shooting. *Time.* Retrieved from http://time.com/4126670/chicago-releases-video-of-laquan-mc donald-shooting/.

Seligman, M. E. P. (1975). *Helplessness: On depression, development, and death.* San Francisco: W. H. Freeman.

Sewell, W., Horsford, C. E., Coleman, K., & Watkins, C. S. (2016). Vile vigilance: An integrated theoretical framework for understanding the state of Black surveillance. *Journal of Human Behavior in the Social Environment, 26*(3–4), 287–302.

Shoichet, C. E. (2016). Keith Lamont Scott: What we know about man shot by Charlotte police. CNN. Retrieved from http://www.cnn.com/2016/09/22/us/keith -lamont-scott/.

Smith, W. A. (2004). Black faculty coping with racial battle fatigue: The campus racial climate in a post-civil rights era. In D. Cleveland (Ed.), *A long way to go: Conversations about race by African American faculty and graduate students* (171–190). New York, NY: Peter Lang.

Smith, W. A., Allen, W. R., & Danley, L. L. (2007). "Assume the Position . . . You Fit the Description": Psychosocial experiences and racial battle fatigue among African American male college students. *American Behavioral Scientist, 51*(4), 551–578.

Smith, W. A., Mustaffa, J. B., Jones, C. M., Curry, T. J., & Allen, W. R. (2016). "You make me wanna holler and throw up both my hands!": Campus culture, black misandric microaggressions, and racial battle fatigue. *International Journal of Qualitative Studies in Education, 29*(9), 1189–1209.

Smith, W. A. (2008a). Campus wide climate: Implications for African American students. In L. Tillman (Ed.), *A handbook of African American education* (297–309). Thousand Oaks, CA: Sage.

Smith, W. A. (2008b). Higher education: Racial battle fatigue. In R. T. Schaefer (Ed.), *Encyclopedia of race, ethnicity, and society* (615–618). Thousand Oaks, CA: Sage.

Smith, W. A. (2010). Toward an understanding of misandric microaggressions and racial battle fatigue among African Americans in historically white institutions. In E. M. Zamani-Gallaher & V. C. Polite (Eds.), *The state of the African American male* (265–277). East Lansing, MI: Michigan State University Press.

Smith, A. (2013). Civic engagement in the digital age. *Pew Internet & American Life Project*. Available at: http://www.pewinternet.org/Reports/2013/Civic-Engage ment/Summary-of-Findings.aspx.

Smith, W. A., Yosso, T. J., & Solórzano, D. G. (2006). Challenging racial battle fatigue on historically white campuses: A critical race examination of race-related stress. In C. A. Stanley (Ed.), *Faculty of color teaching in predominantly white colleges and universities* (299–327). Bolton, MA: Anker Publishing.

Solomon, Z., Mikulincer, M., & Waysman, M. (1991). Delayed and immediate onset posttraumatic stress disorder: II. The role of battle experiences and personal resources. *Social Psychiatry and Psychiatric Epidemiology, 26*(1), 8–13.

Stanley, J. (2013, October). Police Body-Mounted Cameras: With Right Policies in Place, a Win for All. Retrieved 2017, from http://www.urbanaillinois.us/sites/de fault/files/attachments/police-body-mounted-cameras-stanley.pdf.

Steele, C. M., & Aronson, J. (1995). Stereotype threat and the intellectual test performance of African Americans. *Journal of Personality and Social Psychology, 69*(5), 797–811.

Swim, J. K., Hyers, L. L., Cohen, L. L., Fitzgerald, D. F., & Bylsma, W. B. (2003). African American college students' experiences with everyday anti-black racism: Characteristics of and responses to these incidents. *Journal of Black Psychology, 29*, 38–67.

Thompson, C. J. (2004). Civil rights era movers and shakers in higher education: From grassroots to curricular reform at San Francisco State College, 1967–1969. *American Educational History Journal, 31*(2), 109–115.

US Department of Justice, Office of Justice Programs, Bureau of Justice Statistics. (1999). *Police public contact survey.* (DOJ Publication No. NCJ-184957). Retrieved from http://bjs.ojp.usdoj.gov/index.cfm?ty=pbse&sid=18.

US Department of Justice, Office of Justice Programs, Bureau of Justice Statistics. (2002a). *Police public contact survey.* (DOJ Publication No. NCJ-207845). Retrieved from http://bjs.ojp.usdoj.gov/index.cfm?ty=pbse&sid=18.

US Department of Justice, Office of Justice Programs, Bureau of Justice Statistics. (2002b). *Sourcebook of criminal justice statistics.* (DOJ Publication No. NCJ-203302). Retrieved from http://www.albany.edu/sourcebook.

Valenzuela, S. (2013). Unpacking the use of social media for protest behavior: The roles of information, opinion expression, and activism. *American Behavioral Scientist, 57*(7), 920–942. doi:10.1177/0002764213479375.

Volokh, E. (2014). Federal appeals court reaffirms right to videorecord, including at traffic stops. *The Washington Post.* Retrieved from https://www.washingtonpost.com/news/volokh-conspiracy/wp/2014/05/25/federal-appeals-court-reaffirms-right-to-videorecord-including-at-traffic-stops/?utmterm=.1c514ff2e941.

Walton, G. M., & Cohen, G. L. (2007). A question of belonging: Race, social fit, and achievement. *Journal of Personality and Social Psychology, 92*, 82–96.

Watts, R., Griffith, D., & Abdul-Adil, J. (1999). Sociopolitical development as an antidote for oppression: Theory and action. *American Journal of Community Psychology, 27*, 255–272.

Wheeler, R. E. (2016). Michael Brown, Eric Garner, and law librarianship. *Law Library Journal, 107*(3), 467–475.

Whitfield, S. J. (1991). A death in in the delta: The story of Emmett Till. Baltimore: The Johns Hopkins University Press.

Zimmerman, M. A., Ramírez-Valles, J., & Maton, K. I. (1999). Resilience among urban African American male adolescents: A study of the protective effects of sociopolitical control on their mental health. *American Journal of Community Psychology, 27*(6), 733–751. doi:10.1023/A:1022205008237.

Chapter Four

Criminalizing Hope

Policing Latino/a
Immigrant Bodies for Profit

Nayeli Y. Chavez-Dueñas and Hector Y. Adames

Around much of the world, the United States (U.S.) is often called *A Nation of Immigrants*, a phrase that seeks to underscore the history of foreign-born populations in the country. This notion is expressed in many facets of American society including history books, visual arts, and politics. The idea is also depicted symbolically through the Statue of Liberty and national parks such as Ellis Island. More recently, President Barack H. Obama's used the phrase in his 2014 speech on immigration stating that " . . .*we know the heart of a stranger—we were strangers once, too. My fellow Americans, we are and always will be a nation of immigrants . . . Since the founding of our nation, we've weaved a tradition of welcoming immigrants into the very fabric of who we are"* (Obama, 2014, para. 1). While it is factually accurate to say that the U.S. has a long history of immigrants coming to its borders, this phrase renders invisible the contributions and experiences of Native American and African populations who were colonized and enslaved. The phrase also hides the reality of hostility, rejection, and criminalization experienced by many immigrant populations including the 57 million Latino/as who currently are the largest ethnic minority group in the U.S. The immigration of Latino/as continues to be one of the most polarizing issues in the country with a multitude of laws enacted to police and criminalize their presence in these United States.

Esperanza, one of the psychological strengths of Latinos, speaks to the subjective belief that even during the most difficult situations, things will work out for the better (Adames & Chavez-Dueñas, 2017). *Esperanza*, loosely translated, connotes hope, one of the main ingredients that propel immigrants to leave everything behind in search of better economic opportunities, family reunification, or the escapement of violence and political turmoil in their countries of origin. This chapter offers a critical look at the criminalization

of hope with a focus on Latino/a immigrants in the U.S. The central purpose
of the chapter is threefold. One, examine the history and context which has
contributed to the enactment of laws designed to police Latino/a immigrant
communities and criminalize their presence in U.S. territory. Two, describe
how the detention of undocumented immigrants has become a profitable
business which drives the implementation of increasingly aggressive policing
strategies. Three, discuss the impact that aggressive immigration enforcement
tactics has on Latino/a immigrants, their families, and communities. Overall,
this chapter seeks to highlight how the enforcement of immigration policies
has become a profitable business industry in which corporations and politicians benefit from the incarceration of one of the most vulnerable segments
of the U.S. population.

LATINO/AS IN "THE NATION OF IMMIGRANTS"

Latino/as are a group with deeply-seated roots in the U.S. Contrary to commonly held stereotypes, the majority of Latino/as (65% or 36 million individuals) are born in the U.S. (Migration Policy Institute, 2013). The remaining
35% or 19 million individuals of Latino/a descent are immigrants (Migration
Policy Institute, 2013). Moreover, out of the 19 million Latino/a immigrants,
approximately half, or 8.5 million, are undocumented and have either entered
the country without authorization or came with a visa and stayed after their
visas expired. As a result of their legal status, undocumented immigrants are
often susceptible to exploitation, abuse, and deportation, making them one of
the most oppressed segments of the U.S. population. In fact, over the last few
decades the U.S. government has enacted numerous laws and policies seeking to criminalize, incarcerate, and deport undocumented immigrants (Ewing,
Martinez, & Rumbaut, 2015). The next section offers a brief overview on the
context and history that has contributed to the criminalization of immigrants.
  The U.S. has a long history of xenophobia and discrimination against immigrants that is well recorded; however, scholars (Chavez, 2008; Chomsky,
2014) have posited that Latino/as are currently living during one of the most
anti-immigrant and anti-Latino/a periods in modern U.S. American history.
For instance, the number of laws and policies opposing immigration that
disproportionately target Latino/a populations has increased dramatically. To
illustrate, there were approximately 300 bills related to immigration in 2005
(American Immigration Council, 2015). This number increased to 1,500 by
2009. During the same nine-year period, the amount of legislation enacted
increased by approximately 500%, from 38 to 222 new laws (American Immigration Council, 2015). The surge in policies focusing on immigration

control, including punitive laws, has been portrayed mainly as an issue that is necessary to ensure homeland security in the wake of 9/11.[1] As a result, rhetoric describing immigrants as "criminals" who may become a potential threat to the homeland security began to emerge post 9/11 (Ewing et al., 2015). Contrary to the belief that an increase in anti-immigrant laws was necessary to protect the country from additional attacks, historical evidence suggests otherwise. In actuality, the events of 9/11 merely served as a justification to continue a long pattern of policies that have sought to police, criminalize, and deport immigrants from the U.S. For instance, scholars in the social sciences have asserted that " . . . for years, the government has been redefining what it means to be a 'criminal alien,' using increasingly stringent definitions of standards of 'criminality' that do not apply to U.S. citizens" (Ewing et al., 2015, 10). To achieve this goal, new classes of felonies[2] have been created and applied only to immigrants, reinforcing the idea that immigrants are "dangerous criminals." While immigrants have historically been scapegoated, demonized, and feared during times of economic uncertainty in the U.S., the events surrounding 9/11 clearly ignited a new wave of xenophobia, which has exacerbated the public's rejection of undocumented immigrants.

CRIMMIGRATION

Many U.S. Americans hold the belief that they have an inherent right to live in the U.S. because "their ancestors came 'the right' way . . . they assume that their ancestors 'went through the process'" (Chomsky, 2014, 1). Such individuals assume that their ancestors followed the same immigration laws that people are required to abide by today. What is ignored by this assertion is that many immigrants settled in the U.S. before current laws of immigration were established and the concept of "illegality" was created and applied to the unauthorized foreign born population (Chomsky, 2014). The term *crimmigration*, coined by Professor Juliet Stumpf (2006), helps to illustrate the intersection between two bodies of law including criminal law and immigration law. In the U.S. crimmigration can be traced back to the *Immigration and Nationality Act of 1965.*

The Birth of the Southern Border

Throughout U.S. history, laws governing the immigration process have changed. Before 1924, immigrants from Mexico were freely allowed to enter the U.S. and work as seasonal farmworkers in the agricultural industry of the Southwest. During this time, immigration from Mexico was welcomed given the advantages it offered to the country. For instance, Mexican immigrants were willing to work under harsh conditions for very low wages, and they willingly moved from farm to farm following seasonal needs (Chomsky, 2014). They often returned back to their country of origin during off-seasons. Despite the relative ease with which Latino/a immigrants were able to enter the U.S., they often experienced exclusion and rejection, and their status in the U.S. made them easy to exploit and permanently subject to deportation (Chomsky, 2014). The *Appropriation Act of 1924* changed this pattern and officially established the U.S. Border Patrol as a mechanism of immigration control and border security. Soon thereafter the period of the economic slump of the Great Depression began to take hold. During this era, people of Mexican descent experienced massive layoffs, economic hardships, and discrimination. Moreover, a large-scale deportation program was created to repatriate 400,000 Mexicans regardless of their immigration status. Overall, it is estimated that 60% of those who were deported were American citizens of Mexican descent (Chomsky, 2014).

Making Immigration a Crime

The pattern of welcoming and scapegoating Latino/as immigrants continued until the passage of the *Immigration and Nationality Act of 1965, which* established a quota system to limit migration from all countries. This law created a system propitious for corporations to continue benefiting from the cheap labor of Latino/a immigrants, while at the same time making their presence in the U.S. "illegal" (Chomsky, 2014). The 1965 Act was the first of many other laws enacted to police immigrants and criminalize their presence in U.S. soil. Two additional legislations solidified crimmigration including the *Immigration Reform and Control Act* (IRCA) and the *Illegal Immigration Reform and Immigrant Responsibility Act* (IIRIRA).

IRCA was signed in 1986 by President Ronald W. Reagan. The main objective of this legislature was to reduce the number of undocumented immigrants in the U.S. through three mechanisms including: employer sanctions, increased border security, and legalization of undocumented immigrants (Ewing et al., 2015). The employer sanctions made it a crime to knowingly hire workers without checking immigration status. The second component of IRCA increased the number of border patrol officers used to arrest and deport immigrants along the southern border by 50%. Lastly, the third part of this legislation created a path for the legalization of approximately 2.3 million immigrants. While IRCA helped many undocumented immigrants adjust their legal status, this law also reinforced the idea that immigrants trying to enter the country without documents were deserving of less rights and benefits than "lawful" permanent residents and U.S. citizens (Ewing et al.,

2015). Moreover, IRCA prompted the creation of a number of immigration enforcement programs designed to specifically target immigrants. Together, these programs became the foundation of the *Criminal Alien Program* (CAP) designed to identify, detain, and deport immigrants with criminal convictions within federal, state, and local prisons. CAP works by screening the legal status of individuals who are under the custody of law enforcement through the cooperation of local police departments with Immigration and Customs Enforcement (ICE). Overall, CAP encourages local police to engage in ethnic profiling by arresting individuals "suspected" of being undocumented for minor offenses making it easier for law enforcement to screen Latino/as for deportability (Alonzo, Macleod-Ball, Chen, & Kim, 2011; Anti Defamation League, 2008).

IIRIRA, signed in 1996 by President William Jefferson "Bill" Clinton, furthered the criminalization of immigrants becoming part of what scholars call "a system of justice for non-U.S. citizens" (Ewing et al. 2015, 12). This legislation in combination with the *Anti-Terrorism Effective Death Penalty Act* (AEDPA), also signed in 1996, mandated the detention and deportation of documented and undocumented noncitizens convicted of an "aggravated felony." Interestingly the law expanded and modified what constitutes an "aggravated felony" for immigration purposes. In other words, the standard characteristics of "criminality" set for immigrants became more stringent than those for U.S. citizens. Even more damaging for immigrants is the fact that the new standards were applied retroactively to offenses committed before these laws were enacted (Ewing et al., 2015; Stumpf, 2006). IIRIRA went further by establishing streamlined deportation procedures allowing the government to remove immigrants from the U.S. without a hearing before an immigration judge. Instead, immigrants can be processed through what is called expedited removal and reinstatement of removal, where immigration officers serve as both prosecutors and judges often investigating, charging, and making decisions within a very short time frame anywhere between hours to days (Immigration Policy Center, 2014). To further the work done by IRCA, IIRIRA developed a program known as *287g* allowing the Department of Homeland Security to deputize state and local law enforcement officers to perform ICE functions (Alonzo et al., 2011; Ewing et al., 2015).

Crimmigration in the Post 9/11 Era

Following the events of September 11, 2001, a plethora of new laws was enacted in the U.S. that further criminalized the presence of immigrants (Adames & Chavez-Dueñas, 2017; Ewing et al., 2015; Lydgate, 2010). Table 4.1 provides a list of some anti-immigrant legislations and ordinances passed post 9/11. These laws, ordinances, programs, and tactics serve to justify the

Table 4.1. Anti-immigrant Laws, Ordinances, and Programs Passed Since the Events Surrounding 9/11.

Year	Title (Location)	Description
2005	Operation Streamline	Enforces criminal penalty (6 months in prison for 1st attempt and up to 20 years for 2nd attempt) for undocumented immigrants caught trying to cross the southern U.S. border.
2006–2007	Ordinance Hazelton (Pennsylvania)	Legislation seeking to punish landlords and employers accused of renting to and hiring undocumented immigrants.
2007	Save Manassas Prince William County (Virginia)	Local ordinance targeting undocumented immigrants. The ordinance attempted to curb undocumented immigrants access to public services and increased immigration enforcement by local law authorities/police.
2007–present	E-Verify (National)	A program run by the Department of Homeland Security (DHS) and the Social Security Administration which confirms an employee's legal status to work in the U.S. As of 2015, 18 states require the use of the program, as well as public agencies and contractors.
2008–2014	Secure Communities (National)	A program of the DHS designed to identify undocumented immigrants in U.S. jails and prisons. Participating facilities submit fingerprints of individuals arrested to criminal and immigration databases.
2010	SB1070 (Arizona)	Law passed in Arizona in 2010 and upheld by the Supreme Court in 2012 allowing police officers, under the authority of state law to inquire about an individual's immigration status during a routine traffic stop.
2015-Present	Priority Enforcement Program, PEP (National)	Program enabling the DHS to work with state and local law enforcement to take custody of individuals who they determine pose a "danger" to public safety.
2015	HB318 (North Carolina)	Law prohibiting local governments from adopting "sanctuary" ordinances that limit the enforcement of federal immigration law and prohibits some government officials from accepting various forms of identification, and E-verify. The governor of North Carolina signed this law into effect on October 2015.

Note: From "The History of Latinos/as in the United States: Journeys of Hope, Struggle, and Resilience," in *Cultural Foundations and Interventions in Latino/a Mental Health: History, Theory, and Within Group Differences* (p. 69–70), by H.Y. Adames & N.Y. Chavez-Dueñas, 2017. Copyright 2017 by Routledge Press. Adapted with permission.

systematic dehumanization of unauthorized immigrants by taking more of their human rights away (Adames & Chavez-Dueñas, 2017). For instance, *Operation Streamline 2005* made it legal to prosecute immigrants who were arrested while crossing the border in group trials of up to 80 immigrants at a time. Based on this law, immigrants convicted of attempting to enter the country without authorization for the first time were charged with a misdemeanor. Immigrants who tried to cross the border for the second time and are arrested faced convictions of aggravated felonies and up to two years in prison (Lyndgate, 2010).

The new class of crimes specific to immigration developed by IIRIRA and other legislations in the post 9/11 era created a false narrative fomenting the growth of xenophobic beliefs against Latino/a immigrants. Specifically, anti-immigrant lawmakers and organizations can gain public support by highlighting their focus on the detention and deportation of immigrants with criminal records including "aggravated felonies" (Chomsky, 2014). Unfortunately, what is often left out of the picture is the ways in which crimmigration created a system where individuals can be labeled as "criminals" and "felons" for solely crossing the border looking for a better life. The criminalization of immigrants is not slowing down; instead, it is gaining speed. Since 2010 state and local governments have enacted 1,655 laws, policies, and resolutions related to immigration (Jaeger, 2016; National Conference of State Legislators, 2015).

WHITE SUPREMACY MASKED
AS IMMIGRATION CONTROL

Hate groups and other communities with deeply seated white supremacist ideologies contribute to the growing criminalization of Latino/a immigrants in the U.S. These groups are motivated by the creed that the U.S. should remain phenotypically and culturally white. According to the Southern Poverty Law Center (SPLC, 2016a), the number of active hate groups has been growing steadily in the last few years. Between 2000 and 2010, the number of hate groups has grown by approximately 62% from 602 to 1,002. Today, active hate groups are found in 96% of the country or 48 states. The Southern Poverty Law Center (2016a) also reports that many of these groups (e.g., minutemen, white pride groups) believe that specific groups of immigrants (e.g., Latino/as, Muslims) pose a threat to the racial demographic characteristics of the U.S. population and homeland security. Given their rejection of Immigrants of Color, hate groups demonstrate a pathological insistence to secure the southern U.S. border.

Nativists groups believe that native-born U.S. Americans, especially white individuals, should have superior rights to immigrants. Defamation techniques to promote negative stereotypes about immigrants of color are often used by these groups. Of all the different anti-immigrant organizations that exist in the U.S., the most effective are organizations such as the *Federation for American Immigration Reform* (FAIR), *Center for Immigration Studies* (CIS), and *NumbersUSA*, who work inside and outside the government to advance nativist agenda. According to the SPLC, these organizations were founded by John Tanton, an individual they describe as "having white nationalist beliefs" (SPLC, 2016b, para.1). Tanton has made explicit his desire to help keep the U.S. a white country. In some of his writings he states, "I've come to the point of view that for European-American society and culture to persist requires a European-American majority, and a clear one at that" (SPLC, 2016b para. 2; Tanton, 1993). He runs a publishing company that produces reports and articles describing immigrants as criminals who refuse to "assimilate," abuse public benefits, and take jobs away from "deserving" U.S. Americans (Anti-Defamation League, 2008). For instance, in one of Tanton's publications, Harrison (2009) states that Latino/as are not "melting" into the American culture and that traditional cultural values "lie behind Latin America's difficulties in achieving democratic stability, social justice, and prosperity" (para. 1).

Both hate and nativists groups work diligently to support and elect officials who support their ideologies (e.g., the author of SB1070 Chris Koback a policy analyst for FAIR; Nelson, 2011). Another group associated with nativist perspectives known as the *State Legislators for Legal Immigration* (SLLI) has approximately 105 members working at different levels of the U.S. government and representing 40 states (Beirich, 2011). SLLI describes immigrants as being prone to crime, carrying infectious diseases that threaten the public, and costing taxpayers millions of dollars, and seeks to end the 14th amendment. Overall, there is substantial evidence to support how nativists groups use different tactics to create fear among the U.S. general public which garners support for politicians who promise to be tough on immigration (Anti-Defamation League, 2008) by criminalizing and policing immigrants in an effort to "make America great again."

POLICING OF IMMIGRANT BODIES

While it is a fact that immigrants are less likely to engage in criminal activity, and that higher rates of immigration are correlated with lower rates of violent crimes, immigrants are forced to live in constant fear of being detained and separated from their families through deportation. Anti-immigration groups, individuals with white supremacist ideologies, and those who lack an understanding regarding the complexities surrounding the immigration process often foment the cruelty with which immigrants are treated. In recent years, and with the help of various legislations designed to "control" immigration, the U.S. has seen a significant increase in the detention of immigrants. Moreover, there has been a dramatic expansion of programs that seek to prevent and deter immigrants from entering U.S. territory, as well as deport permanent legal residents accused of committing a crime (Loyd, Mitchelson, & Burridge, 2012). The last two decades have seen an increase in communication between local, state, and federal law enforcement agencies and immigration officials (Alonzo et al., 2011; American Immigration Lawyers Association, 2011). Cooperative programs between state and local law enforcement and ICE (e.g., *287g*, Secure Communities and Criminal Alien Program) have been used as tools to enforce immigration law and police immigrant bodies. Table 4.1 describes programs designed to punish and detain "serious criminals." However, evidence demonstrates that such programs rely on racial profiling to identify immigrants who many times have broken minor laws (e.g., traffic violations). In fact, ICE uses a variety of strategies to police, arrest, and detain thousands of suspected (documented and undocumented) immigrants every year. Such operations are part of intensified enforcement activities, including large scale workplace raids, driving checkpoints, and door-to-door operations to arrest immigrants with deportation orders (Capps, Castañeda, Chaudry, & Santos, 2007). Hence, cooperation between ICE and local law enforcement has led to the possibility of immigrants being arrested anytime and anywhere.

Arrests at the Border

Most arrests and detention of Latino/a immigrants occur along the U.S.–Mexican border. The Department of Homeland Security (DHS), one of the largest law enforcement agencies in the world, arrests more than 1.6 million immigrants crossing the U.S.–Mexican border every year (Capps et al., 2007). Immigrants, who make it farther into the interior of U.S. territory, and even those who are permanent legal residents, continue to be at risk of being deported at work, in their communities, and even in their own homes.

Workplace Raids: Working in Terror

The bodies of undocumented immigrants are constantly policed. Despite providing necessary services that benefit society at large, immigrants are made to live in constant fear. They go to work every day knowing that at any given time, ICE may show up and take them away from their families and their homes. For years workplace raids have served as the public face of immigration law enforcement and are also one of the most cruel and inhumane strategies utilized by ICE to arrest unsuspecting undocumented immigrants at their place of employment.

Immigrants arrested through worksite raids are often hard-working individuals who earn low wages and typically do not have a prior criminal history (Capps et al., 2007). During raids, armed agents often wearing SWAT gear enter the workplace and secure the perimeter and the exits to prevent workers from leaving. Once the building is secured, ICE orders immigrants to cease working and begins interrogating people regardless of their legal status. While being questioned, immigrants are typically not informed about their right to get an attorney and remain silent (ACLU, 2011). Immigrants that are unable to provide evidence of their legal status are transferred to remote and out-of-state detention facilities within hours of their arrest. These actions often induce tremendous levels of fear and anxiety in immigrants who are also unable to communicate with their families about being detained. Hence, families are often unable to track the location where the immigrant has been detained creating distress and panic among all family members including children. While detainees are in detention, ICE agents are known to "pressure detainees into signing stipulated removal orders which waive critical due process rights and the opportunity to seek relief, even in cases in which a worker has a valid claim to stay in the United States" (ACLU, 2011, 4). As a result, detained immigrants may be unable to see their family prior to their deportation. Such cruel and inhumane treatment contributes to emotional difficulties (e.g., anxiety, fear, distress) often faced by immigrants and their families (Brabeck & Xu, 2010). Fortunately, under the administration of President Obama, the use of worksite raids declined; with ICE relying more on paperwork audits that verify the identity and employment eligibility of employees (Maurer, 2015).

Living in Fear: Policing in the Community

ICE policy explicitly states, "enforcement actions do not occur at, nor are focused on, sensitive locations such as schools and churches" (Morton, 2011, para. 1). However, during the first weekend of the 2016, a series of raids took place at "sensitive locations." During the raids, ICE officials showed up at the homes of immigrants and arrested them when they opened the door. These series of raids sent shock waves throughout immigrant communities nationwide while creating the fear that immigration officials would show up at schools, churches, barbershops, salons, and the like to arrest children, youth, and families. Such fears and distress intensified when a high school student, named Wildin Acosta, was detained on his way to school in North Carolina. This event created such panic among students that the Board of Education of Los Angeles unified and voted unanimously to bar immigration agents from their campuses (Menas, 2016). In another similar and unsettling case, an immigrant named Raynold Garcia was reportedly lured out of church with fake text messages before being arrested by federal agents. Both of these cases, as well as those of the approximately 336 immigrants who were detained during the 2016 raids, illustrate how immigrant bodies are policed and how the actions of ICE traumatize and terrorize entire communities. Even in spaces that most individuals consider to be safe havens (e.g., home, schools, places of worship), immigrants and their families are made to live in constant fear (SPLC, 2016c).

Policed while Driving

Driving, an activity that has become a necessity for survival in modern society, has become increasingly risky for undocumented immigrants given the current anti-immigrant sentiment and increased concerns about national security (Ewing et al., 2015). Waslin (2013) identifies three main factors that contribute to the probability of undocumented immigrants being arrested and convicted for driving without a license including: (a) increased allocation of resources to immigration enforcement, (b) collaboration programs (e.g., 287g, Secure Communities), and (c) the restriction of driver's licenses to permanent legal residents and U.S. citizens (i.e., only 12 states allow undocumented immigrants to obtain a driver's license). The combination of these elements is described as the "the process of entrapment, in which people and other state agencies impose significant risk of movement on undocumented people" (Nunez & Hayman 2007, 354). Under these circumstances, "any contact with the police, no matter how innocent or trivial, can result in immigration enforcement and removal" (Alonzo et al., 2011, 3). In other words, "police may initiate stops for the sole or primary purpose of enforcing immigration law and may engage in racial profiling or other abusive practices" (Alonzo et al., 2011, 3). Hence, arrests for driving become a "pretext for immigration enforcement" (Waslin, 2013, 3). For instance, the American Immigration Lawyers Association (2011) reports that in over 50% of cases (66 out of 127) reviewed, ICE had initiated removal proceedings against undocumented immigrants who had been cited for minor traffic violations. This reality has led to increased fear of driving while being an undocumented immigrant (A Immigration Lawyers Association, 2015; Lopez & Light, 2009). Overall, fear is exacerbated by other law enforcement tactics such as "sobriety" checkpoints where police inquire about the legal status of drivers (Buiza & Usufi, 2012; Gabrielson, 2010; Waslin, 2013).

DETAINING DREAMS IN PURSUIT OF PROFITS

ICE is the federal agency responsible for overseeing the U.S. detention system where immigrants are incarcerated while they wait for a decision regarding their status. Immigrants held in detention centers include youth, older adults, men, women, families, torture survivors, victims of trafficking and of other crimes, legal permanent residents, individuals with significant health concerns, and other vulnerable populations (Carey, 2011). The detention system consists of a network of more than 200 jails and detention facilities which are located throughout the U.S. (Detention Watch Network & Center for Constitutional Rights, 2015). Currently, the detention system operates under a congressionally mandated quota, which requires ICE to keep approximately 34,000 beds filled by detained immigrants per night (Carson & Diaz, 2015).

The Origin of Bed Quotas

Immigration bed quotas initiated with the approval of the *Intelligence Reform and Terrorism Act* of 2004 that required ICE to increase the immigration detention capacity by 8,000 beds each year from 2006 to 2010 (Carson & Diaz, 2015). During the same year the Chairman of the House Subcommittee on Homeland Security mandated that all detention centers be filled to capacity. In 2007 President George W. Bush added detention beds into the *DHS Appropriations Act*, raising the total of beds to 27,500 (Detention Watch Network & Center for Constitutional Rights, 2015). An even higher bed quota was added to the appropriations bill of 2010 by the Democrat Senator Robert Byrd from West Virginia, a well-known member and recruiter of the Ku Klux Klan (Detention Watch Network & Center for Constitutional Rights, 2015). Senator Byrd raised the quota to 34,000 beds. Although several attempts have been made to erase bed quotas, they have failed. In the 2012 fiscal year, approximately 478,000 immigrants were detained. President Obama has also voiced opposition to the detention quota; nonetheless, the quota remains in place and was recently raised to 34,040 in 2016 (Carson & Diaz, 2015).

Preservation of the bed quota requires an aggressive enforcement of immigration policies (Carson & Diaz, 2015), which is aided by the unprecedented allocation of funds in the form of resources and personnel. Studies demonstrate that the federal government spends more money on the enforcement of immigration policies than any other form of enforcement combined (Meissner, Kerwin, Chishti, & Bergeron 2013). For example, during fiscal year 2012, the U.S. government spent approximately $18 billion on the enforcement of immigration laws, which was 24% more than what it spent on the Federal Bureau of Investigation (FBI), Drug Enforcement Administration (DEA), Secret Service, and U.S. Marshals Service and Bureau of Alcohol, Tobacco, Firearms and Explosives combined (Magaña-Salgado, 2014; Meissner et al., 2013). Moreover since 1986, 187 billion dollars have been used for immigration enforcement alone (Magaña-Salgado, 2014; Meissner, Kerwin, Chishti, & Bergeron 2013). The financial cost of keeping the bed quota is astronomical with the federal government paying $160 per immigrant per night, for a total of $5.4 million a day and $2 billion per year (Carson & Diaz, 2015; Detention Watch Network & Center for Constitutional Rights, 2015; National Immigration Forum, 2013).

While for-profit facilities posit that they provide the detention of immigrants at a cheaper cost than those offered by government-owned facilities, studies have revealed that this is not entirely the case (Venters, Dasch-Golberg, Rasmussen & Keller, 2001; Kunichoff, 2012; Kish & Lipton, 2013). For instance, activists, scholars, and human rights organizations have alleged that the savings result from the delegation of labor (e.g., cleaning facility, cooking) to immigrants in detention who are paid $1 per day instead of the minimum wage required by law for any other worker (Carson & Diaz, 2015; Kunichoff, 2012). Other scholars argue that private companies save money by cutting down on essential needs of detainees such as food and medical care, which leads to inhumane and at times lethal conditions (Venters, Dasch-Golberg, Rasmussen & Keeler, 2001).

The Lucrative Business of Detaining Immigrant Bodies

While the federal government pays the expenses related to the detention of undocumented immigrants, for-profit private companies make the majority of the profits. For-profit private corporations run approximately 62% of all immigration detention centers with nine out of the ten largest detention centers being private (Carson & Diaz, 2015). Correction Corporations of America (CCA) and the GEO group are the largest private for-profit detention corporations in the U.S. (Carson & Diaz, Detention Watch Network & Center for Constitutional Rights, 2015). Together CCA and GEO keep about 14,149 immigrants detained each night (Carson & Diaz, 2015; Detention Watch Network & Center for Constitutional Rights, 2015). The quota served to create a system where the arrest and detention of undocumented immigrant bodies has become a profitable business for privately owned detention facilities. A study conducted by Jaeger (2016) found that the very presence of private correctional facilities increases the average number of deportations. Thus, it is not just anti-immigrant ideologies that drive the high number of deportations but also the financial profits that detention facilities see in the arrests of undocumented immigrants. Hate and anti-immigrant rhetoric are strategies that contribute to the public's support of increasingly aggressive and inhumane immigration tactics. Public support facilities the passage of more stringent immigration laws, which translate into millions of dollars for detention facilities.

Aided by the implementation of the bed quota, the two largest detention facilities (i.e., CCA, GEO) have become billion-dollar industries (Carson & Diaz, 2015; Detention Watch Network & Center for Constitutional Rights, 2015). For instance, CAA's revenue increased from $133,373,000 in 2007 (CCA, 2008) to $195,022,000 in 2014 (CCA, 2015). GEO experienced an even more dramatic profit increase from $41,845,000 in 2007 (GEO, 2008) to $143,840,000 in 2014, an astronomical 244% increase (GEO, 2015). Together these corporations have a combined revenue of about $3 billion annually. Given the fact that each detained immigrant translates into a significant increase in revenue (e.g., CCA reports that filling each empty bed would add $1.00 to earnings per share; CCA, 2014), these corporations have monetary incentives to push for every bed to be occupied. Hence, it is not surprising that there is a positive correlation between the number of immigrants incarcerated and the number of detention beds granted to private prison corporations (Carson & Diaz, 2015). For instance, in 2004 the average daily population in public and private immigration detention facilities was 21,928 (Carson & Diaz, 2015; ICE, 2011). By 2014 the immigration detention system had grown 47% with 32,163 immigrants held in detention each day (Carson & Diaz, 2015; Grassroots Leadership, 2015). As the demand for immigration beds increased so did the percentage of immigrants detained in privately owned immigration facilities. In 2009 about 49% of immigrants were held in privately owned detention centers, this percentage grew to 62% in 2015 (Carson & Diaz, 2015; Grassroots Leadership, 2015). Clearly, these corporations have found that the detention of undocumented immigrants translates into billions of dollars in revenue. As a result, they spend a significant amount of money lobbying and supporting politicians who are proponents of anti-immigrant legislations and are in favor of keeping the bed quotas (Carson & Diaz, 2015). The next section briefly outlines how private for-profit companies use their influences to maintain the bed quota.

Buying Influence

As discussed in the previous section, the quota system has become the driving force behind aggressive immigration enforcement strategies (Carson & Diaz, 2015). State laws and local ordinances are used as strategies to funnel undocumented immigrants arrested for minor violations into jails and privately owned detention centers. These laws and ordinances have produced a surge of lobbyists who spent approximately $45 million over the past decade (2002–2012) in efforts to influence the U.S. congress to increase or, at minimum, maintain the system of bed quotas (Fang, 2013). Money invested in lobbying has paid off by increasing the amount of resources allocated to the enforcement of immigration laws (Fang, 2013). According to Fang, in fiscal year 2012, CCA and GEO, two publicly traded prison companies, made over $441.9 million dollars in federal contracts with ICE and a total combined of $296.9 million in revenue. These contracts came at a cost. For instance, according to Fang (2013), between the years 2011 to 2013, these companies contributed over $380,000 to U.S. Republican candidates and committees. Contributions to the Grand Old Party (GOP) are almost six times the amount they have contributed to politicians from the Democratic National Committee (DNC). Moreover, a report from *Think Progress News* states that "in the past decade, three major private prison companies spent $45 million on campaign donations and lobbyists to push legislation" that advanced their agendas (Shen, 2012, para. 4).

The lobbying influence extends beyond the federal government with states also being incentivized by corporate dollars. As an example, one of the most anti-immigrant laws passed in modern U.S. history, Arizona's SB1070, was heavily influenced by corporate interests (Carson & Diaz, 2015). "By the time S.B. 1070 made it to the floor, 30 out of the bill's 36 co-sponsors had received campaign contributions from private prison companies as well as private prison lobbyists" (Carson & Diaz, 2015, 10). Moreover the 22nd governor of the state of Arizona, Janice Kay "Jan" Brewer, reportedly received significant campaign contributions from CCA before signing SB1070 into law (Carson & Diaz, 2015; Detention Watch Network, 2011). Hence, it is clear that the enforcement of immigration law has become a profitable business where wealthy corporations along with ambitious politicians use the bodies of undocumented immigrants as profitable merchandize (Adames & Chavez-Dueñas, 2017). Unfortunately, while the policing and detention of undocumented immigrants translates into revenue for private companies, it also contributes to the dehumanization of a vulnerable and growing segment of U.S. society. The grave consequences of detention for individuals, families, and communities are discussed below.

THE HUMAN COST OF IMMIGRATION
POLICING AND DETENTION

The policing of immigrant bodies has a devastating effect on Latino/a individuals, families, and the community as a whole. Moreover, aggressive immigration enforcement has a negative impact not only on the immigrants who are arrested and placed in detention, but also on their families. In the U.S.

there are approximately 5.5 million children who have at least one undocumented parent and 80%, or 4.5 million, of these children are U.S. citizens
(Wessler, 2011). Families with documented and undocumented members are
called mixed status. Mixed-status families experience a multitude of challenges including fear of deportation. This fear may lead to symptoms of anxiety and isolation. Symptoms related to abandonment, trauma, and financial
hardship are also common among families who have experienced the process
of detention and deportation (Capps et al., 2007; Yoshikawa, Godfrey, &
Rivera, 2008).

Beyond the common psychological implications associated with immigration detention (e.g., family separation, loss of income), egregious
human rights violations and abuse have become commonplace experiences
for undocumented immigrants held in detention centers across the country
(Furman, Ackerman, Loya, Jones, & Negi, 2012). Immigrants detained
are subject to poor living conditions such as overcrowding, constant noise
(Kotsoni, Ponthieu, & Egidi, 2014), deficient access to outdoor recreation
(e.g., access to sunlight and free-flowing air), and insufficient nutrition, as
well as problems with visitation policies. Moreover, a number of reports
indicate that detention facilities operate with little oversight or accountability (American Civil Liberties Union, Detention Watch Network, &
National Immigrant Justice Center, 2016; Detention Watch Network &
National Immigrant Justice Center, 2015; *New York Times*, 2008; *Washington Post*, 2008; Seattle University School of Law, 2008). One report
concludes that "public and private contractors who run detention facilities continue to make money without adequate oversight, and troubling
conditions of detention persist . . . detailed reviews of six facilities known
to have troubling human rights records suggest that in some cases, ICE
inspections allow facilities to obscure severe conditions" (Detention
Watch Network & National Immigrant Justice Center, 2015, 2). Lack of
accountability creates conditions where little is done to protect the lives
and human rights of the approximately 34,000 immigrants who are held
in detention every night across the country (National Immigrant Justice,
Network & Detention Watch Network, 2015). Conditions that pose a risk
to the lives of immigrants in detention include lack of adequate suicide
prevention, substandard medical care, and deficient standards for sexual
assault prevention and intervention (National Immigrant Justice Center &
Detention Watch Network, 2015). Overall, detention facilities are held to
very low standards in the treatment of detained immigrants. Gross violations of human rights and unexplained deaths of undocumented immigrants held in detention have been publicly documented (American Civil

Liberties Union, Detention Watch Network, & National Immigrant Justice Center, 2016). Nonetheless, facilities where such incidents have allegedly occurred continue to operate and pass inspections, which leads to questions about the value placed on the lives of immigrants.

FROM CRIMINALIZING HOPE TO RADICAL SURVIVAL

Despite all of the challenges described in this chapter, *esperanza* (hope) continues to be the driving force propelling Latino/a immigrants to leave everything behind to settle in the U.S. Even as our Latino/a community braces itself for the presidency of Donald J. Trump, a person who launched his presidential campaign by vilifying Mexican immigrants, Latinx will survive.

In the words of Junot Diaz, a Latino immigrant and Pulitzer Prize winner and 2012 MacArthur "genius grant" Fellow, Latinos are

> *"the only superpower this country will ever know; we survived everything this world threw at us. We survived war, we survived dictators, survived torture and violence, endless violence, and borders all the damn borders, and the loneliness of the newcomers in the new land . . . And we survived the ingratitude of the nation where we settled. The nation we helped build for whom we continuously die. And we survived the infinite heartbreak that is the true story of immigration. And we survived the agony of not knowing how to be bear witness to that story and to ourselves. We survived the hate, the hate that never seems to die. The hate that pretends to be patriotism that pretends to be security that pretends to be leadership. A hate that won't listen to reason, to morality, to compassion. We survived it all . . . We in the Latino community are among the greatest heroes our world has known; and yet despite all we do, and all we are, we find ourselves attacked and demonized . . . and this is why we cannot just survive or live. We have to fight for justice, we have to fight for equality, all of us must be free, all of us must free all, all of us must be free or none."* (Diaz, 2016)

NOTES

1. See Tom Pyszczynski, Sheldon Solomon, and Jeff Greenberg, *In the Wake of 9/11: The Psychology of Terror* (Washington, DC: APA Books, 2003) for research on the social disruption and turmoil that occurred after 9/11.

2. Examples of new classes of felonies include: simple batteries, theft, filing a false tax return, failing to appear in court. See *Aggravated Felonies: An Overview* published by the American Immigration Council (Washington, DC: AIC, 2016).

REFERENCES

Adames, H. Y., & Chavez-Dueñas, N. Y. (2017). *Cultural foundations and interventions in Latino/a mental health: History, theory, and within group differences*. New York, NY: Routledge.

Alonzo, A., Macleod-Ball, K., Chen, G., & Kim, S. (2011). *Immigration enforcement off target: Minor offenses with major consequences*. Washington, DC: American Immigration Lawyers Association.

American Civil Liberties Union. (2011). *ICE worksite enforcement: Up to the job?* Retrieved from https://www.aclu.org/files/assets/ACLU_Statement_re_Worksite_Enforcement.pdf

American Civil Liberties Union, Detention Watch Network, & National Immigrant Justice Center. (2016). *Fatal neglect: How ICE ignores deaths in detention*. Retrieved from https://www.detentionwatchnetwork.org/sites/default/files/reports/Fatal%20Neglect%20ACLU-DWN-NIJC.pdf

American Immigration Council. (2015). The criminalization of immigration in the United States. Retrieved from https://www.americanimmigrationcouncil.org/research/criminalization-immigration-united-states

American Immigration Council. (2016). *Aggravated felonies: An overview*. Retrieved from https://www.americanimmigrationcouncil.org/sites/default/files/research/aggravated_felonies.pdf

Anti-Defamation League. (2008). *Immigrants targeted: Extremist rhetoric moves into the mainstream*. Retrieved from http://www.adl.org/assets/pdf/civil-rights/immigration/Immigrants-Targeted-UPDATE_2008.pdf

Beirich, H. (2011). *Attacking the Constitution: State legislators for legal immigration & the anti-immigrant movement*. Retrieved from https://www.splcenter.org/sites/default/files/d6_legacy_files/downloads/publication/Attacking-the-Constitution.pdf

Brabeck, K., & Xu, Q. (2010). The impact of detention and deportation on Latino immigrant children and families: A quantitative exploration. *Hispanic Journal of Behavioral Sciences, 32*(3), 341–361.

Buiza, C., & Usufi, H. (2012). *Wrong turn: Escondido's checkpoints and impound practices examined*. ACLU San Diego and Imperial Counties: ACLU Foundation.

Capps, R., Castañeda, R. M., Chaundry, A., & Santos, R. (2007). *Paying the price: The impact of immigration raids on America's children*. Retrieved from http://www.urban.org/sites/default/files/alfresco/publication-pdfs/411566-Paying-the-Price-The-Impact-of-Immigration-Raids-on-America-s-Children.PDF

Carey, E. P. (2011). *Outsourcing responsibility: The human cost of privatized immigration detention in Otero County*. Retrieved from https://www.aclu-nm.org/wp-content/uploads/2011/01/OCPC-Report.pdf?556820

Carson, B., & Diaz, E. (2015). *Payoff: How Congress ensures private prison profit with an immigrant detention quota*. Retrieved from http://grassrootsleadership.org/sites/default/files/reports/quota_report_final_digital.pdf

Chavez, L. R. (2008). *The Latino threat: Constructing immigrants, citizens, and the nation*. Stanford, CA: Stanford University Press.

Chomsky, A. (2014). *Undocumented: How immigration became illegal*. Boston, MA: Beacon Press.

Corrections Corporation of America (CCA). (2008). *SEC filing 10-K annual report for the fiscal year ending Monday, December 31, 2007*. Retrieved from https://www.last10k.com/sec-filings/%20CXW/0000950144–08–001419.htm#fullReport

Corrections Corporation of America (CCA). (2014). *SEC filing 10-K annual report for the fiscal year ending Tuesday, December 31, 2013*. Retrieved from https://www.last10k.com/sec-filings/cxw/0001193125–14–072723.htm

Corrections Corporation of America (CCA). (2015). *Form 10-K for the fiscal year ended December 31, 2014*. Retrieved from https://www.sec.gov/Archives/edgar/data/1070985/000119312515061839/d853180d10k.htm#fin853180_1

Detention Watch Network. (2011). *The influence of the private prison industry in the immigration detention business*. Retrieved from https://www.detentionwatchnetwork.org/sites/default/files/reports/DWN%20Private%20Prison%20Influence%20Report.pdf

Detention Watch Network, & Center for Constitutional Rights. (2015). *Banking on detention: Local lockup quotas & the immigrant dragnet*. Retrieved from: https://www.detentionwatchnetwork.org/sites/default/files/reports/DWN%20CCR%20Banking%20on%20Detention%20Report.pdf.

Díaz, J. (2016). *Junot Díaz dedicates Hispanic Heritage Award to Latin@ immigrants and undocumented youth: "We are the children of bridges—bridges made from our backs, our tears, our sacrifice, and from all the ones who never made it across with us."* Retrieved from http://gozamos.com/2016/10/junot-diaz-dedicates-hispanic-heritage-award-to-latin-immigrants-and-undocumented-youth-we-are-the-children-of-bridges-bridges-made-from-our-backs-our-tears-our-sacrifice-and-from-all-the/

Ewing, W. A., Martínez, D. E., & Rumbaut, R. G. (2015). *The criminalization of immigration in the United States*. Retrieved from https://www.americanimmigrationcouncil.org/sites/default/files/research/the_criminalization_of_immigration_in_the_united_states.pdf

Fang, L. (2013). How private prisons game the immigration system. *The Nation*. Retrieved from https://www.thenation.com/article/how-private-prisons-game-immigration-system/

Furman, R., Ackerman, A. R., Loya, M., Jones, S., & Negi, N. (2012). The criminalization of immigration: Value conflicts for the social work profession. *The Journal of Sociology & Social Welfare, 39*(1), 169–185.

Gabrielson, R. (2010). *Car seizures at DUI checkpoints prove profitable for cities, raise legal questions*. Retrieved from http://californiawatch.org/public-safety/car-seizures-dui-checkpoints-prove-profitable-cities-raise-legal-questions

Harrison, L. (2009). *What will America stand for in 2050?* Retrieved from http://www.csmonitor.com/Commentary/Opinion/2009/0528/p09s01-coop.html

Immigration Policy Center. (2014). *Removal without recourse: The growth of summary deportations from the United States*. Retrieved from https://www.americanimmigrationcouncil.org/sites/default/files/research/expedited_removal_fact_sheet_final_0.pdf

Jaeger, J. (2016). Securing communities or profits? The effect of federal-local part-nerships on immigration enforcement. *State Politics & Policy Quarterly, 16*(3), 362–386. doi:10.1177/1532440015626401

Kish, R., & Lipton, A. (2013). Do private prisons really offer savings compared to their public counterparts? *Economic Affairs, 33*(1), 93–107.

Kotsioni, I., Ponthieu, A., & Egidi, S. (2013). Health at risk in immigration deten-tion facilities. In M. Couldrey & M. Herson (Eds.), *Forced Migration Review, 44* (11–13). University of Oxford: Refugee Studies Centre. Retrieved from http://www.fmreview.org/sites/fmr/files/FMRdownloads/en/detention.pdf

Kunichoff, Y. (2012). *"Voluntary" work program run in private detention centers pays detained immigrants $1 a day.* Retrieved from http://truth-out.org/news/item/10548-voluntary-work-program-run-in-private-detention-centers-pays-de tained-immigrants-1-a-day

Lopez, M. H., & Light, M. T. (2009). *A rising share: Hispanics and federal crime.* Retrieved from http://www.pewhispanic.org/2009/02/18/a-rising-share-hispanics -and-federal-crime/

Loyd, J., Mitchelson, M., & Burridge, A. (2012). *Beyond walls and cages: Prisons, borders, and global crisis.* Athens, GA: University of Georgia Press.

Lydgate, J. J. (2010). Assembly-line justice: A review of Operation Streamline. *Cali-fornia Law Review, 98*(2), 481–544.

Magaña-Salgado, J. (2014). *Detention, deportation, & devastation: The dispropor-tionate effect of deportations on the Latino community.* Los Angeles, CA: The Mexican American Legal Defense and Educational Fund; The National Day Laborer Organizing Network; & The National Hispanic Leadership Agenda. Retrieved from http://maldef.org/assets/pdf/Deportation_Brief_MALDEF-NHLA -NDLON.pdf

Maurer, R. (2015). *Workplace enforcement of immigration laws down, data show.* Retrieved from https://www.shrm.org/resourcesandtools/hr-topics/talent-acquisi tion/pages/workplace-enforcement-immigration.aspx

Meissner, D., Kerwin, D. M., Chishti, M., & Bergeron, C. (2013). *Immigration en-forcement in the United States: The rise of a formidable machinery.* Washington, DC: Migration Policy Institute.

Menas, A. (2016). *More schools address student safety as community fears of im-migration raids intensify.* Retrieved from http://educationvotes.nea.org/2016/03/05/undocumented-students-safety-in-public-schools-questioned-as-ice-raids-continue/

Migration Policy Institute. (2013). *Profile of the unauthorized population: United States.* Washington, DC: Migration Policy Institute. Retrieved from http://www.migrationpolicy.org/data/unauthorized-immigrant-population/state/US

Morton, J. (2011). Enforcement actions at or focused on sensitive locations. U.S. Department of Homeland Security, U.S. Immigration and Customs Enforcement. Retrieved from https://www.ice.gov/doclib/ero-outreach/pdf/10029.2-policy.pdf

National Conference of State Legislatures. (2015). *2014 immigration report.* Retrieved from http://www.ncsl.org/research/immigration/2014-immigration-report.aspx

National Immigrant Justice Center & Detention Watch Network. (2015). *Lives in peril: How ineffective inspections make ICE complicit in immigration detention*

abuse. Retrieved from http://www.immigrantjustice.org/sites/immigrantjustice
.org/files/THR-Inspections-FOIA-Report-October-2015-FINAL.pdf

National Immigration Forum. (2013). *The math of immigration detention: Runaway costs for immigration detention do not add up to sensible policies.* Washington, DC. Retrieved from http://immigrationforum.org/wp-content/uploads/2014/10/Math-of-Immigation-Detention-August-2013-FINAL.pdf

Nelson, L. (2011). *When Mr. Kobach comes to town: Nativist laws & the communities they damage.* Retrieved from https://www.splcenter.org/sites/default/files/Kobach_Comes_to_Town_final_web.pdf

Nunez, G. G., & Heyman, J. M. (2007). Entrapment processes and immigrant communities in a time of heightened border vigilance. *Human Organization, 66*(4), 354–365.

Obama, B. H. (2014). *"We were strangers once, too": The President announces new steps on immigration.* Retrieved from https://www.whitehouse.gov/blog/2014/11/20/we-were-strangers-once-too-president-announces-new-steps-immigratio

Pyszczynski, T., Solomon, S., & Greenberg, J. (2003). *In the wake of 9/11: The psychology of terror.* Washington, DC: American Psychological Association. doi: 10.1037/10478-000.

Seattle University School of Law. (2008). *Voices from detention: A report on human rights violations at the Northwest Detention Center in Tacoma, Washington.* Retrieved from https://www.weareoneamerica.org/immigrant-detention-report

Shen, A. (2012). Private prisons spend $45 million on lobbying, rake in $5.1 billion for immigration detention alone. *Think Progress News.* Retrieved from https://thinkprogress.org/private-prisons-spend-45-million-on-lobbying-rake-in-5-1-billion-for-immigrant-detention-alone-b9ef073758be#.d1d68ukzf

Southern Poverty Law Center. (2016a). *Families in fear: The Atlanta immigration raids.* Retrieved from https://www.splcenter.org/20160128/families-fear-atlanta-immigration-raids

Southern Poverty Law Center. (2016b). *John Tanton.* Retrieved from https://www.splcenter.org/fighting-hate/extremist-files/individual/john-tanton

Southern Poverty Law Center. (2016c). *SPLC lawsuit: Federal government withholding records about immigration raids that targeted women, children.* Retrieved from https://www.splcenter.org/news/2016/08/09/splc-lawsuit-federal-government-withholding-records-about-immigration-raids-targeted-women

Stumpf, J. (2006). The crimmigration crisis: Immigrants, crime, and sovereign power. *American University Law Review, 56*(2), 367–419. Retrieved from http://digitalcommons.wcl.american.edu/cgi/viewcontent.cgi?article=1274&context=aulr

Tanton, J. (1993). *John Tanton.* Retrieved from https://www.splcenter.org/fighting-hate/extremist-files/individual/john-tanton

The GEO Group, Inc. (2008). *SEC filing 10-K annual report for the fiscal year ending Sunday, December 30, 2007.* Retrieved from https://www.last10k.com/sec-filings/geo/0000950144-08-001137.htm

The GEO Group, Inc. (2015). *SEC filing 10-K annual report for the fiscal year ending Wednesday, December 31, 2014.* Retrieved from https://www.last10k.com/sec-filings/geo/0001193125-15-062920.htm

The New York Times. (2008). *Immigration agency's list of deaths in custody.* Retrieved from http://www.nytimes.com/2008/05/05/nyregion/05detain-list .html?ref=nyregion

The Washington Post. (2008). *System of neglect: As tighter immigration policies strain federal agencies, the detainees in their care often pay a heavy cost.* Retrieved from http://www.washingtonpost.com/wp-srv/nation/specials/immigration/cwc_d1p1.html

U.S. Immigration and Customs Enforcement (ICE). (2011). *May 2011 ADP by detention facility.* Retrieved from https://www.ice.gov/doclib/foia/dfs/average-daily -pop-by-facility-may2011.pdf

Venters, H., Dasch-Goldberg, D., Rasmussen, A., & Keller, A. (2009). Into the abyss: Mortality and morbidity among detained immigrants. *Human Rights Quarterly, 31*(2), 474–495.

Waslin, M. L. (2013). Driving while immigrant: Driver's license policy and immigration enforcement. In D. C. Brotherton, D. L. Stageman, & S. P. Leyro (Eds.), *Outside justice: Immigration and the criminalizing impact of changing policy and practice*, 3–22. New York, NY: Springer.

Wessler, S. F. (2011). *Shattered families: The perilous intersection of immigration enforcement and the child welfare system.* Washington, DC: Applied Research Center. Retrieved from http://act.colorlines.com/acton/attachment/1069/f-0079/0/-/-/l -sf-cl-70140000000T6DHAA0–000f/l-sf-cl-70140000000T6DHAA0– 000f:11446/file.pdf

Yoshikawa, H., Godfrey, E. B., & Rivera, A. C. (2008). Access to institutional resources as a measure of social exclusion: Relations with family process and cognitive development in the context of immigration. In H. Yoshikawa & N. Way (Eds.), Beyond the family: Contexts of immigrant children's development. *New Directions for Child and Adolescent Development, 121*, 63–86.

Chapter Five

Strengthening the Sanctuary

Institutional Policies to Support DACA Students

Dee Hill-Zuganelli and F. Tyler Sergent

The 2016 US presidential election marked the most public intonation of racist and xenophobic comments against Mexican immigrants on the national stage in several years (Winders, 2016). Trump's rhetoric on the campaign trail echoed that of conservative states' recent anti-immigrant agendas. Proclamations dovetailed neatly with Arizona's defense of officers stopping immigrants based on "reasonable suspicion"; Alabama's limitation of access to secure affordable housing; Michigan's specific denials of emergency relief to undocumented immigrants; the appointment of new border enforcement units in Texas; and Louisiana's attempts to calculate the impact of undocumented immigrants on taxpayers (Morse, Mendoza, & Mayorga, 2015; Winders, 2011, 2016).

With a promise to undo Obama's progress on immigration, Trump vowed to terminate the Deferred Action for Childhood Arrivals (DACA) program and made his plan explicit as part of a ten-point policy statement released in November 2016. Point five reads as follows:

> All immigration laws will be enforced—we will triple the number of ICE [Immigration and Customs Enforcement] agents. *Anyone who enters the U.S. illegally is subject to deportation.* That is what it means to have laws and to have a country. (Donald J. Trump for President, Inc., 2016, emphasis added.)

Trump's immigration policy appears to cite 1990s demographic patterns of Mexican immigrants and steeps language in the rhetoric of the Operation Wetback era in the 1950s (Winders, 2016). We extend this line of thought to an analysis of political structure. Unchecked power and unclear direction mark two problems that occur when racist rhetoric drives immigration policy and enforcement.

Consider Trump's response at a February 16, 2017, press conference. When directly asked whether or not he would continue DACA, he lucidly stated:

> DACA is a very, very difficult subject for me, I will tell you. To me it's one of the most difficult subjects I have. Because you have these incredible kids, in many cases, not all cases. In some of the cases they're having DACA and they're gang members and they're drug dealers, too. But you have some absolutely incredible kids, I would say mostly. They were brought here in such a way; it's a very, very tough subject. We are going to deal with DACA with heart. I have to deal with a lot of politicians, don't forget, and I have to convince them that what I'm saying is, is right, and I appreciate your understanding on that. But the DACA situation is a very, very, it's a very difficult thing for me, because, you know, I love these kids. I love kids. I have kids and grandkids, and I find it very, very hard doing what the law says exactly to do. And you know the law's rough. I'm not talking about new laws. I'm talking the existing law is very rough. It's very, very rough. (Redden, 2017)

This statement is problematic for two reasons. First, it offers sensitivity toward DACA youth in a manner that is inconsistent with the aggressive policy and enforcement stances promoted both on the campaign trail and by members of the Trump administration. Second, and more importantly, Trump's incoherent narrative allows his subordinates to use racism and demonization of brown undocumented bodies[1] as means to fill an operational vacuum. Specifically, the congressional failure to provide pathways to citizenship and legalization for undocumented immigrants (Silva, 2016; Stoll, 2015) has allowed anti-immigrant rhetoric to drive the development of immigration policy. This compels our call in this chapter to contextualize sanctuary cities and campuses around the need to protect today's undocumented youth and their families from increasingly aggressive efforts to surveil, police, and remove brown undocumented bodies by force. Given recent attentiveness to undocumented youth enrolled in higher education (Adams & Boyne, 2015; Figueroa, 2017; Kenworthy, 2016), we call on colleges and universities to assess existing institutional policies related to these student bodies and strengthen them in order to protect against aggressive, anti-immigrant action and racialized policing.

We understand the hesitation to address DACA and undocumented student policies; the fears of economic and political retaliation from the federal government are real (Dinan, 2017; Horwitz & Sacchetti, 2017). Nevertheless, because colleges and universities across the country admitted students with awareness of DACA status, they have a responsibility to assure their safety and to address immigration-related concerns on an ongoing basis, and we offer practical strategies toward this end.

First, we ground today's sanctuary campus movement in its historical origins and existing conceptual frameworks. Second, we describe the vacuum surrounding immigration policy and DACA students by juxtaposing aggressive enforcement actions against contradictory statements from the Trump administration. Third, we assert that colleges and universities are not powerless in the face of such headwinds. In light of high-profile deportations of DACA students, we propose a five-point approach for colleges and universities to follow for strengthening protections for DACA and undocumented students on college campuses.

SEEKING SANCTUARY: HISTORICAL AND CONCEPTUAL FRAMEWORKS

The current-day sanctuary movement takes root in the flight of Salvadorans escaping political violence in the 1980s. Churches and immigrant-based social justice organizations such as Casa El Salvador and the Comité Farabundo Martí in the United States provided material relief for refugees. Providing care and comfort created an opportunity for parishioners and volunteers to not only learn about military suppression, but also call on Congress to enact policy change (Perla & Coutin, 2009). Churches had become key sites for resistance as Mexican immigrants and their families sought a new way of life (Terry & Jiménez, 2007).

Existing scholarship offers macroeconomic explanations for the development of immigration policy. Massey, Denton, and Malone (2002) emphasized trade liberalization. In their view, immigration policy supports agribusiness interests, prioritizing the increase in flow of goods and services across borders even if it means selectively admitting Mexican immigrants to provide necessary labor power. Profit-seeking requires evading labor and pay standards; employers skirt them by hiring undocumented workers off-the-books (Stoll, 2015). Profit not only includes labor exploitation but also the detaining and deporting of Mexican immigrants once legislators deem their presence unwanted. For instance, Corrections Corporation of America (CCA) began housing detainees in 2005; by 2013, CCA earned $215 million, or 13 percent of its total revenue, on this business alone (Silva, 2016). Economic sentiments may fuel voters' support for immigration policies. At a time when recovery from the Great Recession still remains fragile for many Americans, Mexican immigrants face scapegoating from politicians and hard-line anti-immigration activists (Seif, Ullman, & Núñez-Mchiri, 2014). Together, these explanations maintain the profitability and the cultural acceptance of racism. Public, anti-immigrant rhetoric obscures the extent to which employers and private firms exploit immigrant labor for financial self-interest. So long as such rhetoric is vocal and heard by supportive voters, racist sentiments can shape immigration policy in contemporary times (Winders, 2016).

At the same time, macro-level frameworks fail to address the liminal space that today's undocumented youth occupy in the political landscape. This liminal space occurs when existing legislation fails to confer protection to persons targeted by anti-immigrant legislation. DACA provides lawful presence to undocumented youth who entered the United States at a specific age, but denies it to undocumented adults or to persons previously deported. This presence enables eligible youth to acquire work authorization, a Social Security card, and in some states a driver's license, so long as recipients renew their status every two years. Yet, as a legal term, lawful presence has no meaning. Its meaning is inferred in contrast to unlawful presence (i.e., entering the country without admittance or parole) and unlawful status (i.e., removal of lawful status following perpetration of a crime) (Adams & Boyne, 2015). Public statements like Trump's approach to DACA fail to clarify lawful presence any further.

Not only do sympathetic responses fail to address gaps in status, but they also maintain subordinate legal structures that support anti-immigrant enforcement. Even if DACA confers lawful presence on a time-limited basis, the Department of Homeland Security (DHS) has the power to terminate lawful status at any time. Enriquez (2015, 939) described such tenuousness as "a distinct form of legal violence wherein the sanctions intended for a specific population spill over to negatively affect individuals not targeted by [such] laws." Demonizing brown undocumented bodies en masse while providing selective lip service of support to youth fails to change enforcement policies, thus making victims easier to deport through any means necessary (Winders, 2016). We explore how these contradictory dynamics play out through the candidacy and the ascension of the Trump administration below.

HEARTS, SHACKLES, AND HIGH-PROFILE DETENTIONS

On January 25, 2017, Trump signed Executive Order 13768, "Enhancing Public Safety in the Interior of the United States," which declared cities that house undocumented immigrants in violation of national security and public safety interests. The Order referenced 8 USC § 1373, a statute that prevents local and state officials from interfering with federal agents' requests for immigration information (Dunn, 2017).

Section 1373 was the result of an increasingly aggressive enforcement stance crafted by the George W. Bush (Bush II) and Obama administrations.

Under Bush II, Immigration and Customs Enforcement (ICE) shifted away from deportation proceedings at unauthorized workplaces toward home-based apprehensions without warning. Home raids increased from 1,900 cases in 2003 to 34,000 in 2008. If immigrants were unwilling to leave voluntarily, then agents selectively stalled and denied due process. Examples included release with ankle monitoring, issuing expensive bonds up to $10,000 while prohibiting work authorization, and long-term detentions out of state until the hearing (McLeigh, 2010). The sudden nature of home raids and the lack of communication from ICE about apprehension proceedings created a climate of chaos and fear (Capps, Castañeda, Chaudry, & Santos, 2007).

Technologically sophisticated surveillance further magnified the effectiveness of brute enforcement tactics. In 2008, during the Obama administration, the Secure Communities Program led to the creation of data terminals that allowed booking agencies to process criminals' fingerprints against federal work and immigration databases (Seif, Ullman, & Núñez-Mchiri, 2014; Valdez, Coleman, & Akbar, 2017). These terminals automated immigration enforcement to an unprecedented degree, allowing cross-checking of hundreds of thousands of private records with limited discretion over which databases were authorized for use. Furthermore, Secure Communities constrained state and local enforcement prerogatives. Federal legislation (e.g., USA PATRIOT Act, Border Security and Visa Reform Acts) mandated that officials in charge of immigrant admission and deportation responsibilities have unfettered access to state, local, and international data systems to carry out their responsibilities (Richards, cited in Valdez, Coleman, & Akbar, 2017). Secure Communities originally solicited cooperation from cities and local law enforcement through memoranda of agreement (MOAs). However, when local agencies worried that law-abiding immigrants would become more fearful of police presence, DHS terminated all MOAs and declared cooperation to be mandatory (Valdez, Coleman, & Akbar, 2017). Together, technology and policy mandates created extensive enforcement power with DHS conducting self-directed oversight (see Johnson, 2014). Should officials aligned with anti-immigrant interests gain control over these apparatuses, we expect enforcement aggression to increase even in the face of pro-immigrant opposition.

On February 21, 2017, less than a week after Trump's "heart" comments, Press Secretary Sean Spicer addressed reporters' questions regarding two new DHS memos on immigration enforcement and border security. Consistent with Trump's campaign promises, ICE wanted to hire thousands of new agents and support personnel in order to carry out deportations even more swiftly than before. Mexican immigrants also needed to be shamed out of the country; the administration would create a new Victims of Immigration Crime Enforcement office in order to publicize crimes of all magnitude (Office of the Press Secretary, 2017; Redden, 2017). Spicer denied the memos advocated mass deportation; the administration would continue to prioritize deportation of immigrants with criminal records and threats to public safety. When asked how directives would apply to individual cases, Spicer explained:

> And when you're talking about 13, 14, 15, potentially more, millions of people in this country, the President needed to give guidance, especially after what they went through in the last administration where there were so many carve-outs that ICE agents and CBP [United States Customs and Border Protection] members had to figure out each individual whether or not they fit in a particular category and they could adjudicate that case. The President wanted to *take the shackles off* individuals in these agencies and say: You have a mission, there are laws that need to be followed; you should do your mission and follow the law. (Office of the Press Secretary, 2017, lines 626–634, emphasis added)

Newspaper outlets offered critical press after three high-profile arrests, detention, and one deportation of DACA students by ICE. On February 10, 2017, Daniel Ramirez Medina, a 23-year-old resident of Washington state, was arrested and detained during a raid reportedly targeting his father. After six weeks in custody, ICE eventually released Medina on a $15,000 bond (Park, Moshtaghian, & Jarrett, 2017). On February 19, Juan Manuel Montes-Bojorquez, a 23-year-old Californian, was apprehended in Calexico, CA, and within three hours deported to Mexico by US Customs and Border Protection (Gonzales, 2017). CBP issued contradictory reasons for Montes-Bojorquez's detention—initially, caught in midst of a border crossing, with a prior conviction for theft; later amended to no encounter (Gonzales, 2017). CBP also claimed that his DACA status ended in 2015, but in reality his status was valid through 2018 (Gonzales, 2017). Less than two weeks later, on March 1, 2017, Daniela Vargas, a DACA student in Mississippi, was arrested and detained by ICE agents immediately following her public statements about a raid that deported her father and brother and about her own fears as an undocumented immigrant living in the United States (Hauser, 2017). She was given a deportation order without a hearing but eventually was released after immigration attorneys intervened (Jarvie, 2017).

In response, officials in the Trump administration offered unclear justifications. ICE tweeted on March 9, 2017, that "DACA is not a protected legal status, but active DACA recipients are typically lower level enforcement priority." The agency explained in a further sub-tweet that removal is justified after the committing of a crime (ICE, 2017), yet none of these cases had substantiated charges. During the Montes-Bojorquez incident, Attorney General Jeff Sessions could not explain why he was picked up, yet assumed he overstayed his visa (Gonzales, 2017). Sessions continued to assert that "DACA enrollees are not being targeted" in an interview with Fox News despite evidence to the contrary (Shaw, 2017).

Sessions' statement is all the more difficult to parse because DHS Secretary John Kelly removed one of the very few self-checks DHS had conferred unto its agents in the past. Even if ICE asserts that DACA students are low enforcement priority, this designation is not reflected within current operating memoranda (Kelly, 2017). Failure to designate protection also leaves DACA students vulnerable to expansions of expedited removal. Expedited removal (i.e., suspension of due process for border crossers) originally pertained to individuals caught crossing the border within two weeks and 100 miles of their cross point. Kelly expanded the criteria to include anyone, anywhere in the country, who had crossed within two years. The high-profile incidents illustrate that, in practice, officers can detain DACA students *then* justify the right to deport—even if grounds are weak—after the fact. This response compelled Griesa Martinez, advocacy director for United We Dream, to remark: "We've seen Trump . . . and John Kelly say, 'The DACA program is alive and well.' We've seen [House Speaker] Paul Ryan look straight into the eyes of one of our members and say, 'You have nothing to worry about.' And then this happens" (Gomez & Agren, 2017, paras. 10–11).

Regardless of whether or not DACA remains in place, these incidents illustrate the consequence of enforcement agents dictating their own policies without oversight or guidance from legislation or the executive branch. The Trump administration and its surrogates can offer sympathetic and often contradictory statements to the press. So long as DHS asserts that their actions are justified by national security interests, lapses in speech and action can continue unfettered. It is in this chaotic environment that we ask colleges and universities to assess the policies and resources they have in place to protect DACA and undocumented students under their care.

CALLS FOR A NEW SANCTUARY

Hundreds of American colleges and universities have called on the Trump administration to stop these actions and protect DACA students (Heim, 2017). The American Council on Education organized one open letter in March 2017 with more than 560 signatures from colleges around the country (Redden, 2017) and offers from more than 130 college presidents to meet with congressional leaders on DACA matters (Yarbrough, 2016). Parikh and Maciel (cited in Young, 2016) tracked 115 online petitions and 29 sanctuary campuses. Letter signings, press conferences, and joint student-faculty protests signal the need for colleges and universities to move past platitudes and instead clarify university-sanctioned responses (Funke, 2016). Currently, a Google map (2017) identifies schools that have been petitioned to become sanctuary campuses, those that have committed to doing so, and those that have refused.

Some institutions have also pledged not to cooperate with federal agents who may come onto campus seeking these students (American Association of University Professors, 2016) despite threats to cut federal funding to their respective cities (Dunn, 2017; Heim, 2017; Horwitz & Sacchetti, 2017). This is a helpful first step within a comprehensive approach to assess, clarify, and strengthen institutional policies to protect DACA students. We propose appointing a task force of multiple stakeholders to guide this process as follows.

Creating the Task Force

First, a task force composed of faculty, staff, and students should commit to regular meetings for strategizing policies and holding the institution accountable for providing the necessary resources to support DACA students. The task force must first listen to DACA, undocumented, and allied student voices: namely, what *they* see and observe as threats and the types of support and assistance they would like to see from their institution. Participants can then build rapport by discussing their sense of the campus situation and identifying where they see potential for impact. When delegating tasks, aligning members' actions with preexisting research, teaching, or service expertise may bring efficiency and diverse experience to the fore.

The task force can then lay out a strategy for identifying and implementing procedures and policies that best fit the institutional community and its students' needs. An ideal approach will include *several* means of disseminating information and clarifying policies. These may include but are not limited to informational campaigns, hosting discussion forums, networking systems, using rapid-response tools, and aggregating legal resources. The size of the task force and the network of supportive stakeholders can dictate whether it is best to pursue a series of tasks or coalesce around one or two key objectives. The primary objective is to *take action* in line with DACA students' input. No matter the number of tasks pursued, we recommend grounding any work with confidentiality in mind. Protocols and information should be disseminated through a secure cloud-based platform, such as Box (www.box.com). Task force designees can work with campus information systems officials to offer training, if needed. We also explore steps to reduce the risk of "outing" DACA students in a later section.

"Know Your Rights" Campaign

One strategy that both informs the community and helps to garner additional support is a "know your rights" campaign combined with informational forums. Task force members should assess the presence of supportive campus, community, and local agencies to help increase attendees' knowledge and awareness of immigration issues. Clear and explicit designations of support should guide the recruitment process; mission statements and personal relationships can serve as effective means of evaluating helpful parties.

The content of the campaign should reflect a diversity of substantive and legal expertise. Local or regional immigration law centers may present current developments in immigration law, immigrant rights, and common falsehoods many people believe about undocumented populations and their legal status. Faculty members and community organizations can also coach attendees about language and status. For instance, referring to persons with undocumented status as "illegal" or "criminal" mischaracterizes their status because, in reality, being undocumented is not a crime; violations fall under civil law, not criminal. Educating the community on these distinctions can garner additional support for DACA students from peers and even community members outside of the campus (The National Immigration Law Center, 2017).

Another misconception—even among some undocumented residents—is that "illegal aliens" lack legal rights, when in fact everyone who resides even temporarily in the United States has the same constitutional protections under the Bill of Rights that citizens enjoy (Contreras, 2015). These protections include the rights against search and seizure without probable legal cause (US Constitution, Fourth Amendment), self-incrimination (US Constitution, Fifth Amendment), and detention without due process (US Constitution, Fourteenth Amendment). Creating signs that remind individuals of their rights when encountering law enforcement agents provides some level of assurance for DACA students and their families. Such signs provide instruction on individuals' rights pertaining to when agents come to a residence, attempt to forcibly enter it, or detain or arrest an undocumented person. As examples, figure 5.1 shows basic rights, and figure 5.2 is a sign designed to be shown to law enforcement agents. We recommend printing signs in bilingual formats.

Campus Forums

Forums can provide students ongoing, safe space to express fears and concerns and to notify the campus community of current news. In addition, they can communicate how allies may respond in the event of a crisis. Individual participants may be willing to house students or pick up and transport students who have been detained. Other organizations may provide counseling and coping support. Similarly, campus cultural centers and ministries may

KNOW YOUR RIGHTS

EVERYONE in the U.S. has the constitutional right of due process, regardless of documentation status.

IF ICE AGENTS COME TO YOUR HOME:

- DO NOT OPEN THE DOOR, ASK FOR IDENTIFICATION and A WARRANT to be shown to you (through your window or under your door). Read it carefully; a valid search warrant for your home must be signed by a judge and have your address on it (an ICE administrative warrant, form I-200 or I-205, does not permit entry).
- ICE agents may try to trick you or scare you into opening the door, but DO NOT BE FOOLED. An arrest warrant or deportation warrant does not allow them to search your home. ASK FOR AN INTERPRETER IF NEEDED.
- If they have NO WARRANT, say, "YOU MAY NOT ENTER MY HOME. PLEASE LEAVE."
- You have the constitutional right to REMAIN SILENT. Do NOT answer any questions without first speaking to an attorney representing you. Say "I AM EXERCISING MY RIGHT TO REMAIN SILENT."
- DO NOT SIGN ANYTHING without an attorney representing you.

IF ICE AGENTS FORCIBLY ENTER YOUR HOME:

- DO NOT RUN and exercise your right to REMAIN SILENT. State that you do not consent to their entry.
- RECORD the events and remember identities of agents. Write down everything you remember as soon as you can.

IF YOU ARE DETAINED OR ARRESTED:

- DO NOT PHYSICALLY RESIST.
- TRY TO REMAIN CALM.
- ASK FOR AN ATTORNEY.
- REMAIN SILENT. Anything you say or is overheard will be used against you.
- DO NOT DISCUSS YOUR CASE OR STATUS WITH ANYONE BUT AN ATTORNEY.

Figure 5.1. "Know Your Rights" sign.
Image courtesy of F. Tyler Sergent.

ATTENTION LAW ENFORCEMENT AGENTS

- I KNOW MY RIGHTS AND EXERCISE THEM.

- SHOW YOUR IDENTIFICATION BY HOLDING IT UP TO THE WINDOW.

- I WILL NOT OPEN THE DOOR FOR YOU.

- YOU MAY NOT ENTER WITHOUT SHOWING A VALID WARRANT UP TO THE WINDOW.

- IF YOU DO NOT HAVE A VALID SEARCH WARRANT, I REQUEST THAT YOU LEAVE.

- I DO NOT CONSENT TO YOUR ENTRY OR SEARCH.

- I EXERCISE MY RIGHT TO REMAIN SILENT.

- I WILL NOT ANSWER ANY QUESTIONS OR SIGN ANYTHING WITHOUT AN ATTORNEY WHO REPRESENTS ME.

Figure 5.2. "Attention Law Enforcement Agents" sign.
Image courtesy of F. Tyler Sergent.

uphold open-door policies. Task force members reached out to faith-based and advocacy organizations for support. At present, two congregations have been willing to house DACA students in distress (Perla & Coutin, 2009).

In order to keep the campus community at large informed and engaged, a series of information-based as well as discussion-based forums work well. Administrative staff may arrange joint student-staff forums to discuss DACA policies and disseminate internal guidelines for handling situations through campus mail systems. Of course, such meetings and direct involvement of DACA students must also be weighed against protecting their identities and documentation status. Campus officials must not compel DACA students to disclose their immigration status or the status of friends or family members. If disclosure is needed for enrollment or financial aid issues, then it must be done carefully through FERPA-protected individuals and offices at the institution. The Family Educational Rights and Privacy Act (FERPA) is the federal law that protects student school records and personal identifying data from being shared publicly or with any unauthorized individual or agency (*Family Educational Rights and Privacy Act [FERPA]*, 2016; for implications, see also Figueroa, 2017). Depending on the administrative structures at the college or university, this can be accomplished through a centralized office. Administrators should also remind faculty and staff not to inquire about student immigrant status and inform students of their privacy rights. If undocumented or DACA students were to "out" themselves, then faculty and staff must treat that information with absolute confidentiality and sensitivity (Figueroa, 2017).

Contact Cards

Regardless of the type of college or university at which a DACA student is enrolled, the institution's ability to protect a student diminishes the farther away from campus the student travels, whether just off campus property, outside of the municipality, county, state, or country. This does not mean, however, that DACA students must travel at their own risk only without any supportive network. Colleges and universities should develop protocols for informing need-to-know parties regarding DACA students' travel plans. Protocols should also address what-if situations such as what to do if police or ICE stop DACA students or whom to contact if they are threatened with deportation. One useful tool—a contact card—can pair DACA students with faculty and staff members who are willing to be resources and contact persons when the students are traveling away from campus. Individualized wallet-size cards can include the faculty or staff member's contact information on one side and a reminder of the student's rights when encountering law enforcement agents on the other side. Figure 5.3 is an example of what both sides of this card might look like.

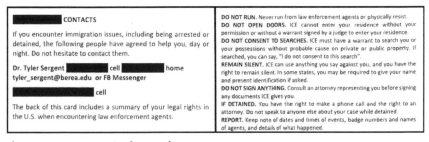

Figure 5.3. Contact Card example.
Image courtesy of F. Tyler Sergent.

We recognize that the willingness to be in touch through a contact card comes with the risk of having one's name, mobile telephone number, and email available to unauthorized parties. Ideally, the task force appoints several persons to share that responsibility and to allow them to revoke that permission at any time. Chaplains and counseling services personnel, may have legal privilege which can mitigate risk to the volunteer and add an additional level of protection for the student. The task force may distinguish public point persons from, for instance, a private telephone tree deployed in an acute crisis situation. Commonsense measures to protect privacy may also include tightly controlling *who* distributes these cards (e.g., a DACA student advisor) and distributing physical copies instead of virtual ones.

The intention is for the DACA student to have a person (or more than one person) that he or she can contact in the event of detention, arrest, or other possible traveling obstacles relating to documentation status. The faculty or staff member must commit to take that call and to help in whatever way possible in that moment. Help might include forwarding calls to the appropriate FERPA-protected institutional office to contact the student's local family or, at the student's request, contacting family members directly; making arrangements for legal representation for the student; or even traveling to where the student is located and helping in person.

Notifica App

Created by a San Francisco–based tech company, Huge, in collaboration with United We Dream, Notifica is designed as a "panic button" phone app for anyone arrested and detained by immigration or other law enforcement agents (Lapowsky, 2017). Once set up and activated, the app sends notification of arrest to pre-selected contacts within two seconds by the press of a single button. Since arrest and detention can come without notice or time to make contact otherwise, even with a contact card and human network, this app can serve the same function without awaiting the opportunity (and right) to make a phone call at the whim of law enforcement agents. Notifica can also serve as an easier-to-remember form of contact in case the contact card is lost or misplaced. A student's contact card person can be among those the app notifies, along with other friends, family, or other support resource person (e.g., immigration lawyer, national consulate, etc.).

Campus Police and Legal Counsel

In addition to determining response in crisis situations, the task force must also assess how campus police and institutional counsel are equipped to respond to demands for cooperating with federal immigration enforcement. The campus-local-state police nexus determination is paramount. Stahly-Butts and colleagues (2015) recommend determining how and to what extent campus police officers are willing to allow outside law enforcement on their campus to conduct enforcement actions. This is especially important with regard to the ICE hold: a 48-hour detention that gives enough time for federal officers to pick up the target. We also recommend that the task force engages in conversation with local police to clarify whether immigration enforcement is a priority for them and how officers would respond to ICE holds. As these details get articulated, college administrators can develop coordinated response plans and dictate how campus police is supposed to act. Response plans can include scripts for fielding ICE calls or in-person appearances, clarifying student information that officers can and cannot disclose, and insistence on warrants before allowing ICE on campus (Kenworthy, 2016).

While developing the response plan, college administrators can address how institutional counsel responds to enforcement actions. At minimum, it can help to ensure confidentiality practices within the campus community. Ideally, institutional counsel may coordinate assistance with immigration law centers, students' private counsel, or even a national consulate. The office of legal counsel can also assist the administration with establishing a legal fund for DACA students. We understand that providing students direct access to institutional counsel may create inadvertent attorney-client relationships or subject institutional attorneys to legal conditions outside of their licensure territory. We also recognize that institutional counsel is primarily responsible for the institution's liability and exposure and not necessarily for the good of DACA students. However, if colleges and universities extend a commitment of educational access for DACA students, then it must follow a commitment to protect students in legal duress. Institutional counsel should be the first legal resource for helping protect DACA students on and off campus.

Beyond the Campus

As faculty, staff, and administrators at institutions of higher education, our main concern, naturally, will be DACA students' safety and well-being. But we must also recognize that as concerned as DACA students are for themselves and their classmates, they are also very concerned about family members with potential mixed immigration statuses. The arguable purpose of policing practices that conduct tens of thousands of raids each year— certainly the result—is to break up families and cut the familial and social support networks for individuals within these families, thus weakening the agency of people under threat.

Although institutions' abilities to support students' families are limited by their resources and obligations, tools and information can certainly be shared with DACA students' families and friends. Colleges and universities should sponsor events for community members who may experience the same fears and concerns as DACA students. Local organizations, businesses, and faith communities can also help with this effort. As a result, the academy becomes integral to the community in support of our undocumented brothers and sisters.

CONCLUSION

Given the political and economic threats made by both the White House (Donald J. Trump for President, 2016) and the US Attorney General against sanctuary cities (Horwitz & Sacchetti, 2017), it is a real possibility that sanctuary campuses could be targeted in the same way (Dinan, 2017). Part of the debate over sanctuary campuses, like sanctuary cities, asks whether or not declaring a public position risks drawing attention from federal authorities that the policy itself attempts to avoid. A college or university campus is far more easily canvassed by law enforcement than an entire city. University presidents may also fear that the claim of sanctuary campus would give false assurance to undocumented students because the label itself holds no legal status (Natanson, 2016). By contrast, our chapter encourages colleges and universities to face such fear by focusing on the development of coordinated responses and non-cooperation tactics to protect DACA students without claiming the public sanctuary campus label.

Ultimately, we must recognize and respond to the racialized and racist bases of these statements, policies, and actions by the US federal government that vilifies Latin Americans—and in particular Mexicans—and that are demonstrated by the discriminating policing that identifies, hunts down, arrests, and deports undocumented brown bodies but does not do the same to undocumented Canadians and Europeans. Homeland Security's own numbers indicate there are 93,035 undocumented Canadians in the United States who have stayed in country beyond their legal visas, and this is well more than twice the number of Mexicans in the same category at 42,114 and is equal to the total number from the whole of South America (Attanasio, 2016; Gomez, 2016). The European number is even higher than Canada at 123,729 (Attanasio, 2016). So why are ICE, CBP, and DHS focusing exclusively on Latinos and Latinas and not the 216,764 Canadians and Europeans who are in the United States illegally? The answer is simple: racism. The Canadians and Europeans by and large look very much like one author of this chapter, and this intentional inclusion of white and exclusion of brown fits all too well with the white nationalist, white supremacist ideology underlying US immigration policy.

Our response to the shifting political winds and policies on immigration and the discriminatory policing of brown bodies is to turn inward and also to reach outward. It is not the public's obligation to decipher the Trump administration's statements on Mexican immigrants or to predict frightfully which sanctuary city is the next target. In our view, time is better spent clarifying how colleges and universities can stand up for DACA students; indeed, this may very well be the first time such institutional policies fall under review. If colleges and universities want to back up their existing, ethically binding commitments to DACA students, whom they have accepted into the student body and campus community, then they must do so by examining their own institutional policies and taking clear steps to correct deficiencies and create policies that support these students. We have provided some strategies and practical approaches to accomplishing these goals. Each institution, public or private, must address and clarify how it would respond if ICE comes for its students.

NOTE

1. The authors acknowledge their assumption that anti-immigrant legislation and aggressive policing implicate a particular subset of brown (i.e., Mexican) bodies even though their potential impact to other racial and ethnic minorities is much more widespread.

REFERENCES

Adams, A., & Boyne, K. S. (2015). Access to higher education for undocumented and "DACAmented" students: The current state of affairs. *Indiana International & Comparative Law Review*, *25*(1), 47–62. doi:10.18060/7909.0004

American Association of University Professors. (2016, November 22). *The atmosphere on–campus in the wake of the elections.* Retrieved from https://www.aaup .org/file/2016-PostElection-Atmosphere_0.pdf

Attanasio, C. (2016, February 4). Canadian immigrants lead world in illegal U.S. visa overstays, according to the first-ever DHS estimates. *Latin Times.* Retrieved from http://www. latintimes.com/canadian-immigrants-lead-world-illegal-us-visa -overstays-according-first-ever-dhs-367906

Capps, R., Castañeda, R. M., Chaudry, A., & Santos, R. (2007). *Paying the price: The impact of immigration raids on America's children.* National Council on La Raza. Retrieved from http://www.urban.org/sites/default/files/ publication/46811/411566-Paying-the-Price-The-Impact-of-Immigration-Raids -on-America-s-Children.PDF

Contreras, R. L. (2015, September 29). Yes, illegal aliens have constitutional rights. *The Hill.* Retrieved from http://thehill.com/blogs/pundits-blog/immigration/255281 -yes-illegal-aliens-have-constitutional-rights

Dinan, S. (2017, January 18). Congress looks to punish "sanctuary campus" colleges that protect illegal immigrants. *The Washington Times.* Retrieved from http://www. washingtontimes.com/news/2017/jan/18/congress-looks-punish-sanctuary-camp us-colleges

Donald J. Trump for President, Inc. (2016). *Donald J. Trump's 10 point plan to put America first.* Retrieved from https://perma.cc/V6VR-8N26

Dunn, C. (2017, May 31). The constitutional wall between Trump and sanctuary cities. *New York Law Journal.* Retrieved from http://www.newyorklawjournal.com/ id=1202787984533

Enriquez, L. E. (2015). Multigenerational punishment: Shared experiences of undocumented immigration status within mixed-status families. *Journal of Marriage and Family, 77*(4), 939–953. doi:10.1111/jomf.12196

Family Educational Rights and Privacy Act (FERPA). (2016, June 26). U.S. Department of Education. Retrieved from https://www2.ed.gov/policy/gen/guid/fpco/ ferpa/index.html

Figueroa, A. M. (2017). Speech or silence: Undocumented students' decisions to disclose or disguise their citizenship status in school. *American Educational Research Journal, 54*(3), 485–523. doi:10.3102/0002831217693937

Funke, D. (2016, December 19). Here's where the sanctuary campus movements stands. *USA Today College.* Retrieved from http://college.usatoday.com/ 2016/12/19/heres-where-the-sanctuary-campus-movement-stands/

Gomez, A. (2016, January 20). Government's failure to track foreign visitors angers Congress. *USA Today.* Retrieved from https://www.usatoday.com/story/news/na tion/2016/01/20/ immigration-visa-overstays-senate-judiciary-committee-hearing/ 79077342/

Gomez, A., & Agren, D. (2017, April 18). First protected DREAMer is deported under Trump. *USA Today.* Retrieved from https://www.usatoday.com/story/news/ world/2017/04/18/first-protected-dreamer-deported-under-trump/100583274/

Gonzales, R. (2017, April 18). DREAMer deportation case raises questions on Trump's deferred action policy. *National Public Radio.* Retrieved from http://

www.npr.org/sections/thetwo-way/2017/04/18/524610150/first-dreamer-protected
-by-deferred-action-program-is-deported

Google.com. (2017). *Sanctuary campuses* [Map]. Retrieved from https://www
.google.com/ maps/d/viewer?mid=1LcIME474-lYWbTf_xQChIhSSN30&hl=en&
ll=36.20397974434345%2C-113.89148250000005&z=4

Hauser, C. (2017, March 2). A young immigrant spoke out about her deportation
fears. Then she was detained. *The New York Times.* Retrieved from https://www
.nytimes.com/2017/ 03/02/us/immigrant-daca-detained.html?_r=0

Heim, J. (2017, February 6). Calls for "sanctuary" campuses multiply as fears grow over
Trump immigration policy. *The Washington Post.* Retrieved from https://www.wash-
ingtonpost.com/news/grade-point/wp/2017/02/06/calls-for-sanctuary-campuses-mul
tiply-as-fears-grow-over-trump-immigration-policy/?utm_term=.99b453281ae0

Horwitz, S., & Sacchetti, M. (2017, March 27). Attorney General Jeff Sessions re-
peats Trump threat that "sanctuary cities" could lose Justice Department grants.
The Washington Post. Retrieved from https://www.washingtonpost.com/world/
national-security/attorney-general-jeff-sessions-repeats-trump-threat-that-sanctu
ary-cities-could-lose-justice-department-grants/2017/03/27/1fa38e2a-1315–11e7–
9e4f-09aa75d3ec57_story.html?utm_ term=.166518d9b893

Immigration and Customs Enforcement. (2017, March 9, 10:37 a.m.) [Twitter mo-
ment]. Retrieved from https://twitter.com/ICEgov/status/839907967692648449

Jarvie, J. (2017, March 10). Mississippi "Dreamer" Daniela Vargas released from
detention but deportation order stands. *Los Angeles Times.* Retrieved from http://
www.latimes.com/ nation/la-na-mississippi-dreamer-20170310-story.html

Johnson, J. C. (2014, November 20). *Policies for the apprehension, detention, and removal of undocumented immigrants.* Department of Homeland Security. Retrieved
from https:// www.dhs.gov/sites/default/files/publications/14_1120_memo_prose
cutorial_discretion_0.pdf

Kelly, J. (2017, February 20). *Implementing the president's border security and
immigration enforcement improvements policies.* Department of Homeland Security. Retrieved from https://www.dhs.gov/sites/default/files/publications/17_0220_
S1_Implementing-the-Presidents-Border-Security-Immigration-Enforcement-Im
provement-Policies.pdf

Kenworthy, J. (2016, November 25). What universities are doing to protect their undocumented students. *The Christian Science Monitor.* Retrieved from http://www
.csmonitor.com/EqualEd/2016/1125/What-universities-are-doing-to-protect-their
-undocumented-students

Lapowsky, I. (2017, March 10). A portable panic button for immigrants swept up in
raids. *Wired Magazine.* Retrieved from https://www.wired.com/2017/03/portable
-panic-button-immigrants-swept-raids/

Massey, D. S., Durand, J., & Malone, N. J. (2002). *Beyond smoke and mirrors:
Mexican immigration in an era of economic integration.* New York, NY: Russell
Sage Foundation.

McLeigh, J. D. (2010). How do immigration and customs enforcement (ICE) practices affect the mental health of children? *American Journal of Orthopsychiatry,*
80(1), 96–100. doi:10.1111/j.1939–0025.2010.01011.x

Morse, A., Mendoza, G. S., & Mayorga, J. (2015). *2015 immigration laws and resolutions by state*. National Conference of State Legislatures. Retrieved from http://www.ncsl.org/documents/statefed/Immig_Laws_state_Feb2016.pdf

Natanson, H. (December 7, 2016). Faust says Harvard will not be a "sanctuary campus." *The Harvard Crimson*. Retrieved fromhttp://www.thecrimson.com/article/2016/12/7/faust-sanctuary-campus-policy/.

Office of the Press Secretary. (2017, February 21, 1:42 p.m.). *Press briefing by Press Secretary Sean Spicer, 2/21/2017, #13*. Retrieved from https://www.whitehouse.gov/the-press-office/2017/02/21/press-briefing-press-secretary-sean-spicer-2212017–13

Park, M., Moshtaghian, A., & Jarrett, L. (2017, March 29). DREAMer to be released after six weeks in ICE custody. *CNN*. Retrieved from http://www.cnn.com/2017/03/29/us/daniel-ramirez-medina-daca-release-ice/index.html

Perla, H., & Coutin, S. B. (2009). Legacies and origins of the 1980s US-Central American sanctuary movement. *Refuge*, *26*(1), 7–19. Retrieved from http://refuge.journals.yorku. ca/index.php/refuge/article/download/30602/28112

Redden, E. (2017, February 17). California dreamers—and their nightmares. *Inside Higher Ed*. Retrieved from https://www.insidehighered.com/news/2017/04/14/dreamers-grapple-increased-stresses-and-challenges

Seif, H., Ullman, C., & Núñez-Mchiri, G. G. (2014). Mexican (im)migrant status and education: Constructions of and resistance to "illegality." *Latino Studies*, *12*(2), 172–193. doi:10.1057/lst.2014.32

Shaw, A. (2017, April 19). Sessions defends immigration policies after reported "DREAMer" deportation. *Fox News*. Retrieved from http://www.foxnews.com/politics/2017/04/19/sessions-defends-immigration-policies-after-reported-dreamer-deportation.html

Silva, A. (2016). Neoliberalism confronts Latinos: Paradigmatic shifts in immigration practices. *Latino Studies*, *14*(1), 59–79. doi:10.1057/lst.2015.50

Stahly-Butts, M., Subramanian, A., Tucker, E., Duffy, J., Kumodzi, K., Sinyangwe, S., . . . & Tucker, J. (2015). Building momentum from the ground up: A toolkit for promoting justice in policing. PolicyLink. Retrieved from http://www.policylink.org/sites/default/ Files/JusticeInPolicing-9.pdf

Stoll, D. (2015). Comprehensive immigration reform and U.S. labor markets: Dilemmas for progressive labor. *New Labor Forum*, *24*(1), 76–85. doi:10.1177/1095796014562232

Terry, D., & Jiménez, N. A. (2007). The new sanctuary movement. *Hispanic*, *20*(7), 42–45.

The National Immigration Law Center. (2017). Retrieved from https://www.nilc.org/

Valdez, I., Coleman, M., & Akbar, A. (2017). Missing in action: Practice, paralegality, and the nature of immigration enforcement. *Citizenship Studies*, *21*, 547–569. doi:10.1080/ 13621025.2016.1277980

Winders, J. (2011). Representing the immigrant: Social movements, political discourse, and immigration in the U.S. South. *Southeastern Geographer*, *51*(4), 596–614. doi:10.1353/ sgo.2011.0035

Winders, J. (2016). Immigration and the 2016 election. *Southeastern Geographer*, *56*(3), 291–296. doi:10.1353/sgo.2016.0034

Yarbrough, B. (2016, November 21). Pomona College prez David Oxtoby signals support for DACA, undocumented students. *Inland Valley Daily Bulletin*. Retrieved from http://www.dailybulletin.com/social-affairs/20161121/pomona -college-prez-david-oxtoby-signals-support-for-daca-undocumented-students

Young, E. (2016, December 2). On sanctuary: What is in a name? *The Huffington Post*. Retrieved from http://www.huffingtonpost.com/entry/on-sanctuary-what-is -in-a-name_us_583f8feae4b0b93e10f8df24

Chapter Six

Sexual Assault (Threat)

Policing Brown Women's Bodies on the Mexico–US Border

Rebecca G. Martínez

"BUILD THE WALL"

On June 16, 2015, Donald J. Trump launched his presidential campaign in New York City. He centered this announcement around what many have described as hate speech toward our neighbors to the south, the people of Mexico. This is obviously a country with which we not only share a 2,000-mile border, but whose social, cultural, political, and economic history is deeply intertwined with that of the United States. Highlighting Mexican—US migration in this way was a clear sign that an austere immigration policy would be a cornerstone of his campaign. The following excerpt is the key part of his announcement, framing his pseudo-immigration policy around xenophobia:

> When do we beat Mexico at the border? They're laughing at us, at our stupidity. And now they are beating us economically. They are not our friend, believe me. But they're killing us economically . . . .When Mexico sends its people, they're not sending their best. They're not sending you. They're not sending you. They're sending people that have lots of problems, and they're bringing those problems with us. They're bringing drugs. They're bringing crime. They're rapists. And some, I assume, are good people. ("Here's Donald Trump's Presidential Announcement Speech," 2015)

And, indeed, one of Trump's biggest rallying cries throughout his campaign, after "Make America Great Again," was "We're going to build The Wall, and Mexico is going to pay for it." This combination of statements was likely a way for him to both tout his "tough on immigration" credentials and his self-described business acumen as a negotiator and dealmaker. He would chant this to raucous applause by the charged majority-white supporters at his rallies. The xenophobia in this country is, of course, nothing new; it's as old as our nation.

In this chapter, I tell the story of my friend's border crossing experience into the United States from Mexico. Her name is Marisol (a pseudonym), and until recently she lived in my same town with her husband and two young children. The part of Marisol's story I will focus on has to do with her experience of being threatened with sexual assault while in the hands of US border patrol agents. In the process, I analyze her story as a critical reflection on the militarization of the border as not only a human right's, but also a women's rights issue. Part of this militarization is a response to specifically gendered and widely circulating US narratives about so-called "anchor babies"—US citizen babies born to undocumented women—who are represented as cultural and racial threats to the nation. Thus, surveillance at the border can also be read, in part, as the policing of "dangerous" "fertile" bodies. In this space of war-like militarization, Marisol's border-crossing story is about the attempts to "control" geopolitical borders on the colonized territory of women's bodies. As feminist activist, artist, and scholar Gloria Anzaldúa (1987) famously remarked in her "Borderlands" poem: "In the Borderlands you are the battleground where the enemies are kin to each other . . . " (194). At the same time, Marisol, who eventually crossed into the United States, struggles to challenge her outsider status, while resisting the dominant "threat narrative" told about her and her family. Drawing on Anzaldúa once more, borderlands theory can be viewed, "as a project of resistance formulated as a set of processes aimed to guide the inner self of a colonized person in its struggle to achieve decolonization and liberation" (Orozco-Mendoza, 2008, 3). Borders divide insider from outsider, but by claiming a borderlands, Marisol challenges exclusion and demands inclusion, as she remains in the United States with her family despite challenges discussed later. These borderlands take on geographical as well as symbolic form in the tensions that exist along the militarized physical border and in the figurative borders related to identity, community, and citizenship. Before focusing on her story, I briefly lay out the demographic shifts occurring in the United States, the militarization of the border, and the accompanying nativist discourses that set the stage for Marisol's experience of *interrogatory sexual threat* at the border.

DEMOGRAPHIC SHIFTS AND FERTILITY THREAT

The Latino population in the United States has experienced rapid growth (Stepler and Brown, 2016). It has tripled since 1980, and Latinos have been the largest minority since 2001. As of 2014 there were 55.3 million

Hispanics in the United States, making up 17.3 percent of the nation's total population (Stepler and Brown, 2016).[1] According to US Census predictions, the number of Hispanics (census terminology) is projected to be at 119 million by 2060 (US Census Bureau, 2016). The largest foreign-born group of Hispanics comes from Mexico, making up approximately 30 percent of all US immigrants as of 2011 (Passel, Cohn, Gonzalez-Barrera, 2012). When it comes to the undocumented population, in particular, Mexicans make up the largest percentage of this population.[2] However, what tends to get missed in the demographic trends is that after four decades, the net migration from Mexico to the United States has stopped and has fallen to zero; this includes both the authorized and unauthorized population (Passel and Cohn, 2011). This fact is important because, although President Trump campaigned on building a border wall, citing the so-called problem of illegal border crossers, the reality is that he proposes spending anywhere from $15 to $25 billion to secure a border with significantly diminished crossings (Isidore & Sahadi, 2017).

Looking at gender and migration patterns, "women make up a substantial share—41 percent—of the adult undocumented population. There are about 4.5 million undocumented men (18 and over) and 3.2 million undocumented women" (Passel, Capps, and Fix, 2004). Research indicates that, along with an increase in women making the journey north, the number of children border-crossers has also grown over the last decade (Rubio-Goldsmith et al., 2016). These demographics indicate that there are also a number of bi-national and bi-status families living in the United States, where family members are composed of un/authorized status, as well as US citizens and other nationalities. Marisol's family is an example of this structure; she and her husband are undocumented immigrants, while their two children are US citizens. Her children represent those targeted derogatorily as "anchor babies," using intersecting racist and sexist images and narratives centered on the bodies of brown women and their offspring. The xenophobia that paints Marisol and her family as threats to the demographics of a "white America" will be explored in the section below.

It is with this backdrop that immigrants in the United States from Latin America, largely from Mexico and Central America, have become what Leo Chavez (2013) calls "the Latino threat." He makes the argument that it is not simply undocumented immigrants from Latin America who are seen as problematic because of their legal status but that legal immigrants and US born citizens of Latino background are threats to a "white" United States. This demographic shift to a "browning of America" as it has become popularly known is, at the very least, a racialized and gendered discourse that conveys nativist concerns over those who are constructed as non-American "others," as outside of American culture. Though racism is rarely overt, references to "cultural difference," what Balibar and Wallerstein (1988) calls a neo-racism, are used to justify practices of exclusion: social, political, economic, medical, educational, and so forth. In outlining these practices of exclusion, Chavez (2013) highlights the work of Dr. John Tanton, a zero population growth advocate in the 1970s, who was well-known for his population control stance, which was also tinged with eugenic sentiments. He later wed this activism with immigration reform and the English-only movement, and he eventually founded the Federation of American Immigration Reform (FAIR), a group known for their nativist and anti-immigrant stance. Latinas are constructed as a problem for population control because they are perceived to be hyperfertile, having "too many" babies of the "wrong" color. By this I mean that Latinas are racialized and culturally othered, and their reproduction is central to the narrative of the so-called "browning of America."

Although Chavez (2013) traces these discourses from the 1970s to the 1990s, they continue to be present and shape a mainstream nativist immigrant discourse. I will highlight just one example that I use in teaching about this topic: a 2006 clip from a Fox News segment by John Gibson. In the clip Gibson tells of demographic shifts in the United States. He notes that while "Hispanics" are producing babies, the white population just isn't keeping up. He links this to the case of Europe and reveals they are "not having enough babies to sustain their population . . . consequently, they are inviting in more and more immigrants every year to take care of things and those immigrants are having way more babies than the native population [read white], hence 'Eurabia.'" He concludes with a vociferous warning to the audience: "So far, we are doing our part here in America, but Hispanics can't carry the whole load. The rest of you, get busy. Make more babies." I then ask my class, "Who is he talking to? Why does the color of babies matter?" My students of color (not just the Latinx ones in the room) know he isn't talking about them. A substantive discussion about who counts as "American," among other things, usually ensues.

This brief account helps to contextualize how Latina sexuality, fertility, and reproduction are central to immigration debates and has resulted in their being targeted as dangerous anchor-baby-producing and resource-sucking drains on US. society. Legislation targeting birthright citizenship, prenatal care for undocumented women, and the like result from these depictions. Words frame images and debates, and the term anchor-baby is used frequently in the media and in pedestrian communication. No other place was this normalization of the term more evident than the first definition of the term included in the *New American Heritage Dictionary.* The entry read as follows:

anchor baby n. A child born to a noncitizen mother in a country that grants automatic citizenship to children born on its soil, especially such a child born to parents seeking to secure eventual citizenship for themselves and often other members of their family.

This entry gave anchor-baby a legitimization by failing to include that the term is, in fact, contested as derogatory and is not neutral (Giovagnoli, 2011). As Mary Giovagnoli explains, " . . . it appears to be a wholly American term, one mired in the politics of anti-immigrant rhetoric. Those who use it are . . . intent on suggesting that people come to the country illegally and deliberately have babies in order to use their children's citizenship to acquire legal status of their own" (para. 4). However, since that initial entry—and likely thanks to Giovagnoli's blog about the dictionary's definition—it has been changed to reflect the offensive and derogatory nature of the term. It now reads:

n.
Offensive
Used as a disparaging term for a child born to a noncitizen mother in a country that grants automatic citizenship to children born on its soil, especially when the child's birthplace is thought to have been chosen in order to improve the mother's or other relatives' chances of securing eventual citizenship (anchor baby, n.d.).

Contestations over language are important because words frame how we think about issues. If lawmakers routinely use this word and back it up by citing a supposedly neutral definition, it can make its way into policies that are inherently biased against populations who are constructed using dehumanizing language. President Trump even used the term "anchor-baby" in the presidential primary against his opponent, Ted Cruz, saying, "Ted Cruz may not be a US citizen, right? But he's an anchor baby. No, he's an anchor baby—Ted Cruz is an anchor baby in Canada" (Diamond, 2016, para. 2). The US president normalizing derogatory language in this way is dangerous. "Anchor-baby" doesn't describe a child; it describes an imagined invader who can then be legitimized as a target. It is imperative to challenge the authoritative power that both President Trump and a dictionary definition imbue with the term "anchor-baby." Its mainstream use and circulation steeped in racism and sexism needs to be made visible and its political bias established. Thus, although language may seem rather inconsequential in a larger scheme of things like sexual assault against migrants, it is part of the base that upholds a racist-sexist-xenophobic-patriarchy, normalizing such violence. As so many acts of history tell us, dehumanization is the first step on the path to violence.

Historically and contemporarily, "controlling images" that circulate about Latinas set the stage for the convergence of diverse groups such as the medical community, social scientists, environmental activists, population control proponents, and anti-immigrant nativists to come together against the perceived problem of the hyper-fertile Latina. Patricia Hill Collins (2002) notes that "controlling images" about black women such as the welfare queen, mammy, and Jezebel have been used to mark and control black women's bodies. Similarly, the image of the Latina as hyper-fertile has established a climate that allows for their reproduction and fertility to become projects of and targets for social, political, and economic policies, particularly as related to US immigration. Historically, such images set the stage for the sterilization without consent of women of color (Roberts 1997; Lopez, 2008; Gutierrez, 2008).

INCREASED MILITARIZATION OF THE BORDER SINCE THE MID-1990S AND SEXUAL ASSAULT

In response to unauthorized border crossing, the border area between the Unted States and Mexico has becoming increasingly militarized since the mid-1990s. This militarization of the border began before this time period, as Dunn (1996) traces it to a low-intensity conflict strategy developed during the Kennedy administration to deal with Central American and other so-called Third World guerrilla tactic insurgencies. However, I focus on the mid-1990s as this period has had particular implications for women because, along with militarization and a tighter border, we have seen a rise in sexual assault in the border area. Before discussing this central point, I outline the militarization of the border over this time period.

Militarization and Low-Intensity Conflict

Briefly, the Border Patrol Strategic Plan 1994 and Beyond, the Secure Fence Act, the Clinton era Illegal Immigration Reform and Immigrant Responsibility Act of 1996, the Defense Authorization Act, Operation Gatekeeper (1994) in California—in addition to other policies—have all contributed to the increased presence of border patrol agents, and a military-style presence at the border. During the mid 1990s the INS budget doubled as did the number of border patrol agents. This surge has continued into the 2000s. The Secure Fence Act of 2006, in particular, was hailed by President Bush saying, "This bill will help protect the American people. This bill will make our borders more secure. It is an important step toward immigration reform" (President

George W. Bush, 2006).[3] Moreover, the White House web link archive for George W. Bush notes a number of heightened border policing policies since his having first taken office up to 2006, including more than doubling funding for border security from 4.6 billion in 2001 to 10.4 billion in 2006 (President George W. Bush, 2006).[4] In effect, post 9/11 US Customs and Border Protection grew by 9,000 agents from 2005 to 2009. It is the second largest police agency in country after the New York City Police Department. At the same time, the border fence, as it is euphemistically referred to (but is in reality a wall in many places) has, as we know, forced many migrants to cross in the desert because urban crossing areas have been practically shut off. Moreover, during this time and in line with its "enforcement only" approach to immigration, the Obama administration increased the number of border patrol agents as part of a $600 million border bill in 2010 (Khimm, 2010). Latino organizations took note of this, and, in fact, criticized the Obama administration for deporting more undocumented immigrants than any other president in history (Marshall, 2016). He was even given the nickname "Deporter in Chief" by these activist groups.[5]

It has been widely documented in both academic and non-academic circles that the militarization of the border has led to many migrant deaths under the harsh conditions of the desert. Specifically, the prevention-through-deterrence strategy implemented in 1994 has redirected migrants from urban area crossings to the desert and the Arizona–Sonoma border (Martinez, 2016). As Daniel Martinez (2016) explains,

> The reality is that there is no definitive or exhaustive count of migrant deaths that have occurred in the region or in any other region. Nevertheless, several studies have empirically demonstrated that the increase in deaths in Southern Arizona has been a direct consequence of the way the United States has chosen to address the issue of undocumented migration—through increased border enforcement. (Station 3, para. 2)

And, because this crossing has become so dangerous, the price of a coyote (someone who guides migrants across the border) now costs roughly between $3,000 and $5,000, whereas when urban crossings were still quite common one might pay around $300. This has also resulted in drug smugglers getting involved in the coyote business, which puts migrants in a more precarious position if those crossing them are not known through trusted social networks. Coyotes have been known to rob, murder, rape, and abandon migrants on their journey (Holmes, 2013).

In addition to the increase in deaths, the militarization of the border is also linked to violence against migrants, including sexual assaults. In her work on border violence, Sylvanna Falcon (2007) utilizes Timothy Dunn's work on war and low-intensity conflict to analyze this process of border militarization, connecting it to sexual assaults perpetrated by border patrol agents. This framing is useful because it allows for both a psycho-social and material understanding of how border crossers become targeted as enemies of the United States and, as such, violence against them routinized. Dunn defines low-intensity conflict (LIC) as:

> . . . a limited political-military struggle to achieve political, social, economic, or psychological objectives. It is often protracted and ranges from diplomatic, economic, and psycho-social pressures through terrorism and insurgency. Low-intensity conflict is generally confined to a geographic area and is often characterized by constraints on the weaponry, tactics, and level of violence. (1996, 20)

Given that undocumented immigration and drug trafficking were constructed as issues of national security, Dunn (1996) further argues that this policy of LIC was effectively implemented on the US–Mexico border. As a result, unauthorized border crossers, who largely come in search of economic opportunities—are transformed into enemies of the state. Falcon (2007) argues that this psycho-social turn to see migrants from a lens of civil enforcement to military enforcement, where the mentality is to protect the nation at all costs, has led to a hyper-aggressive mode of interaction with migrants. The idea that the United States is "at war" with unauthorized border crossers also opens up a space for understanding sexual assaults by border patrol agents within the context of a low-intensity conflict. With border patrol given both the weapons of war and the mindset of war, the stage has been set for the now well-known and well-established hyper-masculinity of sexual assault during war.

Sexual Assault, War, and Low-Intensity Conflict at the Border

Articulating the concept of "militarisation of sexual violence," Josh Cerretti (2016) argues that a significant change in late-twentieth century warfare is the "recognition that sexual violence during times of war is a particular manifestation of gender inequality and gendered violence" (794). The rape of women by soldiers has been documented in the former Yugoslavia, Rwanda, Liberia, Sierra Leon, Kosovo, Iraq, and Afghanistan, to name a few. United Nations organizations that focus on the problem of sexual violence during war are demanding that it be treated as a war crime that is systematically implemented for political or military objectives. Rape, as a weapon of war, is used to " . . . terrorize the population, break up families, [and] destroy communities . . . (Outreach Program on the Rwanda Genocide and the U.N., n.d.)." As I argue below, these objectives can be applied to the experiences of unauthorized women migrants who have been constructed as economic, social, cultural, and political enemies, particularly because they represent the embodiment of the reproduction of people of color.

Understanding the US–Mexico border as a geographical space of low-intensity conflict, the interrogatory sexual assault threat that Marisol experienced at the hands of border patrol agents acting as military personnel—as well as the actual sexual assaults of women—helps us to make sense of the routinization of violence as a deterrence strategy and militarized act. Women crossing the border, particularly for those crossing unaccompanied by a trusted male partner—like a relative—run a greater risk of being sexually assaulted. As an aside, this, of course, does not mean that men are not sexually assaulted (Holmes, 2013). For women, there is increasing documentation as to the dangers that they face in this regard. According to a UN Development Fund for Women Report, violence against migrant women along the border is not isolated or random. They estimate that at least 60 to 70 percent of undocumented women migrants who cross the border alone experience sexual abuse. They highlight the greater danger for migrants from Central American countries, as they must pass through two militarized borders—"between Guatemala and Mexico and between Mexico and the U.S. Sexual violence often occurs while being robbed, as 'payment,' or in exchange for not being apprehended or detained by immigration authorities" ("Immigration Policing and Border Violence," n.d.). Moreover, according to the US government Office for Victims of Crimes: "For the increasing numbers of women who make the journey across the Mexico-U.S. border, rape has become so prevalent that many women take birth control pills or get shots before setting out to ensure that they won't get pregnant" (Watson, 2006). Even with the risks, women migrate for a number of reasons, some the same as men and some different: single mothers looking for work to support their children; financially supporting parents or other relatives; family reunification; and migrating to escape abusive relationships and controlling paternalistic environments, among other things (Dreby, 2010; Menjivar, Abrego, & Schmalzbauer, 2016). If they have few other options for work and can secure enough money or a loan to cross the border, they may take the risks. For many of these women, the needs of their families outweigh the dangers they face (O'Leary, 2016).

Not only are women victims (and survivors) at the hands of smugglers, but also at the hands of border patrol agents. Falcon (2007) has documented cases in which border patrol agents have been charged in the sexual assault of women migrants. In analyzing "the interconnections between militarism, hyper-masculinity, colonialism, and patriarchy" and how they "contribute to violence against women," she notes that an US vs THEM "ideology contributes to the construction of a racialized enemy—that is associated with women's bodies, which symbolize a nation (and its future)" (207). Recent reports in the media also point to the dangers of sexual assault that women face when trying to cross. A 2010 *Los Angeles Times* article notes that, "In the last 18 months, five Border Patrol agents have been accused or convicted of sex crimes, including one agent who pleaded guilty in January to raping a woman while off duty, and another who is accused of sexually assaulting a migrant while her young children were nearby in a car" (Dilanian, 2010). The article also cites Tony Payan, political scientist at the Univerity of Texas, El Paso, who studies the agency. He states: "They see themselves as a quasi-military body defending the country. Add to that the fact *that* they are expanding rapidly, and you have thousands of rookies who have very little experience" (Dilanian, 2010, para. 12). This story about border patrol agents is not an anomaly; a more recent 2015 CBS News Report documents sexual misconduct among US Customs and Border Protection (CBP) (Werner and Strickler, 2015). The report found that between 2012 and 2014 there were more than 35 "sexual misconduct" cases against agents, a rate significantly higher than other law enforcement agencies according to James Tomsheck, chief of Internal Affairs at US Customs and Border Protection. Additionally, the CBS investigation documented 21 customs or border patrol agents indicted or pleading guilty to sexual offenses between 2009 and 2015. This number of cases being prosecuted, let alone leading to convictions is un-usual, as sexual assault cases are less likely to be prosecuted compared to other crimes (Bulman, n.d.). In policing cases there is the added threat of retaliation and officers protecting each other with a code of silence (Falcon, 2007). Thus, sexual assault cases against police officers are even more rare. A report by the Associated Press found that over six years, approximately 1,000 officers had lost their badges due to rape, sexual assault, and sexual misconduct. Yet, they also note this number is "unquestionably an undercount" because even several of the nation's largest law enforcement agencies don't have mechanisms for decertifying officers (Sedensky & Merchant, 2015). When it comes to CBP having higher purported rates of sexual assault and misconduct cases than other policing agencies, it's important to recognize that even these numbers are also most certainly underreported and undercounted as well.

Moreover, women make up just 5.4 percent of the Border Patrol agent workforce. This is not to say that a totalizing solution to a hyper-masculine agency is simply "add women and stir" so to speak. The issue centers around a border practice that is directed to a border war. As Falcon (2007) notes, "National security policy making is left to a largely masculinized policy elite; and the police and military security apparatuses are male-dominated (Enloe 2000, 124)" (205). It is precisely this hyper-masculinity that explicates sexual assault at the border; a conscious and systemic rejection of this polic-ing culture is necessary to challenge the imaginary threat of migrants and the war-like approach that it engenders. As long as the US–Mexico border is militarized, the war-like consequences will continue to place women in particular danger as gendered threats and targets. Trump's ramped-up deportation policy is yet another way his administration further marginalizes and puts women's physical and mental health at risk.

Marisol's Border Crossing Story

And, finally, this brings us to Marisol's story. Marisol described her first attempt at crossing without documents into the United States in 2005. She was afraid of crossing over the desert and opted for a safer route traveling by bus and hoping to cross with the fake documents she had obtained. She was well aware of the dangers that the desert presented, including death. However, the story she told me—that influenced her decision to risk fake documents rather than the desert—was about women who she had heard who had been kidnapped by narco-traffickers and held in a house near Laredo, Texas on the border. She said they had been raped and then killed. These news stories circulate among migrants. They serve as a warning of the dangers that could be faced. It is with this backdrop that Marisol told me the story of how she tried to cross. She nervously gave her documents to the border agent when her bus was stopped at a second checkpoint in the United States at Falfurrias, Texas. She said, "I practiced not looking nervous because they can tell a lot by how you carry yourself. But they pulled me off. They said my documents were fake." She said she was nervous and frightened and at first insisted to them that they were real. She said she was brought into a building with a series of small rooms, finger printed, and then interrogated by two male border patrol Latino Spanish-speaking agents. That is when they pointed through a window to a van and threatened her. Marisol explains: "They said, 'See that van over there?' It's full of men. If you don't tell us your real name we are going to put you in there. Then just see what happens. We won't be responsible for what happens to you." That is when Marisol finally relented and gave her true identity to the border patrol agents. She said they looked serious, and the threat was enough to get her to relent. Marisol also said the agents told her it would be her "castigo" (punishment) for lying to them. So, although it was also an interrogatory sexual assault threat, it was also described as punishment. What is also of importance in this experience is the way in which threat is transferred through a third party, undocumented men, another vulnerable group in Immigration and Customs Enforcement (ICE) custody. The sexual assault threat, of course, pits one vulnerable population against another with the embodiment of potentiality clearly on the undocumented men and, therefore, an all the more powerful tool of the border patrol, as they remove themselves while manipulating and controlling the situation. Importantly, the fact that the agents who threatened Marisol were Latinos represents the uses of people of color to uphold policies of white supremacy. Their privileges of citizenship, class, and masculinity were in turn used by them to both further exploit the narrative of the dangerous brown man and also to terrorize a brown woman of color. The use of Latinos to police other Latinos because of cultural familiarity and language is a horrid, if masterful, example of Gloria Anzaldúa's statement of kin being enemies on the borderlands, quoted at the beginning of this piece.

Marisol's experience of interrogatory sexual assault threat is likely not a unique one. I have discussed the sexual assault and rape that migrant women face by both border patrol agents and coyotes, and while Marisol's experience is not of that level, it is still a form of sexual violence in the form of sexual assault threat. And it is one that is likely routinized and normalized as a reinforcement of order. Unlike sexual violence that is somewhat less visible, the interrogatory sexual assault threat, as described by Marisol, was done in the open with more than one agent around. This implies a certain confidence in the legitimacy of the tactics used and that are gendered to target the vulnerability that women share. That she could be threatened this way, in a relatively open manner, speaks to the institutionalization of sexual threat by the border patrol as an everyday tool of interrogation. Erika Sanchez, who writes for AlterNet, describes the physical and verbal abuse experienced by a woman she calls Morena:

> Morena, who crossed the Tijuana border when she was 21, says that before she left for the border, people advised her to look like a man to avoid getting raped. In preparation, she cut her hair very short. She said that when she was caught by Border Patrol, she felt most threatened by the *pocho* (Americanized Mexican) agents. "The *pochos* were the worst," she said. "One grabbed me by the neck and dragged me across the floor. He laughed and called me *mugre gallina mojada* ('dirty wetback chicken'). He asked me if I was lesbian because of my haircut." (2012, para. 10)

Both Marisol's and Morena's interactions with agents involved Mexican American men. This is not unusual given that as of 2008 52 percent of border patrol agents are Latinos due to aggressive recruiting of this population, as funding for border enforcement has grown dramatically in the last decade (Pinkerton, 2008). However, I find it significant that Morena specifically stated that she thought they treated her "the worst" (presumably as compared to white non-Latino agents), although she does not provide an explanation as to why she believes they are generally more abusive. One might assume the ability to communicate in Spanish or having the same ethnic background would make for better interactions because of greater cultural knowledge. In fact, this has been a theory in policing since the urban unrest of the 1960s: more minority officers in the community will lead to less conflict between police and residents (Smith, 2003). However, on at least one extremely violent measure—police-caused homicides—research indicates that diversified departments don't have significantly lower levels.

Surprisingly, not much is known about what role diversity might play in easing less violent interactions, but policies focusing on increasing minorities in policing are based on taken-for-granted assumptions about relatability rather than empirical evidence (Smith, 2003). Efforts placed on diversity, without attention to systemic issues like militarization, are misplaced, but this type of obfuscation may be precisely the goal. Border patrol agents are not the same as police, but they are now experiencing greater militarization like that which has been taking place among border enforcement for decades (Dansky, 2016; Gamal, 2016; Doherty, 2017; Radil, Dezzani, & McAden, 2017). Moreover, militarization not only undergirds all types of US policing practices, but is also a globally occurring phenomenon not likely to be easily reversed (Bolduc, 2016). As I have argued throughout, the deep entrenchment of this policy in the United States has its roots not only in politics, but in economic, social, and cultural spheres as well. Policy makers who have built their careers on both the subtle and overt narrative of brown and black bodies being threats to all aspects of (white) American society are not interested in the evidence pointing to the systemic problem of militarization. I suggest this is an important reason why micro-level solutions, like greater diversity in departments and agencies, are offered up to ameliorate abusive policing and are many times uncritically received as legitimate. I am not arguing conspiracy, but only that diversity has become such a buzzword that communities of color buy into its unexamined use as well, while institutions have learned how to incorporate it to uphold institutional whiteness and to deflect claims of racism (Ahmed, 2012).

As a result of racialized militarization, I suspect that in our Latino-threatened society, joining the border patrol is a concrete way for some Latinx to resist racialization and to feel incorporated at the top of the hierarchy, as they straddle a military/policing career that highlights both patriotism and protection of the United States against othered people who look just like them. In a recent news story on Mexican American border patrol agents, it was noted that President Trump, who called Mexicans rapists and criminals, would end up relying on many Latino border patrol agents (a majority of Mexican background) to enforce his sweeping promise to deport all unauthorized immigrants. The implication is that Latinos will have divided allegiances (Carroll, 2016). Ironically, I suggest that quite the opposite may actually occur; the focus on patriotism within the border patrol—which is likely not as emphasized in community policing—can heighten an internalized psycho-social mission to prove allegiance. As the news story notes, "Patriotism—an America-first, beware-all-threats brand of patriotism—is the first thing to understand about the Border Patrol. The agency sees itself as the nation's first line of defense, frontier sentinels on perpetual guard" (Carroll, 2016, para. 5). The US CBP website is quite telling in this regard. The section on "Veterans" highlights the following: "CBP Hires Veterans. CBP values the experience, commitment, and discipline that Separating Service Members and veterans bring to the job. That's why CPB is proud to offer rewarding careers and unique benefits to veterans seeking employment with CPB" (CPB, para. 1). Even the image on the webpage looks to be a Latino male wearing a half military/half border patrol uniform. Moreover, there is a special Veteran Recruitment Appointment (VRA) to streamline the hiring process, which takes into account recent military fitness and medical tests. The relationship between military experience and border protection is quite evident, and it is not surprising that patriotism plays a central role, easily digestible with policing the south of the border constructed "enemy." For example, "Paco, an agency spokesman, said that would not be a problem [in reference to the theory of divided ethnic allegiance]. 'We have a mission. I'll never jeopardize my job. Heritage is not to be confused with patriotism . . . '"(Carroll, para. 12). His emphasis on patriotism is central and propels him to make a strong statement in support of his US allegiance; it is difficult to imagine any other ethnic heritage being similarly questioned.

Thus, Latinos, particularly those with military backgrounds, seem to be the ideal agents from a militarization perspective; they may be especially motivated to prove their patriotism, not only for job security, but as reinforcement of their American identity. The use of Latino agents to police other(ed) brown bodies—women's bodies—reflects the hegemony of sexism and internalized racism in upholding white supremacist immigration policies. These Latino border agents, with the privilege of citizenship, are invited to separate themselves from the brown faces across the border that look just like them. Although my intent is not to provide a psychological analysis, it's important to recognize the motivation that the promise of power given to the powerless can engender. And, brown men policing brown women adds another intersectional element of gendered power and control. The ability to claim a higher rung on a ladder can be seductive for those who refuse to recognize a common marginalization; brown bodies without badges are targets of white supremacist policies just the same.

These are just a few examples of the abuse women experience in being interrogated at the hands of the US Border Patrol. The specific forms of gender violence serve to reinforce the idea that immigrant women from south of the border represent a particular type of threat to the hegemony of a white, patriarchal United States that is fearful of being outnumbered and losing power in the face of an imagined homogenous "American-ness." All of these experiences highlight a form of "punishment" for transgression on the colonized bodies of women. It's not simply enough to obtain information from the women, but they must be punished. They must know that they are receiving a *castigo*. As discussed earlier, sexual violence in war has long been documented, and given the transformation of the border area to a war zone through militarization, it is important to make visible the sexual assaults that occur and also the everyday tactics of interrogatory sexual assault threat that are inextricably linked to acts of sexual assault. We need to investigate incidents of interrogatory sexual threat and to document, for a social justice politics, the ways in which these methods are routinized and become part of the systemic treatment of migrants.

FASHIONING A SENSE OF BELONGING
IN THE AGE OF DEPORTATION

Although the xenophobic and nativist discourses presented here would construct Marisol as a threat requiring military-like action, she sees herself and her husband, José, as hard workers who only want to better themselves. As stated earlier, she and José have two children who were born in the United States, children who are popularly disparaged through "controlling images," as "anchor babies." When asked what she imagined for herself and her family she said, "My children have an advantage. They are from here. What I want is a good job so that my kids can study at the university. What I want is that they study and have a better future. That they live better." She ended our conversation by adding, "We don't want to take anything away [from Americans]. They point their fingers at us but all we want to do is work."

Marisol is sacrificing a lot to make this a reality for her children. Because of the militarized border she cannot risk traveling back to Mexico, and as a result hasn't seen her mother in years. She teared up when she said that her mother did not know her children. Later I learned that José had been in a minor car accident and was deported back to Mexico when he couldn't produce a driver's license and his unauthorized status was discovered. This was a terrifying experience for Marisol who didn't have family support in town. As a result, Marisol moved to Texas, where her mother-in-law lived, and José eventually managed to cross back into the United States. When I contacted her shortly after she had resettled in Texas she said that she felt particularly alone and imprisoned there, even with having her mother-in-law in town. This was because border patrol agents regularly patrolled the area, and she said she was afraid to go out and felt trapped. After experiencing José's deportation (and her family being separated), as well as her own inter- rogatory sexual assault threat, her fear was heightened. Marisol's experience exemplifies this everyday stress as, "Research has shown that militarization of communities contributes to a collective feeling of being under siege" (Sabo et al., 2014, 67). A recent news story about towns along the US–Mexico border in Texas and New Mexico reports on a complaint submitted to US Department of Homeland Security accusing border patrol agents of using excessive force, and physically and verbally abusing, harassing, and intimi- dating residents (Contact Reporter, 2016). With good reason, Marisol's fear of being harassed, deported, and/or detained has weighed on her and has severely restricted her movement in the highly policed border town. Success- fully crossing the border was one incredibly intense and stress-filled hurdle for her, but living day-to-day feeling imprisoned in her home with two young children kept her in a state of stress and insecurity. For Latinx, living under constant surveillance in the geographical region of the border is now norma- tive with militarization policies.

Marisol's desire for belonging to provide a better future for her children is no different from millions of undocumented immigrants in bi-national fami- lies who fear being separated from their US-born children and violence at the hands of policing. Ultimately, Marisol's story speaks to the high costs of migration for women. Not only do women risk sexual violence as unauthor- ized border crossers, but for those who are heads of households in the United States, being deported can have grave material and emotional consequences for any children residing with them: mothers and their children become sepa- rated, and loss of income from the head of household also leaves children economically vulnerable (Dreby, 2010; Menjívar et al., 2016). Given the ways that unauthorized brown women are policed, I echo Lozano and Lopez (2013) who argue that, " . . . governments need to consider the gender impli- cations of their immigration policies, as well as ensure that women's rights, in particular, are protected when moving across borders" (106). In telling Marisol's story, she and I hope to elucidate the micro- and macro-level injus- tices that women like her face. Her testimonial of threat and fear illustrates the way in which systematic violence functions as an integral part of immi- gration policy, even as there are purported efforts to eliminate it. I argue that militarizing the border region, in particular, brings with it systematic gender violence that is not a by-product of low-intensity conflict, but rather integral to it. The continued criminalization of migrant women, through the circula- tion of gender-specific "controlling images" and dehumanizing discourses, both within policy and public arenas, incite hostile responses to an "enemy."

Thus, combatting sexual assault threat at the border, like that experienced by Marisol, requires, at least in part, dismantling the dehumanizing narratives that invite and sustain it.

NOTES

1. This number represents a nearly nine-fold increase in the Latino population from the 1960s when the number was at 6.3 million (Stepler and Brown, 2016).

2. Because of proximity, it makes sense that Mexicans represent the greatest proportion of the undocumented population. Approximately 58 percent of the undocumented population comes from Mexico (Passel and Cohn, 2011).

3. This 2006 legislation laid out the following platform: (1) Authorizes the construction of hundreds of miles of additional fencing along our Southern border; (2) authorizes more vehicle barriers, checkpoints, and lighting to help prevent people from entering our country illegally; and (3) authorizes the Department of Homeland Security to increase the use of advanced technology like cameras, satellites, and unmanned aerial vehicles to reinforce our infrastructure at the border.

4. From the President George W. Bush website additional policing accomplishments and goals for the border were laid out: (1) Increased the number of Border Patrol agents from about 9,000 to more than 12,000—and by the end of 2008, we will have doubled the number of Border Patrol agents since the President took office; (2) deployed thousands of National Guard members to assist the Border Patrol; (3) upgraded technology at our borders and added infrastructure, including new fencing and vehicle barriers; (4) apprehended and sent home more than 6 million people entering America illegally; and (5) we are adding thousands of new beds in our detention facilities, so we can continue working to end "catch and release" at our Southern border.

5. The Obama administration removed more than 2.5 million people through immigration orders between 2009 and 2015 (Marshall, 2016).

REFERENCES

Ahmed, S. (2012). *On being included: Racism and diversity in institutional life.* Durham: Duke University Press.

Anchor Baby (n.d.). In *The American Heritage Dictionary.* Retrieved from https://ahdictionary.com/word/search.html?q=anchor+baby&submit.x=0&submit.y=0

Anzaldua, G. (1987). *Borderlands/La Frontera: The new Mestiza.* San Francisco: Aunt Lute Books.

Balibar, E., & Wallerstein, I. (1988). *Race, nation, class: Ambiguous identities.* London: Verso.

Bolduc, N. S. (2016). Global insecurity: How risk theory gave rise to global police militarization. *Indiana Journal of Global Legal Studies,* 23(1), 267–292.

Bulman, P. (n.d.). *Increasing sexual assault prosecution rates*. Retrieved from https://www.ncjrs.gov/pdffiles1/nij/228384.pdf

Carroll, R. (2016, December 12). *Life as a Mexican-American on the Border Patrol: 'The system is not broken.'* Retrieved from https://www.theguardian.com/us-news/2016/dec/12/mexican-american-border-patrol-agent-vincente-paco

Cerretti, J. (2016). Rape as a weapon of war(riors): The militarisation of sexual violence in the United States, 1990–2000. *Gender & History*, 28(2), 794–812.

Chavez, L. R. (2013). *The Latino threat: Constructing immigrants, citizens, and the nation*. Stanford: Stanford University Press.

Contact Reporter. (2016, May 17). *Complaint: U.S. border and customs officers abusing residents along Texas, New Mexico*. Retrieved from http://www.chicagotribune.com/news/nationworld/ct-border-customs-abuse-complaint-20160517-story.html

Dansky, K. (2016). Local democratic oversight of police militarization. *Harvard Law & Policy Review*, 10, 59–75.

Diamond, J. (2016, January 29). *Donald Trump: Ted Cruz is an 'anchor baby.'* Retrieved from http://www.cnn.com/2016/01/29/politics/donald-trump-ted-cruz-gop-debate-pummeled/

Dilanian, K. (2010, September 7). *Border Patrol is grappling with misconduct cases in its ranks*. Retrieved from http://articles.latimes.com

Doherty, J. B. (2017). Us vs. them: The militarization of American law enforcement and the psychological effect on police officers & civilians. *Southern California Interdisciplinary Law School*, 25, 1–52.

Dreby, J. (2010). *Divided by borders: Mexican migrants and their children*. Berkeley: University of California Press.

Dunn, T. J. (1996). *Militarization of the U.S.-Mexico border, 1978–1992*. Austin: University of Texas Press.

Falcon, S.M. (2007). Rape as a weapon of war: Militarized rape at the U.S.-Mexico border. In D.A. Segura & P. Zavella (Eds.), *Women and Migration in the U.S.-Mexico Borderlands* (203–223). Durham: Duke University Press.

Gamal, F. (2016). The racial politics of protection: A critical race examination of police militarization. *California Law Review*, 104, 979–1008.

Giovagnoli, M. (2011, December 2). *Anchor baby added to New American Heritage Dictionary*. Retrieved from http://immigrationimpact.com

Gutierrez, E. (2008). *Fertile matters: The politics of Mexican-origin women's reproduction*. Austin: University of Texas Press.

Hill Collins, P. (2002). *Black feminist thought: Knowledge, consciousness, and the politics of empowerment*. London: Routledge.

Holmes, S. M. (2013). Is it worth risking your life?: Ethnography, risk and death on the U.S.—Mexico border. *Social Science & Medicine*, 99, 153–161.

Immigration Policing and Border Violence. (n.d.). Retrieved from http://www.incite-national.org/page/immigration-policing-border-violence

Isidore, C., & Sahadi, J. (2017, January 26). Here's how much Trump's border wall will cost. Retrieved from http://money.cnn.com/2017/01/25/news/economy/trump-mexico-border-wall-cost/

Khimm, S. (2010, September 9). *Border patrol charged with sexual abuse, assault, and torture*. Retrieved from http://www.motherjones.com

Lopez, I. (2008). *Matters of choice: Puerto Rican women's struggle for reproductive freedom*. New Brunswick: Rutgers University Press.

Lozano, F. A., & Lopez, M. J. (2013). Border enforcement and selection of Mexican immigrants in the United States. *Feminist Economics*, 19(1), 76–110.

Marshall, S. (2016, August 29). *Obama has deported more people than any other president*. Retrieved from http://abcnews.go.com/Politics/obamas-deportation-policy-numbers/story?id=41715661

Martinez, D.E. (2016). Migrant deaths in the Sonora Desert: Effects of unsuccessful border militarization efforts from southern Arizona. In R. Rubio-Goldsmith, C. Fernandez, J.K. Finch, & A. Masterson-Algar (Eds.), *Migrant Deaths in the Arizona desert: La vida no vale nada* (station 3, para. 2). Tucson: The University of Arizona Press.

Menjívar, C., Abrego, L. J., & Schmalzbauer, L. (2016). *Immigrant families*. Cambridge: Polity Press.

O'Leary, A. O. (2016). 'Con el Peso en la Frente': A gendered look at the human and economic costs of migration on the US–Mexico border. In R. Rubio-Goldsmith, C. Fernandez, J. K. Finch, & A. Masterson-Algar (Eds.), *Migrant deaths in the Arizona desert: La vida no vale nada* (station 2, Crossings). Tucson: The University of Arizona Press.

Orozco-Mendoza, Elva Fabiola. *Borderlands Theory: Producing Border Epistemologies with Gloria Anzaldua*. Thesis submitted to the Faculty of Virginia Polytechnic Institute and State University In partial fulfillment of the requirement for the degree of Master of Arts in political science. April 24, 2008 Blacksburg, Virginia.

Outreach Program on the Rwanda Genocide and the U. N. (n.d.). *Background information on sexual violence used as a tool of war*. Retrieved from http://www.un.org/en/preventgenocide/rwanda/about/bgsexualviolence.shtml

Passel, J. S., Capps, R. & Fix, M. E. (2004). *Undocumented immigrants: Facts and figures*. Immigration Studies Program. Retrieved from http://www.urban.org/publications

Passel, J. S., Cohn, D., & Gonzalez-Barrera, A. (2012, April 23). *Net migration from Mexico falls to zero—and perhaps less*. Retrieved from http://www.pewhispanic.org

Pinkerton, J. (2008, December 30). *Latinos now make up 52% of Border Patrol agents*. Retrieved from http://www.sfgate.com/news/article/Latinos-now-make-up-52-of- Border-Patrol-agents-3178850.php

President George W. Bush, fact sheet: The secure fence act. (2006). The White House. Retrieved from https://georgewbush-whitehouse.archives.gov/news/releases/2006/10/ 20061026–1.html

Radil, S. M., Dezzani, R. J., & McAden, L. D. (2017). Geographies of U.S. police militarization and the role of the 1033 program. *The Professional Geographer*, 69(2), 203–213.

Roberts, D. (1997). *Killing the black body: Race, reproduction and the meaning of liberty*. New York: Pantheon Books.

Rubio-Goldsmith, R., Fernandez, C., Finch, J. K., & Masterson-Algar, A. (2016). Introduction: No vale nada la vida? (La vida no vale nada) (Does life have no worth? [life has no worth]). In R. Rubio-Goldsmith, C. Fernandez, J. K. Finch, & A. Masterson-Algar (Eds.), *Migrant deaths in the Arizona desert: La vida no vale nada* (introduction, para. 1). Tucson: The University of Arizona Press.

Sabo, S., Shaw, S., Ingram, M., Teufel-Shone, N., Carvajal, S., Guernsey de Zapien, J., Rosales, C., Redondo, F., Garcia, G., Rubio-Goldsmith, R. *Social Science & Medicine 109* (2014) 66–74.

Sanchez, E. L. (2012, June 26). *Ripped off by smugglers, Groped by border patrol: The nightmares women migrants face.* Retrieved from http://www.alternet.org

Sedensky, M. & Merchant, N. (2015, November 1). *A.P.: Hundreds of officers lose licenses over sex misconduct.* Retrieved from https://www.washingtonpost .com/news/post-politics/wp/2017/02/23/trump-touts-recent-immigration-raids -calls-them-a-military-operation/?utm_term=.a7e06969e790

Smith, B. W. (2003). The impact of police officer siversity on police-caused homi- cides. *The Policy Studies Journal,* 31(2), 147–162.

Stepler, R., & Brown, A. (2016, April 19). *Statistical portrait of Hispanics in the United States.* Retrieved from http://www.pewhispanic.org

Time Staff. (June 16, 2015): http://time.com/3923128/donald-trump-announcement -speech/.

U.S. Census Bureau. (2016, August 6). *Profile America facts for features, Hispanic heritage month 2012: Sept. 15—Oct. 15* (Report No. CB12-FF.19). Retrieved from https://census.gov/newsroom/facts-for-features/2016/cb16-ff16.html

U.S. Customs and Border Protection (n.d.). *Veterans: CBP hires veterans.* Retrieved from https://www.cbp.gov/careers/veterans

Watson, J. (2006, April 27). *Women risk rape, death in U.S. journey.* Retrieved from www.washingtonpost.com

Werner, A., & Strickler, L. (2015, May 4). *"Disturbing" sex abuse within agency that patrols U.S. border, says former top official.* Retrieved from http://www.cbsnews .com

Chapter Seven

"They Don't Really Care about Us"

Policing Black and Brown Lives and Futures

Derrick R. Brooms

Between me and the other world there is ever an unasked question: unasked by some through feelings of delicacy; by others through the difficulty of rightly framing it. All, nevertheless, flutter around it. . . . How does it feel to be a problem? —Du Bois (1903/2005, 1)

In establishing a context for this chapter, I draw from pop singer icon Michael Jackson's song, "They Don't Really Care about Us" and preeminent scholar and black sociologist W. E. B. Du Bois's (1903/2005) classic literary work *The Souls of Black Folk*. In his song, Jackson focuses on the pain and anger that people extract from how they are treated—by each other and by institutions and governments. I situate Jackson's song within the current #BlackLivesMatter movement and the ongoing killing of black and brown men, women, and children in public by police and other paraprofessional individuals. And, Du Bois's work is important as well given his aim to unpack and reveal the experiences of blacks in the United States and also center their humanity. I conceptualize "policing" in a broad sense to account for the ways that government-sanctioned authorities (i.e., police officers) and everyday citizens surveil, criminalize, and condemn black and brown life.[1] Du Bois deemed that there existed two different and distinct worlds within the United States: one black, to which he belonged, and one white, "the other world." The main chasm between these two worlds was their inability to relate to each other; yet, as Du Bois relates, the presence and existence of the black world (and the brown world by extension) was a problem. In pondering the meaning of blackness at the dawn of the twentieth century, he offered that being a problem is "a strange experience" (1903/2005, 1). The concern that I offer here speaks to black and brown lives and communities, and I pay particular attention to the targeting, policing, and the estrangement from and within society that they experience. There is a long historiographical record for the "strange experience" that black and brown communities have endured and for which Jackson's song resonates with how these communities, and people, are policed.

The flagrant disregard for black and brown lives reflects a continuation of what scholar bell hooks (1984) calls "imperialist, capitalist, white supremacist patriarchy" in a way that diminishes and denigrates these communities. In particular, the killings of black and Latinx[2] youth—such as Trayvon Martin (aged 17), Tamir Rice (12), Darnesha Harris (16), Aiyana Stanley-Jones (7), Hector Morejon (19), and Anthony Nuñez (18), to name but a few—demonstrate how policing tactics that can be deadly also victimize youth. In fact, data continues to show a rather discernable pattern of policing and violence that lead a number of citizens to assert that, "they don't really care about us." One needs only to examine the disturbing and troubling trends regarding police shootings. For instance, the Mapping Police Violence organization reports that over 300 blacks were killed each year by police officers in 2014, 2015, and 2016. Additionally, over a 42-month period, from January 2013 through June 2017, 894 Latinx and 1,504 blacks were killed by police as well (Mapping Police Violence, 2016). Collectively, these data reveal that many of the killings of black and Latinx people are not isolated incidents, and simplified narratives of respectability politics cannot diminish them to individual encounters. As sociologist Victor Rios (2011) has argued, many young men of color experience state surveillance, and multiple institutions in their lives (e.g., schools, community organizations, and courts) collude in a process of hyper-criminalization and over-punishing them regardless of their actual behaviors. For instance, in detailing some of the youth's experiences of being criminalized, Rios noted that, "For Jose and most of the other boys, their perceptions of being watched, managed, and treated as criminals began at a young age and became exacerbated after their first offense" (2011, 83). Additionally, Rios maintained that, "Their minor transgressions branded them with a mark that would make their one-time criminal act into a permanent criminal identity" (2011, 83). Overwhelmingly, Rios found that black and Latino boys were caught in a spiral of punishment and incarceration that entangled them in harassment, stereotyping, profiling, and labeling (as deviant or "bad") that ultimately led to them being surveilled, disciplined, criminalized, and pipelined through the criminal justice system.

As others have argued, violence against black and brown bodies at the hands of police, or state-sanctioned authorities, is just one form of violence levied against their communities (see Muhammad, 2013; Shabazz, 2015; Weissinger, Mack, & Watson, 2017). For example, Shabazz (2015) revealed that the prison industrial complex "represents the massive economic, discursive, and political shifts that changed the way prisons contributed to social and economic order" (71). In analyzing the use and availability of housing in Chicago, Shabazz contended that housing projects were linked intimately with the prison industrial complex, as they are sites infused with carceral power. Additionally, representations and portrayals of people of color in the media are problematic as well, often relying on stereotypes, misrepresentations, and controlling images. These portrayals play a significant role in public imagination and popular narrative because they often castigate people of color while at the same time exposing their bodies to invasions and gross inequities and repositioning them as subjects of a carceral state. Even further, Collins (2000) argued that these stereotypes allow gendered racism and unequal power relations to permeate, which helps maintain subordination and restricts the responses of marginalized groups. Importantly, these projections easily can be used as justification and rationale for surveilling, policing, and controlling black and brown bodies and communities. These representations and projections also can be used to commodify racism and misinform perspectives that allow for the scarring, maiming, and killing of black and brown bodies (see Henderson, 2002; Roberts, 1998).

Thus, paying attention to how black and brown communities are policed can help provide greater clarity on the health, vibrancy, and possibilities (and limitations) of our communities. For instance, during a weekly radio appearance, former New York City mayor Michael Bloomberg asserted that the New York Police Department did not use the "stop-and-frisk" tactic enough on people of color, particularly black and Latino males. He offered that people of color were stopped "too little" and that whites were stopped "disproportionately" (Yakas, 2013). Here, Bloomberg's rationale supported these policing tactics, yet his justification and reasoning about stops were unsubstantiated by the data. According to the New York Civil Liberties Union's analysis, which was based on police department data, 88 percent of the nearly 5 million stop-and-frisk encounters between 2002 and 2015 were of innocent people who were not arrested and did not receive a citation. Although only nine percent of the stops involved white citizens, Bloomberg still attributed the disproportionality to "those who witnesses and victims describe as committing murders" and also added that, "most serious crimes in this city are committed by male minorities 15 to 25" (Yakas, 2013). Thus, Bloomberg and other elected officials (such as mayors and police captains) rely on overgeneralizations and controlling images in asserting that being men of color is synonymous with being murderers and serious criminals. In taking cues from how people of color are projected in mass media, and the stereotypes and profiling levied against them, policing and over-policing these communities can be "justified" through these rationales.

WHERE ARE WE?

On March 4, 2015, the Department of Justice released reports of two investigations in the aftermath of the officer-involved shooting death of Michael Brown in Ferguson, Missouri. The Department found a pattern or practice of racial bias in both the Ferguson Police Department and municipal court:

> The harms of Ferguson's police and court practices are borne disproportionately by African Americans and that this disproportionate impact is avoidable.
>
> Ferguson's harmful court and police practices are due, at least in part, to intentional discrimination, as demonstrated by direct evidence of racial bias and stereotyping about African Americans by certain police and municipal court officials (Department of Justice, 2015).

This report is important for a variety of reasons and is particularly germane to community-police relations that have garnered widespread attention throughout the United States. Overwhelmingly, reports, recollections, and testimonials from individuals and communities continue to detail fissures and disconnects in interactions and engagement with police. Without a doubt, much of these tensions are due to the ways in which people feel that they are always already under surveillance. The surveilling techniques used to "police" communities are connected across multiple social institutions (e.g., schools, police, courts) and some of the social disorganization of a number of our communities.

In too many instances, our history shows a disparate treatment of individuals, groups, and communities based on their intersecting race, gender, and class identities. All too often, members of black and brown communities have their lives narrowed down through extra-punitive treatment by policing and court systems that seem more inclined to punish them as opposed to protecting and serving them (e.g., see Alexander, 2010; Muhammad, 2013; Rios, 2011). In fact, the disparate treatment of individuals from different racial and ethnic groups continues to be cause for concern for many communities. If all people were treated and policed equally, how do we explain the disparities between the care and attention given (and not given) to individuals like Freddie Gray and Dylann Roof? These two instances stand at polar opposite ends of the spectrum for valuing and respecting life. Gray, a 25-year-old black man, was arrested in Baltimore, Maryland, for allegedly carrying an illegal knife on April 12, 2015. Police reported to having found a "switchblade" in Gray's possession, which is illegal according to Maryland state law; however, the knife was not a switchblade and found to be legal according to Baltimore chief prosecutor Marilyn J. Mosby. Video footage and witness accounts asserted that Gray screamed in pain during his arrest. Just 45 minutes later, after being transported in a Baltimore Police Department van, he was found unconscious and not breathing. According to reports, 80 percent of Gray's spine was severed from his neck and he sustained massive injuries to his larynx and vertebrae during the transport, as he was not secured safely in the police van. After a seven-day coma, Gray succumbed to his injuries on April 19 (see Peralta, 2015).

Roof, a 21-year-old white male, killed nine black worshippers during a bible study session at Emmanuel African Methodist Episcopal Church in Charleston, South Carolina, on June 17, 2015. According to reports, police officers bought him a fast food meal while he was in custody as he "complained he was hungry" (McCormack, 2015). These two incidences, just weeks apart, raised a number of questions about police conduct, policing, and police malfeasance in addition to continued questions about how lives are valued in US society. In some ways, many of our communities remain constrained by Du Bois's (1903/2005) burgeoning and troubling inquiry, which he quipped over a century ago: "How does it feel to be a problem?"

Still, the examples provided are not simply about individuals but rather are representative of a larger cultural ethos that delimits and denigrates black and brown life. In fact, these examples, and many others (as discussed below), continue to remind us about the permanence of race and racism in our society and how some of us remain positioned as "faces at the bottom of the well" (see Bell, 1992). And, yet, this example is not a new phenomenon; indeed, as many have argued, there are two nations within the United States. Dr. Martin Luther King, Jr. (1968), in a speech: "The Other America," asserted, "I use this title because there are literally two Americas. Every city in our country has this kind of dualism, this schizophrenia, split at so many parts, and so every city ends up being two cities rather than one." Dr. King continued and, in describing these differing Americas, added, "One America is beautiful for situation. . . . But there is another America. This other America has a daily ugliness about it that transforms the buoyancy of hope into the fatigue of despair." One of the main points of Dr. King's speech was to reveal the inherent racial inequalities and inequities that severely limited black life and their ability to garner better life qualities. Not only does the dualism of US life show people's plight, it also, in some ways, prescribes the limitations of their lives. Primarily, many policing practices, and the effects of these practices, not only have criminalized people but also have criminalized entire communities and neighborhoods. In fact, some communities have been designed for greater ease in policing and surveilling people's movements and activities (Shabazz, 2015). As a result, how communities are policed can be tied to how we think about, perceive, and value these spaces and the lives within them.

PERCEPTIONS OF RACE IN THE UNITED STATES

As data and research continue to reveal, race and racism remain prominent features and components of US society. From residential racial segregation and inner city communities (Massey & Denton, 1993; Wilson, 2012) to differing job opportunities and prospects (Pager, 2007) to different types of engagement in schools and politics (Dawson, 2011; Nelson & Monforti, 2006), each of these phenomenon individually and collectively inform us about the circumstances and possibilities for different groups within society. Much of the recent data, interactions, experiences, and testimonies regarding race and policing clearly confirm that we have a great deal more work to do in improving how people are policed and treated.

A 2016 CNN poll conducted found that 54 percent of respondents offered that relations between blacks and whites worsened during the Obama presidency, including 57 percent of whites and 40 percent of blacks. These data are starkly different from responses in 2009 when blacks and whites almost uniformly thought that relations had stayed the same at rates of 61 and 60 percent, respectively. There also were differences within the responses regarding how blacks are treated in society, how they are perceived, and how respondents viewed the criminal justice system. For instance, while 34 percent of whites thought that racial discrimination against blacks in the United States was a serious problem, 73 percent of black respondents thought it was a serious problem. Similarly, 48 percent of whites thought that the US criminal justice system favors whites over blacks while 74 percent of blacks thought that inequality persisted in the criminal justice system. These differences in opinion reveal the chasms and gaps between how people perceive and experience various events, interactions, and institutions. That is, these differences reaffirm how some may believe that "they"—institutions, political figures, government agencies, people, etc.—don't really care about "us." Additionally, these differences in perceptions are connected to how people label and stereotype particular types of behaviors, how these behaviors are survielled and policed, and some people, especially blacks and Latinos, are repositioned and constituted as criminals within society (see Brooms & Perry, 2016; Muhammad, 2013; Rios, 2011). Black and Latino criminality are central to contemporary conceptions of urban America as dangerous, the need for "get tough" on crime laws and rhetoric, and for policing these communities.

In their quantitative study of 2,000 Latinx in four urban counties in the United States, Theodore and Habans (2016) found that many Latinx reported a fear of police. In particular, a significant number of their participants reported that they would be less likely to contact the police voluntarily if they were victimized by crime or to provide information about a crime. According to the researchers, the participants' fear contributed to their social isolation and exacerbated their mistrust of law enforcement authorities because they feared negative encounters with police. These encounters involved questions regarding immigration status, perceived unfair treatment, and vulnerabilities due to documentation status. These community tensions are critical given the current political climate and the increased use of local police authorities in immigration enforcement. Similarly, Theodore (2013), in reporting survey findings regarding Latinx perceptions of law enforcement, found that 44 percent of Latinx and 70 percent of those who are in the country without documentation surveyed said they were less likely to contact police about crimes. Additionally, when asked about their perceptions of police stopping Latinx without good reason or cause, 62 percent said that it occurred very often or somewhat often.

RECENT HISTORY KEEPS US INFORMED

In October 2014, 17-year-old Laquan McDonald was shot and killed by police in Chicago. A few notes about this event are noteworthy. First, it took more than 400 days for police to release dash cam video to the public. Second, the narrative offered at the time of the shooting was that McDonald, who was holding a 4-inch knife, swung the knife in an "aggressive, exaggerated manner" while also ignoring police orders to drop the knife (The Guardian, 2015). Video footage easily revealed that the narrative offered was grossly false and inaccurate; in fact, McDonald was moving *away* from police cars when a single officer opened fire and shot him 16 times—using and connecting with every bullet in his gun, including a significant number while McDonald was on the ground and not moving. The shooting, of all 16 rounds, took 15 seconds (Sanchez, 2017).

On July 10, 2105, Sandra Bland was pulled over for failing to use her signal while changing lanes. After refusing to put out her cigarette, she was ordered out of her car and was later arrested for assaulting a police officer. Three days later, Bland was found dead in her cell in Prairie View (TX); medical staff ruled her death a suicide. In the aftermath of her death, a #SayHerName social media campaign exploded to voice concerns over her death and bring greater awareness to the lack of attention given to black women who were killed by police officers.[3]

During July 2016, police shot and killed Philando Castile and Alton Sterling in two separate incidents. Castile, a 32-year-old black man, was shot during a traffic stop for a broken tail light in Falcon Heights (MN) while his girlfriend and daughter were in the car on July 6, 2016. Diamond Reynolds,

Castile's girlfriend, reported that when Castile reached for his license and registration, at the officer's request, he also informed the officer that he had a gun in the car and was licensed to carry. The officer opened fire and shot Castile four times.[4]

A day prior to Castile's killing, on July 5, 2016, Alton Sterling, a 37-year-old black man, was shot multiple times by police while being held down on the ground in Baton Rouge (LA). During the same week, with no high-profile headlines or national media attention, six Latinos were shot and killed by police: Fermin Vincent Valenzuela, Vinson Ramos, Melissa Ventura, Anthony Nuñez, Pedro Villanueva, and Raul Saavedra-Vargas. Valenzuela, a 32-year-old Latino man, went into cardiac arrest on July 2, 2016, after police used a stun gun on him in Anaheim (CA). Valenzuela attempted to move past police officers when he was confronted about following a civilian; he was bipolar and, according to Patricia Gonzalez (his ex-wife), was on and off his medication for years (Haire, 2016). He died July 11, days after being placed in a medically induced coma. In San Jose (CA), where one in six gun deaths in 2015 was attributed to police shootings (Department of Justice, 2016), 18-year-old Anthony Nuñez was shot and killed on July 4, 2016, on the front porch of his family's home while suffering from a suicidal episode. According to the Mapping Violence research project, although they account for one-third of the population, blacks and Latinos made up more than two-thirds of those killed by police in San Jose since 2013 (Mapping Police Violence, 2016).

In response to these shootings, and in the context of many others, then-president Barrack Obama offered, "When incidents like this occur, it's a big chunk of our fellow citizens that feel as if because of the color of their skin they are not being treated the same, and that hurts." He concluded, "This is not just a black issue. It's not just a Hispanic issue. This is an American issue that we should all care about. All fair-minded people should be concerned" (Hannon, 2016). President Obama's appeal to understanding the interconnectedness of these experiences beyond racial lines is important, as it reveals the ways in which police actions—including those that do not result in killings—affect the lives of civilians a great deal. The differences between how some people and communities are policed create stark disconnects in people's responses to their interactions with police officers. As opposed to teaching people, especially youth, to acquiesce to overly intrusive policing—which often is denigrating and dehumanizing, as has been explored throughout this volume—we must demand a more humanistic approach from our police officers and community policing. "Fair-minded-ness" has not resulted in enough empathy, coalition building, truth telling, and equity for it to be a plausible belief or hope for many people of color. Too often we condone youth for being youth and too often we see our youth treated as if they were adults. In far too many cases we are told to allow the court system to run its course so that the facts and justice will be served. However, too often, we have seen the exact opposite.

The racial disparities between arrests and incarcerations, the inequities of how people are treated by police, and the barrage of damage-centered, deficit narratives continue to remind us that, "We are made to fit descriptions that have been designed to contain us" (Brooms, 2016). These racial disparities not only belie notions of color blindness, but they also reveal racial privileges within the criminal justice system. The most recent cases centered on officer-involved shooting continue to reveal that police officers have a wide latitude in discerning guilt and innocence in their interactions with citizens. In too many instances courts excuse police officers for violating our citizenship rights—and killing us in the street. For instance, in her research on the Cook County courthouse in Chicago (IL), Van Cleve (2016) asserted that, "I saw the [official court] record not as a source of protection that accurately documented court proceedings, but as a tool of censorship that protected the mainstays of court culture and its brand of racial abuse (92)." In particular, this censorship "transforms what should be a device that protects defendants into a device that actually violates their rights. Professionals literally have the power to abuse defendants and then rewrite history" (92). These messages inform black and Latinx folks that what they wear makes them look suspicious (e.g., a hoody), that they are guilty until proven innocent, and instances of open court humiliation are all additional forms of policing their actions and behaviors that easily can be translated as a punitive state. These sentiments are expressed most urgently by coalitions within the #BlackLivesMatter organization. Founded by Patrisse Cullors, Opal Tometi, and Alicia Garza, #BlackLivesMatter is a chapter-based national organization intended to build connections between black people and their allies to fight anti-black racism, spark dialogue among black people, and encourage social action and engagement.[5]

On September 16, 2016, 40-year-old Terence Crutcher was shot fatally by Betty Shelby, a Tulsa, Oklahoma, police officer. Unarmed during the encounter, in which he was standing near his vehicle in the middle of the street, Crutcher reportedly failed to comply with Officer Shelby's instructions and posed a threat to her. In her first public statements about the encounter, Shelby offered, "I'm feeling that his intent is to do me harm, and I keep thinking, 'Don't do this. Please don't do this. Don't make this happen'" (Edwards, 2017).

Two recent incidents are noteworthy as well.

On May 7, 2017, Jordan Edwards, a 15-year-old in Balch Springs, Texas, was shot and killed by a police officer while riding in the passenger seat of a car on the way home from a party. In the immediate aftermath of the event, police reported the vehicle was moving "aggressively" toward police, which then led to the officer to shoot. However, the report was retracted after video footage and witness accounts contradicted this narrative.

On May 14, 2017, Tashii Brown, a 40-year-old black male, was tasered repeatedly while lying on the ground by a Las Vegas police officer. He was placed in a chokehold for over a minute, lost consciousness, and pronounced dead after being rushed to the hospital.

There is much to be learned from these accounts and, undoubtedly, these accounts join a throng of others that recount deferential treatment and policing of black and brown bodies. Research shows police use force (or the threat of force) in less than 2 percent of interactions with civilians each year (Eith & Durose, 2011) and, importantly, most of these incidences do not result in a death (Klinger et al., 2015). Though rare, deaths caused by police are cause for concern for many families and communities. For instance, in analyzing 900 police fatal shootings using data compiled by *The Washington Post* in 2015, Nix and colleagues (2017) found evidence of implicit bias by using multivariate regression models. They found that blacks were more than twice as likely as whites to have been unarmed when they were shot and killed by police. Their findings also suggested that, "officers may have been more likely to experience perception failures in fatal shootings that involved minority civilians. That is, officers subconsciously perceived minority civilians to have been a greater threat than they were" (329; see also Fachner & Carter, 2015). In fact, Voigt et al. (2017) found that police use more favorable language in speaking with motorists who are white. Their findings stemmed from analyzing over 36,000 utterances of policy-civilian interactions. In particular, in their data, even after controlling the effect of driver age and gender; officer race; the crime rate and density of business of the neighborhood; whether the stop resulted in some form of a citation (e.g., a search, warning, citation, or arrest); and the severity of the offense (if one occurred), they found that more respectful language was used with white drivers than with black drivers. Examining these two studies together yields deep insights regarding how biases inform interactions, which ultimately affect police-community relations.

In his grand jury testimony in the shooting death of Michael Brown, officer Darren Wilson described Brown through overly exaggerated brute-like terms, much of which has been referred to as "superhumanization" bias—the attribution of supernatural, extrasensory, and magical mental and physical qualities to humans (see Waytz, Hoffman, & Trawalter, 2015). Wilson, in speaking about Brown, testified, "He looked up at me and had the most aggressive face. That's the only way I can describe it, it looks like a demon, that's how angry he looked" and, after mentioning the first shots, added, "At this point it looked like he was almost bulking up to run through the shots, like it was making him mad that I'm shooting at him" (Bouie, 2014; Calamur, 2014; Department of Justice, 2015). This account, and many others, attests to the damning effects of race prejudice, explicit bias, and anti-black and anti-Latino violence. In his testimony, Wilson's detailing of Brown as "almost bulking up to run through the shots" relies on the black-male-as-superhuman narrative in an effort to amplify the interaction and his reading of Brown's body. Additionally, Wilson's account also reveals how Brown is dehumanized as Brown is referred to as "it" twice in the quotes provided and also is referenced as demon-like.

Scholars have argued that blackness and brownness have been projected and contorted as synonymous with criminality, which has resulted in exponential increases in their incarceration (see Alexander, 2010; Muhammad, 2013). For instance, Rios (2006) found that youth had to contend with the pressure of adults who often held negative and deficit views about their ability to do well. Jr., a 15-year-old Latino youth in his study, reported that teachers at his school had direct contact with the school officer and his probation officer. His probation officer was stationed at the local community center, which resulted in a combining of social services with state surveillance in one location. Here, "the punitive arm of the state, the criminal justice enterprise, had percolated itself into traditionally nurturing institutions like the family and the community center" (49), which allowed youth to be created, labeled, and treated as criminals "not only by police, courts, and probation, but also by teachers, community centers, and even parents" (50). Similarly, Smiley and Fakunle (2016) argued that the negative media imagery of black men as "brutes" and "thugs" is part of the descriptors that allow them to be posthumously criminalized. They asserted that using negative images (e.g., picture of victim in mug shot), previous criminal convictions or charges, and allegations of criminal behavior are typical ways that media depictions of black bodies remain dependent upon and compliant to white supremacist structures. Further, in pondering reasonable questions regarding the potential influence of microaggressions in media, Smiley and Fakunle (2016) concluded that, "The only contributions they potentially provide are a triggering of negative misconceptions that will be unconsciously and unjustifiably attached to these individuals" (363).

CONCLUSION

The policing of black and brown communities has been cause for concern continuously throughout the history of the United States. This policing happens well before police authorities show up in communities and well before there are statistics to document police-civilian interactions. This policing occurs in everyday interactions as black and brown lives routinely are scrutinized by a white gaze that positions them as outsiders—or some form of unwanted or unwelcomed guests. It means, as Du Bois (1903/2005) quipped, that one ever feels his/her two-ness. Additionally, it means that many of our black and brown communities still ponder and work to discern how it feels to be problematized in US society.

Of course, the policing of these communities is not a new phenomenon. While much progress has been made throughout society, there still remains a long way to go to alleviate many of the inequities and inequalities that continue to grip, arrest, and imprison our development and possibilities. How black and brown lives and communities are imagined and projected matters a great deal in how they are perceived and policed. There remains much work to do in repairing relationships between police and our communities. However, grave difficulties remain in repairing how black and brown lives and communities are perceived in wider society. The pre- and re-criminalization of our lives and communities started in the Colonial era and continue centuries later. This history re-positions us as always already under surveillance and, in many ways, threatens our humanity and freedoms.

NOTES

1. My conception of policing is informed through a historical lens that connects the colonial enslavement and slaving practices (e.g., slave codes) of peoples of African descent in the United States to the legal and extra-legal measures that developed in its aftermath, such as the black codes, Jim Crow era polices, and modern day practices of surveilling people of color (also see Alexander, 2010; Bell, 1992; Du Bois, 1903/2005; Muhammad, 2013).

2. I use the term *Latinx* as a gender-neutral alternative to Latino, Latino, and Latin@. Importantly, the aim is to move this racial identifier beyond gender binaries while at the same time being mindful of intersecting identities of people of Latin American descent. Additionally, Latinx is inclusive of people who are transgender, queer, non-binary, or gender non-confirming.

3. In June 2017, Texas Governor Greg Abbott signed the Sandra Bland Act into law, which mandates that county jails divert people with mental health and substance abuse issues toward treatment and requires that law enforcement agencies investigate jail deaths. The law took effect September 1, 2017.

4. At the time of writing this chapter, Jeronimo Yanez, a St. Anthony, Minnesota, police officer was acquitted of all charges in the shooting death of Philando Castile on July 6, 2016. He was found not guilty of second-degree manslaughter on June 16, 2017; he also was acquitted of two counts of intentional discharge of a firearm that endangered the safety of others. Similarly, Dominique Heaggan-Brown was acquit-

ted on June 21, 2017, of the shooting death of Sylville K. Smith in Milwaukee (WI). Heaggan-Brown's second shot, at point blank range, after he was on the ground after having the first shot hit him in the arm, pierced Smith's heart and lung. These rulings join the throng of others—such as Darren Wilson, George Zimmerman, and the Baltimore Police Department, to name a few—that continue to diminish and degrade black and brown lives, even posthumously.

5. #BlackLivesMatter was created in 2012 in response to George Zimmerman's acquittal of killing 17-year-old Trayvon Martin. A significant component of the trial, which ignited activism and outrage, was that Trayvon was placed on trail posthumously for his own murder.

REFERENCES

Alexander, M. (2010). *The new Jim Crow: Mass incarceration in the age of color-blindness*. New York, NY: The New Press.

Bell, D. A. (1992). *Faces at the bottom of the well: The permanence of racism*. New York, NY: Basic Books.

Bouie, J. (2014, November 26). Michael Brown wasn't a superhuman demon: But Darren Wilson's racial prejudice told him otherwise. *The Slate*, retrieved from: http://www.slate.com/articles/news_and_politics/politics/2014/11/darren_wilson_s_racial_portrayal_of_michael_brown_as_a_superhuman_demon.html

Brooms, D. R. (2016). "Innocent until proven black: A eulogy for black males . . . but, can we live?" In T. Richards (Ed.), *I can't breathe: Mass extinction & mass incarceration. ReImagining Magazine: Education—Culture—World*, retrieved from http://reimagining.chicagowisdomproject.org/2016/07/14/innocent-proven-black-eulogy-black-males-can-live/

Brooms, D. R., & Perry, A. R. (2016). "It's simply because we're black men": Black men's experiences and responses to the killing of black men. *Journal of Men's Studies, 24*, 166–184.

Calamur, K. (2014, November 25). Ferguson documents: Officer Darren Wilson's testimony. *National Public Radio*, retrieved from http://www.npr.org/sections/thetwo-way/2014/11/25/366519644/ferguson-docs-officer-darren-wilsons-testimony

Collins, P. H. (2000). *Black feminist thought: Knowledge, consciousness, and the politics of empowerment* (Revised 10th Anniversary 2nd ed.). New York, NY: Routledge.

Dawson, M. C. (2011). *Not in our lifetimes: The future of black politics*. Chicago, IL: University of Chicago Press.

Department of Justice. (2015). Justice department announces findings of two civil rights investigations in Ferguson, Missouri. Press Release Number 15–263, retrieved from https://www.justice.gov/opa/pr/justice-department-announces-findings-two-civil-rights-investigations-ferguson-missouri

Department of Justice. (2016). California: Offenses known to law enforcement by city, 2015. Retrieved from https://ucr.fbi.gov/crime-in-the-u.s/2015/crime-in-the

-u.s.-2015/tables/table-8/table-8-state-pieces/table_8_offenses_known_to_law_en-forcement_california_by_city_2015.xls

Du Bois, W. E. B. (2005). *The souls of black folk.* New York, NY: Dover. Originally published, 1903

Edwards, B. (2017, March 30). Tulsa, Okla., officer who killed Terence Crutcher says race had nothing to do with it. *The Root*, retrieved from http://www.theroot.com/tulsa-okla-officer-who-killed-terence-crutcher-says-r-1793868121

Eith, C., & Durose, M. R. (2011). Contacts between police and the public, 2008. Washington, DC: Bureau of Justice Statistics, U.S. Department of Justice. Retrieved from bjs.gov/index.cfm?ty= pbdetailandiid= 2229.

Epp, C. R., Maynard-Moody, S., & Haider-Markel, D. P. (2014). *Pulled over: How police stops define race and citizenship.* Chicago, IL: University of Chicago Press.

Fachner, G., & Carter, S. (2015). Collaborative reform initiative: An assessment of deadly force in the Philadelphia police department. Washington, DC: Community Oriented Policing Services, U.S. Department of Justice. Retrieved from ric-zai-inc .com/ric.php?page= detailandid= COPS= W0753.

The Guardian. (2015, December 5). Laquan McDonald swung knife aggressively, claim newly released Chicago reports. *The Guardian*, retrieved from https://www .theguardian.com/us-news/2015/dec/05/laquan-mcdonald-swung-knife-aggres sively-claim-newly-released-chicago-police-reports

Haire, C. (2016, July 11). Man injured by police stun gun taken off life support, dies. *Orange County Register*, retrieved from http://www.ocregister.com/2016/07/11/man-injured-by-police-stun-gun-taken-off-life-support-dies/

Hannon, E. (2016, July 7). President Obama addresses fatal police shootings of Alton Sterling and Philando Castile. *The Slate*, retrieved from http://www.slate.com/blogs/the_slatest/2016/07/07/obama_speaks_on_fatal_police_shootings_of_alton_sterling_and_philando_castile.html

Henderson, C. E. (2002). *Scarring the black body: Race, representations in African American literature.* Columbia: University of Missouri Press.

hooks, b. (1984). *Feminist theory: From margin to center.* Boston, MA: South End Press.

Jackson, M. (1996). They don't really care about us. On *HIStory: Past, present and future, book I* [CD]. New York, NY: MJJ Productions, Epic Records.

King, M. L. (1968). The other America. Speech, retrieved from http://www.crmvet .org/docs/otheram.htm

Klinger, D., Rosenfeld, R., Isom, D., & Deckard, M. (2015). Race, crime, and the micro-ecology of deadly force. *Criminology & Public Policy, 15*(1), 193–222.

Mapping Police Violence. (2016). *2016 Police violence report.* Retrieved from http://mappingpoliceviolence.org

Massey, D., & Denton, N. (1993). *American apartheid: Segregation and the making of the underclass.* Cambridge, MA: Harvard University Press.

McCormack, S. (2015). Cops bought Dylann Roof Burger King hours after Charles-ton shooting. *The Huffington Post,* retrieved from http://www.huffingtonpost .com/2015/06/23/dylann-roof-burger-king_n_7645216.html

Muhammad, K. G. (2013). The condemnation of blackness: Race, crime, and the making of modern urban American. Cambridge, MA: Harvard University Press.

Nelson, W. E., & Monforti, J. L. (Eds.). (2006). *Black and Latino/a politics: Issues in political development in the United States*. Miami, FL: Barnhardt & Ashe Pub Inc.

Nix, J., Campbell, B. A., Byers, E. H., & Alpert, G. P. (2017). A bird's eye view of civilians killed by police in 2015. *Criminology & Public Policy, 16*(1), 309–340.

Pager, D. (2007). *Marked: Race, crime, and finding work in an era of mass incarceration*. Chicago, IL: University of Chicago Press.

Peralta, E. (2015, May 1). Timeline: What we know about the Freddie Gray arrest. *National Public Radio*, retrieved from http://www.npr.org/sections/thetwo-way/2015/05/01/403629104/baltimore-protests-what-we-know-about-the-freddie-gray-arrest

Roberts, D. E. (1998). *Killing the black body: Race, reproduction, and the meaning of liberty*. New York, NY: Vintage.

Rios, V. (2006). The hyper-criminalization of black and Latino male youth in the era of mass incarceration. *Souls, 8*(2), 40–54.

Rios, V. (2011). *Punished: Policing the lives of black and Latino boys*. New York, NY: New York University Press.

Sanchez, R. (2017, March 23). Laquan McDonald death: Officer indicted on 16 new charges. *CNN*, retrieved from http://www.cnn.com/2017/03/23/us/laquan-mcdonald-case-hearing/index.html

Shabazz, R. (2015). *Spatializing blackness: Architectures of confinement and black masculinity in Chicago*. Urbana, IL: University of Illinois Press.

Smiley, C., & Fakunle, D. (2016). From 'brute' to 'thug:' The demonization and criminalization of unarmed black male victims in America. *Journal of Human Behavior in the Social Environment, 26*(3–4), 350–366.

Theodore, N. (2013). Insecure communities: Latino perceptions of police involvement in immigration enforcement. Report retrieved from http://www.policylink.org/sites/default/files/INSECURE_COMMUNITIES_REPORT_FINAL.PDF

Theodore, N., & Habans, R. (2016). Policing immigrant communities: Latino perceptions of police involvement in immigration enforcement. *Journal of Ethnic and Migration Studies, 42*(6), 970–988.

Van Cleve, N. G. (2016). *Crook county: Racism and injustice in America's largest criminal court*. Chicago, IL: University of Chicago Press.

Voigt, R., Camp, N. P., Prabhakaran, V., Hamilton, W. L., . . . Eberhardt, J. L. (2017). Language from police body camera footage shows racial disparities in officer respect. *PNAS* 1–6, retrieved from http://www.pnas.org/content/early/2017/05/30/1702413114

Waytz, A., Hoffman, K. M., & Trawalter, S. (2015). A superhumanization bias in whites' perceptions of blacks. *Social Psychology and Personality Science, 6*(3), 352–259.

Weissinger, S., Mack, D. A., & Watson, E. (Eds.). (2017). *Violence against black bodies: An intersectional analysis of how black lives continue to matter*. New York, NY: Routledge.

Wilson, W. J. (2012). *The truly disadvantaged: The inner city, the underclass, and public policy*, 2nd edition. Chicago, IL: University of Chicago Press.

Yakas, B. (2013, June 29). Bloomberg thinks NYPD stops-and-frisks too many white people, not enough minorities. *Gothamist*, retrieved from http://gothamist.com/2013/06/29/bloomberg_thinks_nypd_stops-and-fri.php

Chapter Eight

To Protect and Serve

Examining Race, Law Enforcement Culture and Social Work Practice

Shakira A. Kennedy, Folusho Otuyelu, and Warren K. Graham

There continues to be a pervasive criminalization within communities of color in spite of the numerous studies (Smiley & Fakunle, 2016; Associated Press-NORC Center for Public Affairs Research, 2016), journal articles (Otuyelu, Graham, & Kennedy, 2016; Tolliver, Hadden, Snowden, & Brown-Manning, 2016; Moore et al., 2016; Barthelemy, Chaney, Maccio, & Church, 2016), news reports (Smiley, 2015; The Guardian, 2016; The Guardian, 2017; Hudson, 2014; Mathias, 2014) and eyewitness accounts of the treatment and murder of people of color. According to The Guardian (2016) database, both Native Americans and blacks have the highest rates of deaths within the United States at the hands of the police. Native Americans are being killed by the police at a rate of 7.6 deaths per million and blacks with a rate of 5.54 deaths per million, whereas whites at a rate of 2.9 per million. In 2015, the number of officers charged for deadly on-duty shootings was one of the highest in years reported. However, even though 1,134 young black men in 2015 (The Guardian, 2017) were killed by police officers, none of these officers were convicted of murder or manslaughter (Elinson, 2015).

The lack of police accountability speaks to the predatory nature and socialization of police along with the continued invisibility of communities of color within police departments across the country. This invisibility of communities of color has given birth to "Black Lives Matter"; this movement is an adjudication of that invisibility with demands for justice and impartiality within the justice system. Therefore, predatory policing that targets specific communities for arrest can lead to feelings of distrust, making people less likely to report crimes within their communities (US Department of Justice, 2003). The issue of racism, community distrust, discretionary policing and racial profiling contributes to a racialized law enforcement culture. If policing reform does not occur, the potential for more anti-police sentiments expressed through racial uprising in urban settings will continue for years to come (Palmer, 2012), similar to what has been seen in Milwaukee, WI, in 2014 and 2016; Charlotte, NC, in 2016; Ferguson, MO, in 2014; and Baltimore, MD, in 2015 (Workneh & McLaughlin, 2016; Price, 2016; Taibbi, 2015; Buchanan et al., 2015).

The profession of social work has a mission that focuses on addressing the needs of the most vulnerable in society and addressing social injustices (National Association of Social Workers [NASW] Code of Ethics, 2008). The profession of social work can play a pivotal role with many of the negative police and community encounters by adhering to the core values of service, social justice, dignity and worth of individuals along with the importance of human relationships. Working side-by-side within police departments, this group of professionals understands the dynamics of difference and the power of inclusion. Social workers are skilled in the areas of assessment, intervention, problem solving, collaboration, cultural awareness and attuning to organizational structures and functions. These critical skills are essential in addressing police-community relations particularly when there is community distrust.

POLICING WITH COMMUNITY DISTRUST

"Trust" is a vital component to any interpersonal relationship as it dictates how people respond to each other. Trust becomes more critical and central during periods of uncertainty due to a crisis (Mayer, Davis, & Schoorman, (1995); McAllister, 1995). Therefore, the absence of "trust" is "distrust." According to Dunn (1988), distrust is the doubt that makes people find other means or ways of addressing a problem. Thus, the community's perception of the police will directly influence its interaction with them. For example, in the 2015 investigation into the behavior of the Ferguson, Missouri, police department's handling of the Michael Brown police shooting on August 9, 2014, the Department of Justice found a community that was deeply polarized, where deep distrust and hostility often characterized interactions between police and area residents (US Department of Justice Civil Rights Division, 2015).

This perception normally comes from negative personal interactions with law enforcement, negative media portrayal (US Department of Justice, 2003) of communities of color and the unnecessary use of excessive force (Reisig, 2010), the lack of accountability of police officers for the violations of civilian civil rights, racial profiling and the lack of acknowledgment of how race affects who is arrested and how communities of color are approached (Smiley & Fakunle, 2016). All of the above leads to police distrust, and many black and brown communities view this treatment as an unavoidable and inevitable part of their American experience. This can be seen in the 2013 ruling on the New York Police Department's "stop, question, and frisk." It was concluded that this practice violated the constitutional rights of minority citizens within the City. Between January 2004 and June 2012, New York City conducted 4.4 million stops, 88 percent of which resulted in no further action, and 83 percent of the stopped population were black or Latino, despite the fact that those minority groups, together, made up just over half of the city's overall population (Floyd v. City of New York, 2013). Within the social work profession, trust between the social worker and client is the cornerstone for establishing a working relationship. Social workers understand the importance of trust, thus they are equipped with the skills needed to address the problem of distrust between communities of color and law enforcement.

People of color are often stereotyped and perceived to be guilty before the judicial system proves them to be innocent as compared to their white counterparts (Hall, Hall & Perry, 2016). This puts people of color, more specifically, black and brown youths, at greater risk of experiencing harsh policing when engaged by law enforcement as well as being more likely to be engaged due to over-surveillance tactics. The over-surveillance of black communities has existed since the 1950s, when the federal government targeted black Americans fighting against segregation and structural racism (Kayyali, 2014). Concrete examples of this engagement can be seen across the country when we examine the treatment of people of color and the aggressive reactions of police during various encounters. In New York it was Eric Garner, Abner Louima, Amadou Diallou, Sean Bell and Randolf Evans. In Ferguson it was Michael Brown; in Maryland it was Freddie Gray; and in Los Angeles, it was Rodney King. In addition, there was also the fatal experiences of Sandra Bland and Walter Scott in 2015, and the controversial arrest of black Harvard professor Henry Louis Gates in 2009. These individuals were profiled by police officers and were the subject of immense media coverage spotlighting what profiling looks like and the dire consequences thereof (Smiley & Fakunle, 2016).

Henry Louis Gates's police encounter deserves to be referenced as an encounter with racial undertones as racism does not need to be blatant and overt to be psychologically and emotionally traumatic. Responding to a call of a possible break-in, white Cambridge Police Sergeant James Crowley arrested Gates outside of his home after verifying his identity and scrutinizing his State credentials (Goodnough, 2009). This encounter would have been minimized if social workers were community partners with law enforcement. According to Wood and Beierschmitt (2014), law enforcement officers continue to serve on the front lines as mental health interventionists, so utilizing principles of engagement from clinical social work to reduce confrontational behavior is a skill that can be developed by officers trained with, working next to or influenced by social work practice. In addition, the significant focus on cultural competence in social work curriculum would have helped shape the officer's response, having been exposed to concepts of microaggression, social location, and the impact of power and privilege.

Social workers are trained in de-escalation techniques, which are helpful tools in bridging the gap of misunderstanding and distrust between police and communities of color. The power of inquiry, careful individual assessment and situational awareness when engaging a person of color are vital to de-escalate and defuse tense situations and preserve safety. To further describe techniques promoting peaceful resolution, officers can minimize the reliance on handguns, slow a situation down by asking for a supervisor on scene, use alternative tactics like "words instead of guns, questions instead of orders, and patience instead of immediate action" (Wexler, 2002).

Often, misunderstandings between the police and the community can be explained away due to various factors in an encounter. Within racial environments of distrust, communities of color have to racially socialize their children through having "the talk" (Whitaker & Snell, 2016) to address law enforcement perceptions. These talks, both sensitive and painful, help children of color not only understand how they are perceived, but also remind communities of color that they are powerless. This powerlessness is also demonstrated through these communities' inability to effectively mobilize for justice; hence, the emergence of Black Lives Matter. Communities of color can organize (rallies, vigils, news briefs), but they can't always get justice. Black Lives Matter attempts to broaden the conversation around state violence to include all of the ways in which black people are intentionally left powerless at the hands of the State (Black Lives Matter, n.d).

The critique with "the talk" is, while tailored messages address the perception of black youth toward law enforcement, it does not address law enforcement bias toward black communities. This parallel process of "the talk" can be seen in the recruiting of police officers and within the culture of the police department. When police officers are recruited, they come to the police department with their own implicit bias.

Research on implicit bias, conducted primarily by sociologists and social psychologists, finds that racism persists in the United States because people discriminate due to non-conscious stereotypes regarding persons of color (Hutchinson, 2015). Police officers, as members of the public, are not immune to this level of programming. Examples of these are noted in 2016 by the news of recent cop killings becoming national news. An off-duty New York Police Department (NYPD) police officer murdered Delrawn Small in Brooklyn in front of his girlfriend and children in an incident classified as "a road rage incident" (Colon, Mongelli & Fears, 2016). On July 5, 2016, two Baton Rouge police officers held down and shot Alton Sterling for selling "bootleg" CDs (Shoichet, Berlinger & Almasy, 2016). On July 6, 2016, in Minnesota, a police officer pulled over a family for a broken tail light. Philando Castle was shot dead while reaching for his wallet after advising the officer he has a permit to carry a concealed weapon (Hobbs, 2016). The repeated exposure to negative media coverage of black and brown communities speaks more to young black boys being at risk for complex trauma.

Complex trauma is chronic or includes multiple exposure to traumatic events in childhood often involving a caretaker or someone whom the child has a close interpersonal relationship with (Lawson & Quinn, 2013). Complex trauma is also noted in children who live in oppressive environments such as homes with familial or partner violence, rigid oppressive political and religious settings, environment under constant acts of terrorism or war, and living in refugee like situations. Thus, it is conceivable that black children in low income communities are at higher risk for developing complex trauma, which may be further compounded by tense police-community relations.

Social workers can mediate these processes by providing trainings that will help officers understand, appreciate and interact with persons from different cultures and/or belief systems. Social workers understand that conflict is a part of human development on the micro, mezzo and macro practice levels. Additionally, social workers can develop techniques and provide appropriate conflict resolution options for non-violent community confrontations (Yanoov, 1996). Social workers are trained to understand child developmental processes and variations based on cultural experiences. Therefore, they are needed to aid in civility and constructive discourse on both sides. As communities of color increase their comfort with police, this can result in more accurate community reporting of crime and address other social ills when incidents occur, which, in turn, enhances trust between the community and law enforcement. Furthermore, as noted in Wilson and Bennett (1994), when officers feel competent in community policing efforts, and acknowledged for these efforts by the community, they have the highest job satisfaction.

TO PROTECT AND SERVE WHITENESS

The police uniform, the badge, are like white skin, and the person who wears that skin is allowed to enforce laws which they do not intend to follow.

Therefore, whomever wears the uniform feel protected, which may lead to the exploitation of people who obey the law and who respect his or her power as a police officer (Newitz & Wray, 1997). Complaints of officer abuse, including use of lethal force, prompted a federal investigation in Los Angeles in the 1990s; agents found a rough-and-tumble culture where force was all but encouraged (Williams, 2016). The failure of police to be governed by the law is indicative of a double-standard system and hypocrisy, as well as an imbalance of expectations between citizens and police officers; this is an example of impunity (Goldsmith, 2005). An example of this double-standard can be seen in the Tennessee v. Garner case of 1985. The court found that an officer cannot use deadly force against a fleeing suspect unless the suspect is a threat to the officer or to bystanders. However, in the case of Graham v. Connor in 1989, the courts ruled that investigators cannot criminally charge an officer if they conclude that a "reasonable" cop would have done the same thing in the same situation (Williams, 2016). The trial of Officer Betty Jo Shelby in the death of Terence Crutcher demonstrated both the increased pressure to hold officers responsible for using lethal force and the difficulty of convicting them of a crime (Walinchus & Perez-Pena, 2017). Officer Betty Jo Shelby asserted that she had a reasonable fear that Mr. Crutcher was reaching for a gun and that she simply followed her training and killed him.

Incidents of police abuse of authority cost local communities tens of millions of dollars in legal damages, and as municipalities make payments for restitution, tax dollars are wasted. Of the 15 high-profile cases from the last three years that rose to national prominence, eight have settled through civil lawsuits (2014, Tamir Rice—$6 million; 2014, Eric Garner—$5.9 million; 2015, Samuel DuBose—$4.85 million; 2015, Sandra Bland—$1.9 million; 2015, Freddie Gray—$6.4 million; 2015, Walter L. Scott—$6.5 million; 2014, Akai Gurley—$4.1 million; 2014, Laquan McDonald—$5 million). While criminal convictions are uncommon, many families of victims have agreed to settlements which have totaled $40.65 million tax dollars (Lee & Park, 2017).

The absence of equal protection under the law contributes to distrust and even cynicism among communities of color, resulting in the protecting of whiteness (*privilege*) and policing of blackness (*threat that requires policing*). McIntosh (1989) describes this privilege as an invisible package of unearned assets like an invisible weightless backpack of special provisions, maps, passports, codebooks, visas, clothes, tools and blank checks. An example of blackness can be seen in New York's previous stop-question-and-frisk program. Not only were black women routinely the target of physical brutality and killed during police encounters, they also experienced forms of physiological and psychological punishment that were distinct from those typically enacted against black men, who are more likely to be seen as immanently threatening. Black women and other minorities were often the target of this aggressive policing (Burton, 2015).

Over-policing can lead to a fear response from these communities; when seeing a law enforcement officer and trying to avoid the officer, it may lead the officer to engage what he or she perceives as "suspicious" behavior. Protecting whiteness can be seen throughout the history of the United States indicated in the 1790 fugitive slave laws, which made it a criminal offense to assist fugitive slaves; the 1790 Naturalization Act, which allowed an individual to apply for citizenship if he or she was white, of good character, free and living in the country for two years; the Indian Appropriation Act in 1871 ending recognition of tribes; followed by the 1942 executive order 9066, the internment of Japanese Americans (Pickus, 2007; Park, 2008).

These are all examples of laws designed to protect and serve whiteness. Whiteness, as a social construct, is the summation of culture, values and identity that benefit the quality of being white. There has been no change in the messages conveyed about the insignificance of blackness in the United States when the laws are viewed as a microaggressive tool and an extension of blatant racist policies, outdated and illegal. We understate the importance of these messages, that blacks have always been insignificant. To understand the phenomenon of aggressive policing, one must acknowledge systems of inequality, marginalization, racism, elitism, and power and privilege, particularly, as it relates to the support of the law (Kirabo, 2015).

Questions regarding elitism and privilege in the administration of policing led to a confidential July 5, 2016, interview with the authors and a Nassau County police officer who identifies as African American. Due to the sensitive nature of the subject matter, the officer and military veteran wished to remain anonymous since he is currently working for the predominantly white Nassau County Police Department with under five years of active service. The interview provided a law enforcement perspective that most officers operate from a "god complex, as former victims of bullying who grew into their authority with a badge and a gun to punish others." That is a profound assertion from someone familiar with the inner workings of police department culture. Former Chicago Police Officer Juan Antonio Juarez discusses this abuse potential in his 2004 book, *Brotherhood of Corruption: A Cop Breaks the Silence on Police Abuse, Brutality, and Racial Profiling.*

The "god complex" is privilege both inside and outside of the police system. For example, a white police officer benefits from the intersectionality of being white and a police officer, while a black police officer doesn't benefit from those same privileges. Black police officers may often find themselves on the receiving end of microaggressions in the form of racist jokes, commentary and offenses in station houses and precincts. In some instances, black police officers may even find themselves profiled by white peers (Barlow & Barlow, 2002). In the community, these same officers face a double marginalization for being black and a police officer (Wilson & Henderson, 2014), seen as a representative of a broken system oppressing communities of color. Sociologists Bolton and Feagin's (2004) book, *Black in Blue: African American Police Officers and Racism*, provides an in-depth accounting of the daily experiences of black officers and their challenges working within an institution steeped in racist practice ideology while balancing a desire to serve the public and manage being branded a traitor to the black community (Bolton & Feagin, 2004). The literature supports the experiences validated by the black Nassau County police officer, even over the course of a relatively short law enforcement career, and reinforced by similar military experiences as a veteran (Bolton & Feagin, 2004; Wilson & Henderson, 2014).

The intrinsic value of difference in society becomes lost in the black-white binary where the context of power and privilege is based on public perceptions and elitism. Former St. Louis, Missouri, Police Officer Redditt Hudson worked for the National Association for the Advancement of Colored People (NAACP) and chairs the board of the Ethics Project. In a 2014 *Washington Post* article entitled "Being a cop showed me just how racist and violent the police are—there's only one fix," the author discussed an incident of institutional racism whereby an officer maintained a website designed to create a sense of camaraderie and social support among law enforcement. The website wound up temporarily shut down due to racist content. The experience of being black, and an officer, otherwise perceived as a member of a criminal group can undermine the common mission or mutual goal of protecting communities, especially when deviance is systematically linked to people of color (Russell-Brown, 2009). In addition, white officers' perception of color elicited cops to routinely call anyone of color a "thug," whether they were the victim or just a bystander (Hudson, 2014), in part due to a tendency to remain stuck in earlier cultural configurations regarding race and policing (Conti & Doreian, 2014).

Social workers are able to provide clinical interventions, provide crisis management, address childhood trauma and provide cultural and educational trainings. It is also essential that law enforcement view social workers as assets and resources in addressing social problems, youth culture, child development, trauma, community culture and engagement. For example, when a young black man is approached about a situation and he raises his voice, this may be a symptom of anxiety or fear, not disrespect. However, a law enforcement officer calling a young man "boy" or being told not to talk can be viewed by the young man as being disrespected and judged as committing a crime. A trained social worker is able to understand critical communication skills in highly tensed situations. Having a social worker intervene by using active listening and reflective and clarifying skills can de-escalate this situation; hence, training law enforcement in identifying cultural nuances and subtle communication patterns that escalates situations.

THE CULTURE OF THE "BRAND"

In February 1955, the Los Angeles Police Department, through the pages of the internally produced *BEAT Magazine*, conducted a contest for a motto for the police academy. The winning entry was the motto, "To Protect and to Serve" submitted by Officer Joseph S. Dorobek. "To Protect and to Serve" became the official motto of the Police Academy, and it was kept constantly before the officers in training as the aim and purpose of their profession. With the passing of time, the motto received wider exposure and acceptance throughout the department (Los Angeles Police Department [LAPD], 2016). The significance of the police motto suggests a focus on public safety, as not overseers of a broken system, but collaborators and facilitators of safety, protecting the public. This motto has been popularized in pop culture, media and film, even though there appears to be ambiguity over exactly what constitutes "protecting" or "serving" (Burg, 1998).

From 1955 to the 2000s, the police department has evolved significantly from an environment where their motto suggests a focus on community service to one where broken window policing has contributed to the proliferation of policies that deny rights and profile people of color and other marginalized communities. Popularized in the 1980s, broken windows policing is an outgrowth of criminological theory which suggests that aggressively policing low-level crimes prevents more serious infractions (Corman & Mocan, 2002; Harcourt & Ludwig, 2006). It is this theoretical framework which served as the foundation supporting stop-question-and-frisk procedures, already proven to be unconstitutional in practice (Goldstein, 2013).

Under NYC Mayor Michael Bloomberg and Police Chief Ray Kelly, the mission of the New York City Police Department (NYPD) was described as enhancing the quality of life in New York City by working in partnership with the community to enforce the law, preserve peace, reduce fear and maintain order (New York Police Department Patrol Guide, 2005). The 2013 New York Civil Liberties Union's briefing on stop-question-and-frisk practices yielded valuable information specific to these inequities:

> In 71 out of 76 precincts, black and Latino people accounted for more than 50 percent of stops, and in 36 precincts they accounted for more than 90 percent of

stops. In the 10 precincts with the lowest black and Latino populations blacks and Latinos accounted for more than 70 percent of stops in six of those precincts. Though they account for only 4.7 percent of the city's population, black and Latino males between the ages of 14 and 24 accounted for 40.6 percent of stops in 2012. The NYPD often seeks to justify the high percentage of stops of black and Latino New Yorkers by contending that those high percentages merely reflect the concentration of stop-and-frisk activity in high-crime precincts that are black and Latino. While there are many responses to this contention that are beyond the scope of this report, the 2012 data are striking in what they reveal about the large percentages of blacks and Latinos being stopped in precincts that have substantial percentages of white residents. (New York Civil Liberties Union, 2013)

Ignoring police procedure has allowed a grand jury to review cases against multiple New York City officers facing misconduct in the fatal encounters with black men. In Staten Island, NYPD officer Daniel Pantaleo used a chokehold banned under police department guidelines which contributed to Eric Garner's death. The practice for policing black communities is inconsistent with NYPD departmental policy, evidenced by not only the illegal chokehold that killed Eric Garner, but Officer Peter Liang's fatal shooting of Akai Hurley in 2014, as he patrolled a NYC housing project stairwell (Mathias, 2014).

According to the NYPD's March 2, 2015, departmental memo (New York Police Department Patrol Guide, 2005), an encounter between a police officer and a civilian constitutes a stop whenever a reasonable person would not feel free to disregard the officer and walk away. Having internalized the degradation of what it means to be black (Duke & Berry, 2011) and bearing witness to the changing landscape of policing in black communities, a reasonable black person may never feel free to disregard an officer. The power differential between ordinary citizens and police officers is magnified when a person of color is involved as community contempt of officers' increases based on the continued negative characterization of blacks.

Social work has a long history and tradition of social justice and political advocacy, so much so that there are specific fields of practice within graduate social work programs that teach students the intricacies of community organizing and mobilization. Having the conversation regarding the merits of why social work is concerned about aggressive policing, racism and social justice is par for the course because of decades of effort rooted in historical context. The branding of a militarized police force seen as minimizing the rights of others based on superficial categorizations like race, ethnicity or religious orientation conflicts with the social work standards of cultural competence, cross-cultural knowledge and ethical treatment.

BUILDING TRUST THROUGH
EFFECTIVE COMMUNITY POLICING

Addressing communities of color concerns regarding distrust infers the need for confidence-enhancing experiences that challenge the negativity of pre-existing public attitudes (Goldsmith, 2005). Cultivating accountability, as a part of changes to the police departmental structure, is vital to the challenge of building trust and can be accomplished via the utilization of police social workers, or social workers allowed to engage officers through learning paradigms. The standards to which accountability will occur must reflect the endorsement of protective *(assessing before shooting)* rather than regime *(shooting before assessing)* policing (Goldsmith, 2003).

Accountability further extends to openness. Silence and secrecy within police work are both unwelcome and unwarranted. Accountability means being transparent, responsive and, most importantly, being respectful of differences. Meaningful change starts from the top down; thus, it is incumbent on the police department to set up an organizational culture that is conducive for innovation and change. Organizational culture plays an important role in organizations, regulating the behavior of their employees, through a system of values, norms and symbols resulting in the establishment of best practices (Szczepańska-Woszczyna, 2014).

A departmental organizational culture that fosters anti-corruption practices, encourages informal community contacts (US Department of Justice, 2003) especially in communities and neighborhoods disproportionately affected by crime that aims to reduce crime by improving relationships are the most effective ways to foster cooperation within communities (President's Task Force on 21st Century Policing, 2015; Barthelemy, Chaney, Maccio & Church, 2016). There is also a need to improve recruitment using a number of methods, such as sending law enforcement to a diverse group of community leaders and setting up a table at community meetings, shopping malls, schools, colleges and community gathering places (US Department of Justice, 2003). Social workers can facilitate the establishment and maintenance of these relationships. Building trusting relationships anchored in dignity and respect for individual and groups is a cornerstone of social work making it an invaluable resource for bridging the relationship between law enforcement and low-income communities, as evidenced by the work, done in the Rochester, New York, police department where social workers and counseling specialists were employed in this capacity.

Peaslee's (2009) review of police–social service partnership provides examples of how shifting attention to prevention and intervention initiatives humanizes police and sends a message to community residents that police care about the youth in their community. Working with social service agencies enhanced capacity to refer individuals to resources and social services without engaging the legal system. The study also highlighted Boston's Youth Service Providers Network (YSPN) and its use of full-time, licensed clinical social workers in police precincts to connect children and families with partnering agencies, thus streamlining referral for services while building relationships between police officers, communities and social workers. A similar partnership in New Haven, Connecticut, utilized mental health practitioners in a consultation service with the police department, thus providing law enforcement the ability to call mental health practitioners 24 hours a day when encountering trauma cases (Peaslee, 2009). The child development-community policing headed by Colleen Vadala of the Yale child study in New Haven, Connecticut, is an example of collaborative community–police services that addresses these issues. The program focuses on providing trainings on child development to law enforcement. It also has a collaboration consortium involving police, probation officers, juvenile detention and mental health professionals. This program currently serves as a national model for police and social service partnership and is being replicated in other cities. These are promising interventions that can alter young black boys' perception of being treated as criminals by law enforcement.

Best practices in identifying issues of power, privilege and oppression within the law enforcement system must be comprehensive and realistic in order to restore public trust in the system. One of the most underexamined issues shaping law enforcement members is the effect implicit biases have on an officers' effectiveness from a qualitative perspective. Focus groups and investigations, not with the intent to be punitive, but with an agenda to solicit honest emotions and feelings, will help shape future policy and improve community–police relations (Otuyelu, Graham, & Kennedy, 2016).

Social service organizations within black communities also play a viable resource for building positive relationships, yet few social service organizations work collaboratively with law enforcement organizations. Social service organizations often staffed by social workers are aware of the needs, struggles and barriers to resources within these communities. Many have strong positive relationships with parents and youth that is essential to positive policing. There should be a concerted effort between law enforcement organizations and social service organizations to bridge the gap of discourse that is a result of negative stereotyping and racial prejudice often propagated in black communities.

The prejudicial attitude toward blacks has been officially decreed, sanctioned, supported organized violence and paid for by our tax dollars (Schafer,

1976). Before we can address aggressive policing in its entirety, we need to remove legal barriers proving to be the foundation supporting racist, behaviors and attitudes.

It is beneficial for officers to live or spend as much time as possible in the community they are serving in. It is difficult to expect a community to trust officers if they are not a part of the community. According to US Department of Justice Community Relations Toolkit (n.d), recommendations for improving relations include involvement in local school activities, police athletic leagues, ride along with police and police-led community activities. Also recommended is that police officials view themselves as part of the community they serve. Effective policing involves programs that mandate officers' engagement in community activities, thus removing the "us" versus "them" feeling. Engaging young black men in community events and activities fosters a feeling of trust for youth and law enforcement. Engaging in community activities with law enforcement before a crime is committed is a way of building positive capital with the community, and it has the power to change negative perception of law enforcement by young black men and vice versa. The approach for addressing these must be multi-pronged and modified when needed.

REFERENCES

Associated Press-NORC Center for Public Affairs Research. (2016). Law enforcement and violence: The divide between black and white Americans. Retrieved from http://www.apnorc.org/projects/Pages/HTML%20Reports/law-enforcement-and -violence-the-divide-between-black-and-white-americans0803–9759.aspx

Barlow, D.E, & Barlow, M.H. (2002). Racial profiling: A survey of African American police officers. *Police Quarterly*, 5(3), 334–358.

Barthelemy, J. J., Chaney, C., Maccio, E. M., and Church II, W. T. (2016). Law enforcement perceptions of their relationship with community: Law enforcement surveys and community focus groups. *Journal on Human Behavior in the Social Environment*, 26(3/4), 413–429.

Black Lives Matter. (n.d.). About the Black Lives Matter Network. Retrieved from http://blacklivesmatter.com/about/

Bolton, K. H., & Feagin, J. R. (2004). Black in blue: *African American police officers and racism*. New York: Routledge.

Buchanan, L., Fessenden, F., Lai, K.K.R., Park, H., Parlapiano, A., Tse, A., Wallace, T., Watkins, D., & Yourish, K. (2015). What happened in Ferguson? *New York Times*. Retrieved from https://www.nytimes.com/interactive/2014/08/13/us/ ferguson-missouri-town-under-siege-after-police-shooting.html

Burg, M. (1998). To serve and protect? Retrieved from http://www.policemag.com/ channel/patrol/articles/1998/12/to-serve-and-protect.aspx

Burton, O. (2015). To protect and serve whiteness. *North American Dialogue*, 18(2), 38–50

Colon, S., Mongelli, L., Fears, D. (2016). Video surfaces of NYPD cop's road-rage shooting. *New York Post*. Retrieved from http://nypost.com/2016/07/08/video -surfaces-of-nypd-cops-road-rage-shooting/

Conti, N., & Doreian, P. (2014). From here on out, we're all blue: Interaction order, social infrastructure, and race in police socialization. *Police Quarterly*, 17(4), 414–447.

Corman, H., & Mocan, N. (2002). *Carrots, sticks and broken windows*. Cambridge, MA: National Bureau of Economic Research.

Duke, B. (Producer/Director), & Berry, C. (Producer/Director). (2011). *Dark girls*. United States of America: Duke Media & Urban Winter Entertainment.

Dunn, M. H. (1988). *Trust and political agency. Trust: Making and breaking cooperative relations*. New York: Blackwell.

Elinson, Z. (2015, September 23). More police go to trial in killings, but convictions remain rare. *The Wall Street Journal*.

Floyd v. City of New York, No. 12 Civ. 2274, Dkt. No. 112. (2013).

The Guardian. (2016). The counted. People killed by police in the United States. Retrieved from https://www.theguardian.com/us-news/ng-interactive/2015/jun/01/ the-counted-police-killings-us-database

The Guardian. (2017). U.S. policing. The counted. Retrieved from https://www .theguardian.com/us-news/2015/dec/31/the-counted-police-killings-2015-young -black-men

Goldsmith, A. (2003) Policing weak states: Citizen safety and state responsibility. *Policing and Society* 13, 3–21.

Goldsmith, A. (2005). Police reform and the problem of trust. *Theoretical Criminology*, 9(4), 443–470.

Goldstein, J. (2013). Judge rejects New York's stop-and-frisk policy. *New York Times*. Retrieved from http://www.nytimes.com/2013/08/13/nyregion/stop-and -frisk-practice-violated-rights-judge-rules.html.

Goodnough, A. (2009). Harvard professor jailed; Officer is accused of bias. *New York Times*. Retrieved from http//www.nytimes.com/2009/07/21/us/21gates .html

Hall, A.V., Hall, E.V., & Perry, J. L. (2016). Black and blue: Exploring racial bias and law enforcement in the killings of unarmed black male civilians. *American Psychologist*, 71, 175–186.

Harcourt, B. E., & Ludwig, J. (2006). Broken windows: New evidence from New York City and a five city social experiment. *The University of Chicago Law Review*, 73, 271–320.

Hobbs, A. (2016). The power of looking, from Emmett Till to Philando Castile. *The New Yorker*. Retrieved from http://www.newyorker.com/news/news-desk/the-power-of -looking-from-emmett-till-to-philando-castile

Hudson, R. (2014). Being a cop showed me just how racist and violent the police are—There's only one fix. *Washington Post*. Retrieved from https://www.washing

tonpost.com/posteverything/wp/2014/12/06/i-was-a-st-louis-cop-my-peers-were
-racist-and-violent-and-theres-only-one-fix/?utm_term=.2ac1de823e79

Hutchinson, D. L. (2015). Continually reminded of their inferior position: Social dominance, implicit bias, criminality, and race. *Washington University Journal of Law & Policy*, 46(18), 23–115.

Kayyali, D. (2014). The history of surveillance and the black community. Electronic Frontier Foundation. Retrieved from: https://www.eff.org/deeplinks/2014/02/history-surveillance-and-black-community

Kirabo, S. (2015). Want to help end systemic racism? First step: Drop the white guilt. Retrieved from http://thehumanist.com/commentary/want-to-help-end-systemic-racism-first-step-drop-the-white-guilt

Lawson, D.M., & Quinn, J. (2013). Complex trauma in children and adolescents: Evidence-based practice in clinical settings. *Journal of Clinical Psychology*, 69, 497–509.

Lee, J., & Park, H. (2017). Few police officers have been convicted in high-profile cases involving death of blacks. *The New York Times*. Retrieved from: https://www.nytimes.com/interactive/2017/05/17/us/what-happened-to-offi cers-in-police-involved-deaths-of-blacks.html

The Los Angeles Police Department (2017). The Origin of the LAPD motto. Retrieved from: http://www.lapdonline.org/history_of_the_lapd/content_basic_view/1128.

Mathias, C. (2014). NYPD officer shoots and kills unarmed man in Brooklyn. *Huffington Post*.

Mayer, R. C., Davis, J. H., & Schoorman, F. D. (1995). An integrative model of organizational trust. *Academy of Management Review*, 20, 709–734.

McAllister, D. J. (1995). Affect- and cognition-based trust as foundations for interpersonal cooperation in organizations. *Academy of Management Journal*, 38, 24–59.

McIntosh, P. (1989). White privilege: Unpacking the invisible knapsack. *Peace and Freedom*, July/Aug, 10–12.

Moore, S. E, Robinson, M. A., Adedoyin, A. C., Brooks, M., Harmon, D. K., & Boamah, D. (2016). Hands up—don't shoot: Police shooting of young black males: Implications for social work and human services, *Journal of Human Behavior in the Social Environment*, 26(3–4), 254–266.

National Association of Social workers (NASW). (2008). Code of ethics. Retrieved from http://socialworkers.org/pubs/code/code.asp

New York Civil Liberties Union. (2013). Analysis finds racial disparities, ineffectiveness in NYPD stop-and-frisk program: NYCLU briefing.

New York Police Department Patrol Guide. (2005). Retrieved from http://www.nyc.gov/html/ccrb/html/nypd-patrol-guide/nypd-patrol-guide.shtml

Newitz, A., & Wray, M. (1997). *White trash: Race and class in America*. New York: Routledge.

Otuyelu, F., Graham, W., & Kennedy, S. A. (2016). The death of black males: The unmasking of cultural competence and oppressive practices in a micro-aggressive environment. *Journal of Human Behavior in the Social Environment*, 26(3/4), 430–436.

Palmer, S. (2012). 'Dutty babylon': Policing black communities and the politics of resistance. *Centre for Crime and Justice Studies*, 87, 26–24.

Peaslee, L. (2009). Community policing and social service partnerships: Lessons from New England. *Police Practice and Research*, 10, 115–131.

President's Task Force on 21st Century Policing. (2015). *Final report of the President's task force on 21st century policing*. Washington, DC: Office of Community Oriented Policing Services.

Price, M. (2016). Charlotte's racial troubles bring scorching responses from vast corners of the web. *The Charlotte Observer*. Retrieved from http://www.charlot teobserver.com/news/local/article104844231.html

Reisig, M. D. (2010). Community and problem-oriented policing. *Crime and Justice* 39, 33–36.

Russell-Brown, K. (2009). *The color of crime: Racial hoaxes, white fear, black protectionism, police harassment, and other macroaggressions*, 2nd ed. New York: New York University.

Schafer, S. (1976). *Introduction to criminology*. Reston, VA: Reston Publishing Company.

Shoichet, C. E., Berlinger, J., Almasy, S. (2016). Alton Sterling shooting: Second video of deadly encounter emerges. Retrieved from http://www.cnn.com/2016/07/06/us/ baton-rouge-shooting-alton-sterling

Smiley, C. J., & Fakunle, D. (2016). From "brute" to "thug": The demonization and criminalization of unarmed black males victims in America. *Journal of Human Behavior in the Social Environment*, 6(3/4), 350–366.

Smiley, T. (2015, May 11). It's a dignity thing—Democracy is threatened by racism and poverty. *Time Magazine*.

Szczepańska-Woszczyna, K. (2014). The importance of organizational culture for innovation in the company. *Forum Scientiae Oeconomia*, 2(3), 27–39.

Taibbi, M. (2015). Why Baltimore blew up. *Rolling Stone Magazine*. Retrieved from http://www.rollingstone.com/politics/news/why-baltimore-blew-up-20150526

Tolliver, W. F., Hadden, B. R., Snowden, F., & Brown-Manning, R. (2016). Police killings of unarmed black people: Centering race and racism in human behavior and the social environment content. *Journal of Human Behavior in the Social Environment*, 26(3–4), 279–286.

United States Department of Justice. (n.d.). Importance of police-community relationships and resources for further reading. Retrieved from https://www.justice.gov/ crs/file/836486/download.

United States Department of Justice. (2003a). Office of justice programs. Factors that influence public opinion of the police. Retrieved from http://www.ojp.usdoj .gov/nij

United States Department of Justice. (2003b). Principles of good policing: Avoiding violence between police and citizens Retrieved from www.usdoj.gov/crs

United States Department of Justice Civil Rights Division. (2015). Investigation of the Ferguson Police Department. Retrieved from https://www.courts.mo.gov/file .jsp?id=95274

Walinchus, L., & Perez-Pena, R. (2017). White Tulsa officer is acquitted in fatal shooting of black driver. *New York Times*. Retrieved from https://www.nytimes

.com/2017/05/17/us/white-tulsa-officer-is-acquitted-in-fatal-shooting-of-black
-driver.html?_r=0

Wexler, C. (2002). An integrated approach to de-escalation and minimizing use of
force. Retrieved from http://www.policeforum.org/assets/docs/Critical_Issues_Series/
an%20integrated%20approach%20to%20de-escalation%20and%20minimizing%20
use%20of%20force%202012.pdf

Whitaker, R.T., & Snell, C. L. (2016). Parenting while powerless: Consequences
of "the talk." *Journal of Human Behavior in the Social Environment*, 26(3/4),
303–309.

Wilson, D. G., & Bennett, S. F. (1994). Officers' response to community policing:
Variations on a theme. *Crime & Delinquency*, 40, 354–370.

Wilson, F. T., & Henderson, H. (2014). The criminological cultivation of African
American municipal police officers: Sambo or sellout. *Race and Justice*, 4(1),
45–67.

Williams, J. P. (2016). Why aren't police prosecuted? *U.S. News & World Report*.
Retrieved from https://www.usnews.com/news/articles/2016–07–13/why-arent
-police-held-accountable-for-shooting-black-men

Wood, J.D., Beierschmitt, L. (2014). Beyond police crisis intervention: moving
"upstream" to manage cases and places of behavioral health vulnerability. *International journal of law and psychiatry*, (37) 5, pp. 439-447.

Workneh, L., & McLaughlin, M. (2016). Milwaukee uprisings reflects Wisconsin's
terrible treatment of black lives. Retrieved from http://www.huffingtonpost.com/
entry/milwaukee-uprisings-reflect-wisconsins-terrible-treatment-of-black-lives
_us_57b39627e4b04ff8839957be

Yanoov, B. C. (1996). *Social work approaches to conflict resolution: Making fighting
obsolete.* New York: Routledge.

Chapter Nine

Leaders are Dealers in Hope

A Look at the Intentional Actions Called for in the Forward through Ferguson Report

Sandra E. Weissinger

"The officer has to have a heart for what he (or) she is doing, and at the same time the community has to understand that we are there to do that corny phrase, 'to serve and protect' them, that is our purpose, and we do it at the best of our abilities. . . . I just don't know that mandating more training (will work) . . . If you've got someone that's a problem, get rid of them." (Sheriff Dennis Martin, as quoted by Marshall Griffin, 2015). On the surface, what Sheriff Martin is saying makes sense: if a department has a problem officer, the department has the responsibility to terminate the employment of the individual. But to leave the issue at the individual level is short-sighted. Problem officers are hired—passing all screening and entry hurdles. They are then trained and, arguably, do what their training has informed them to do (Gilbert, 2017). That alone indicates an issue with the procedures that allowed them entry to the profession. It indicates a larger, and looming, discrepancy with the institution itself.

One way to address the issue of problem officers is to research and make changes to policing as an institution. In Missouri, this is being done through officer training. As observed in the words of, then governor, Jay Nixon, it is irresponsible to send officers into the field without effective, community interactions informed, training. It does not help to put the blame of problem policing on the officer alone. They are products of their training. It does not help the affected community to scapegoat the officer either, for this further instills the fear of random, undetectable (until someone dies), "bad apples." Training in community de-escalation, however, provides uniform standards—alleviating the need for scapegoats and the deep entrenchment of fears. Such training mandates are a direct result of the tragedies Ferguson unearthed. In this chapter, I examine the lessons Ferguson continues to offer law enforcement and citizens.

In the aftermath of Michael Brown Jr.'s sudden death in August 2014, Governor Jay Nixon formed a commission of sixteen volunteer civic leaders. These leaders designed a recommendation report by focusing, heavily, on the lived experiences of people in the Saint Louis region. Report writers argue that the wounds of Ferguson cannot heal and equity will not come unless " . . . intentional action to build positive relations between community members and police" occur (Ferguson Commission, 7). To this end, this chapter examines the content of the report and supporting information as found on the companion website, *Forward through Ferguson*.[1] Certainly, it is important to understand how residents and political leaders within the region have moved to give life to these policy suggestions. Of key concern, in this chapter, are the changes policing agencies have engaged in because of community outcry (as captured in the Ferguson report and in news reports following the death of Michael Brown). Ferguson represents a moment in which to grow and develop new tactics for police and community engagement. It is a learning example for communities and policing agencies in other cities. But if actions are not taken to implement the well-researched policy suggestions found in the Ferguson report, the question must be asked: are we, as a society, ready to do the work to end racial injustices (especially where it is found within law and order)—to organize differently in the age of Black Lives Matter? Alternatively, is it just business as usual?

In November 2014, Missouri Governor Jay Nixon formed a commission of sixteen (volunteer) community and industry leaders. This commission authored a living report and helped birth the after commission accountability group, *Forward through Ferguson* (Ferguson Commission, 14; Rosenbaum, 2016). The report is a living document that changes often. When community actors purposefully address items listed on the internet-housed document, members of *Forward through Ferguson* make note (Ferguson Commission, 6).

As stated by the report architects, "This report is not meant to be the end of the discussion. . . . It is meant to raise questions and offer important, community-informed calls to action on these topics" (Ferguson Commission, 11). This wording is purposeful, as most recommendations developed by similar commissions are rarely implemented (Ferguson Commission, 8–11). Similar commissions have attempted to deal with the aftermath of violence and racism. For example, commissions in cities like Cincinnati, Detroit (the Kerner Commission), and Los Angeles (the Christopher Commission and McCone Commission) serve as predecessors to Ferguson. Commonly, residents and leaders fail to implement the calls for changes as suggested by commission members (see Dawsey, 1990; *Los Angeles*

Times, 1991; Lupo, 2010). This would be disastrous for the Saint Louis area—eroding what small fragments of public trust still held by community members for policy makers, elected bodies, and policing agencies—those with the power to enact the regional changes needed (Ferguson Commission, 7). As uncovered by the Ferguson Commission and by the Department of Justice (as led by Attorney General Eric H. Holder, Jr.), systemic and interlocking forms of violence (in the forms of racism, classism, and youth marginalization) organize the entire region in a quiet, and sophisticated, type of way. If local leaders are unwilling to do the work—leaving citizens and the institution of policing in a state of unchecked denial—real progress simply will not happen. It will be a fast-track ticket back to the institutionalized and recalcitrant forms of racism—masked as diversity, within police departments and the affected community, for the sake of diversity, without the grit of real equity and anti-racism work.[2]

Rather, collaborations and partnerships will not be optional as the region tackles deep-seated issues in a mature and unflinching way. These clearly stated issues take the form of 189 policy recommendations outlined in the report. The items illuminated are a result of 17 open community meetings across the Saint Louis region (Ferguson Commission, 14–15) and the efforts of the following four working groups on citizen–law enforcement relations; economic inequity and opportunity; municipal courts and governance; and racial equity and reconciliation (Ferguson Commission, 15–17). This chapter addresses the findings related to citizen–law enforcement relations.

Within the report, the Ferguson Commission names four "signature priorities" that are in need of urgent attention (Ferguson Commission, 26). They concern the use of force; the need for additional police training; the importance of civilian review of police; and police responses to demonstration. The goal of this chapter is to highlight what these urgent items are, and how people in the Saint Louis region have addressed them. In order to do this, the report by the Ferguson Commission (and additional documents made available on the Forward through Ferguson website) was analyzed. This data is triangulated by examining reports from Saint Louis Public Radio—an organization that was on the forefront of reporting about the events in and surrounding Ferguson, as they were uncovered.[3]

CITIZEN–LAW ENFORCEMENT RELATIONS: THE PROBLEM

As a nation, images of police engaged in violent altercations with people of color has bombarded conscientious people. Viewing recordings of these

interactions is traumatic for all, leaving lay people of color to fear that some-
day they may end up on a similar recording too.[4] Non–law enforcement are
left asking important questions, one of which includes asking about bias in
policing. Several well-researched studies speak to the existence of implicit
bias and racial profiling (for example, see Alexander, 2010; Davidson, 2016;
The President's Task Force on 21st Century Policing, 2015). So prevalent are
the issues of implicit bias and racial profiling that, since 2000, Missouri police departments have been required to report information about their traffic
stops—this information includes demographics like race (Lippman, 2014).
Scholars have found that whether an officer engages, actively, in racial profiling or, unconsciously, in implicit bias, the results are the same: people of
color are overrepresented as engaging in criminal activities (consider Blow,
2014). Purposeful anti-racist training illuminates both forms of discrimination and allows officers to engage in the policing as "guardians" (and not
"warriors") mindset (The President's Task Force on 21st Century Policing,
2015).

Civilians and social critics also ask another question concerning alternatives to force that officers can engage in. There is a use-of-force continuum
by which officers of the law are to reconcile their actions against (Ferguson
Commission, 26). When officers abuse their power, through excessive use
of force (when a less violent tactic would have accomplished the job of
apprehending the suspect), public trust falls apart—as exemplified in fast-
moving social media exchanges and at the committee meetings held by the
Ferguson Commission (additional examples of public trust in police falling
apart include Alexander, 2010; Gilbert, 2017; Graham, 2016). Excessive
force is about more than bad judgment by an officer. It is about the resulting
violation of rights (of the person who is on the receiving end of increased
forced), reduced levels of community trust, and decreased safety within
neighborhoods (full of individuals who no longer trust the police). It is also
about training. Arguably, along the continuum of force, departments can
spend greater effort training officers on de-escalation tactics (Gilbert, 2017;
Lippmann, 2015). Said another way, even a perception of irrational or abusive police threatens the entire body of the community for which officers
are charged with protecting. This makes the officers' jobs harder. It makes
being a community member harder too—living with a double consciousness[5]
or understanding that the police view you as a threat, regardless of your actions. A solution lies in institutional reform—reform that squarely deals with
systemic inequalities.

This double consciousness appeared in the face-to-face discussions Commission members had with black citizens in the Saint Louis region. Those
residents who spoke shared the same, uniform, criticism: these citizens felt

regularly silenced and disrespected in the justice process—referred to as procedural justice. These individuals believed that bias, in the system and among those who served as the arms of the system (officers), lead to unnecessary and/or excessive use of force. Such bias appears during day-to-day interactions and in extraordinary events, like that of a demonstration (Ferguson Commission, 30). Strategic work to limit bias among officers and the institution of policing will address the concerns of both the citizens and officers in the field. To accomplish the dual tasks of safety and trust, new training modules and on-the-job socialization[6] are necessary.

CITIZEN–LAW ENFORCEMENT RELATIONS: THE PRIORITIES

Restoring public trust, after continuous examples of excessive force and human rights violations, is a timely process. A process that needs to start with police, as they are the ones with the means and legal authority to end the lives of those who oppose them. This proposition is quite different from that of pro-police activists or by some Trump supporters (for example, see Nunberg, 2016). Claims to "restore law and order" have a racial past that those who parade the words around for show may be ignorant of—despite the fact that several educational resources are available on the topic (for example, see Michelle Alexander's book (2010) or *Fresh Air* interview (Davies, 2012); also consider Michael Tonry's (2011) book.

Just the same, if we take the idea of "restoring law and order" as one without racist underpinnings and take the words at face value, the Ferguson Commission demonstrates that what is in need of restoration lies with the thinking and bias of the policing institution. No amount of black respectability (not letting one's pants sag) or brown respectability (having legal documents to prove one's citizenship) can fix a system that is broken and biased toward people of color (see Butler, 2017; Joseph, 2017; Samuelsohn, 2016). Simply put, the oppressed cannot fix what the oppressor maintains. It does not matter if the oppressed co-sign in order to receive favorable treatment or protest vehemently. Until the oppressor recognizes their role and starts doing some work to change, inequality not only continues but also becomes sophisticated (hegemony). Starting on this work requires changes and a departure from denial that the old ways of interacting with communities are sustainable. To this end, the report names three areas in need of change, if not an overhaul. These include changes to use-of-force policies, officer training, and the overall culture of police departments (Ferguson Commission, 26).

USE OF FORCE

Different groups create their own norms, rules, and culture. Just as this is an accurate observation of the larger society, it is also a correct observation within specific contexts, like that of a policing agency. An overarching call of the report is for a change in policing culture. Such a change will affirm a value in human life and rights. This is illuminated through the ideal that a change in the shared values regarding use of force must be developed (Ferguson Commission, 27). When force is used, the culture will affirm that the least amount is used to secure a situation. When force is used, the culture will also value fair and rigorous investigations to ensure that the community is healthy, safe, and sustainable.

An example of questionable use of force was observed in the days following the death of Michael Brown Jr. A " . . . clear lack of an appropriate plan for dealing with demonstration . . ." (Ferguson Commission, 30) led to reports of an overtly militaristic response (for example, the use of military grade equipment and tear gassing of protestors as well as reporters) to citizens demonstrating on the streets of Ferguson and the larger issue of law enforcements' use of surplus property from the US Defense Department (Howard, 2014a; Howard, 2014b).[7] Demonstration is a right that people have. But when the culture of the responsive police unit is one that does not prioritize human life and rights, as argued by the architects of the Ferguson Report, a revision and sharp change is needed in the training and policies in which officers are tasked with adherence to.

On the part of the Senate and US House of Representatives, programs to audit and provide oversight into the military-grade capabilities of local policing agency are needed—this includes "rein[ing] in the 1033 program" in which the Department of Defense provides materials to law enforcement organizations (Howard, 2014b). Such programs, though only addressing the tools used by agencies, can effectively encourage changes in the culture of local agencies. Without military-grade equipment, a shift in focus—for example, to interact with those who are policed (rather than engage in force)—is much more likely.

OFFICER TRAINING

New training standards, which followed the Ferguson Commission's report, rely less on force and more on interaction with potential suspects and the public at large (Griffin, 2015). The Missouri Peace Officers Standards and Training Commission voted, unanimously, to expand the number of training hours mandated for law officers (Griffin, 2015). In line with the report (as will be discussed more in the sections which follow), the Commission mandated that training academies provide two hours, yearly, on the following four subject areas:

- Fair and impartial practices—for example, implicit bias recognition
- Tactical training that includes de-escalation, crisis management, critical thinking, and social intelligence skills
- Training to interact with those who have mental health and cognitive impairment issues
- Officer well-being—including mental health awareness and support (Griffin, 2015)

Fair and rigorous investigations, when deadly force is used, take the form of external reviewers (Ferguson Commission, 27). External reviewers can include, but do not have to be limited to, a civilian review of law enforcement activities (Ferguson Commission, 29–30). Creating this new culture means providing tools whereby the external reviewers and police can both know and access the shared rules. This serves as a way to renew community trust in law enforcement (Ferguson Commission, 29). To this end, the report calls for updating statutes and policies where needed and establishing a use of force database that is also available to the public (Ferguson Commission, 27–28). It also calls for revisions in officer training.

CULTURE OF DEPARTMENTS

The language of the report is very clear: the current training for officers in the Saint Louis region (and perhaps in other vicinities) is insufficient and inconsistent as communication skills are not at the center of this education (Ferguson Commission, 28) and officers do not always receive the same type or quality of training[8] (Ferguson Commission, 28–29). Communication, in this sense, addresses gaps in diversity training—which can lead to the very disrespect community members reported to members of the Commission. More than diversity training, education cannot be reduced to seeing difference (or saying one does not see difference, as stated by a well-meaning Officer Gronewald [Lecci, 2015]). Instead, seeing and understanding difference is at the core of advanced training. This means that knowing about, and understanding the current day ramifications of historical trauma, is necessary—even as it is currently missing. Such a training will prove to enhance the cultural competence and responsiveness of law enforcement members charged with interacting with the community at large.

In response to the calls from the Ferguson Commission, the state of Missouri's Peace Officers Standards and Training Commission mandated 24 hours of training per year (Griffin, 2015). While some, like Lane Roberts (the director of the Department of Public Safety), see the new training standards as relevant and necessary, others, like Dennis Martin (sheriff of Atchison County), see the additional training as a financial burden (for example, see Lippmann, 2015). Regardless of the varying opinions, there is a race by departments across the country (and with encouragement of bi-partisan Congressional supporters) to develop new training for officers (Freivogel, 2014). This call for more training is also supported by organizations like the NAACP, or National Association for the Advancement of Colored People (Phillips, Kellogg, and Rosenbaum, 2015).

CITIZEN–LAW ENFORCEMENT RELATIONS: A DISCUSSION

The Saint Louis grand jury decided not to indict Darren Wilson, but the US Department of Justice proceeded in conducting an investigation against him—questioning whether the former officer had violated Michael Brown's civil rights. While it is hard to prove civil rights violations, as reported on by William H. Freivogel (2014), it is important to put such questions in front of the courts. Such a gesture opens the door to conversations about the discrepancy between race, use of deadly force, and policing practices.

In a compelling report, by journalist Curtis Gilbert (2017), states without (or with very little) de-escalation training were examined. Within these states, 34 officers shot unarmed people, like Michael Brown, in 2015 and 2016. Gilbert found that all, except one, had fewer than 2 hours of de-escalation training since 2012. The argument is that such training can save lives. This is not a fruitless argument. Those who have received de-escalation training or who receive recognition for not using force in tumultuous circumstances have saved lives, as shown by the same reporter. There are 18,000 police departments in the United States and there are no uniform standards for training (Gilbert, 2017). This includes standards for de-escalation training hours. Moreover, while this discrepancy strikes some observers as a crucial problem in need of addressing, for others, uniform standards are a non-issue. In fact, those of this later cadre call for "fewer restrictions on law enforcement" (Phillips, 2015a).

With Ferguson and the St. Louis metropolitan area at the center, cultural critics have observed that a cadre of citizens are rebelling against the findings of the Department of Justice. These protestors lament the protests of their fellow citizens in Ferguson. In the wake of Darren Wilson's shooting of Michael Brown, months of unrest ensued. Pro-police protestors rallied in St. Louis, crying that police officers are "handcuffed" and unable to do their jobs. This inability to police as usual, without the scrutiny of the world and federal agencies, was a "public safety" issue, according to protestors. Such individuals, as reported by Phillips (2015a), do not mention use of force practices and death as public safety issues of concern. Pro-police protestors, like rally organizer Leisa LaBelle, made no statements about what the job of policing entailed. LaBelle simply made mention of a generalized fear that more crime was occurring since Brown's death and that Ferguson protesters were at fault (Phillips, 2015a).

When asked about the Department of Justice report, which found that the Ferguson Police Department had engaged in a pattern of racial bias, activist Leisa La Belle called the findings of qualified and established policing and legal professionals "absolutely asinine" (Phillips, 2015a). The sentiment that the police officers are to be supported at all costs (regardless of data proving that a problem exists) was supported by other residents, as the March 28, 2015, rally had an estimated 80–100 protestors attendance. What was present in each statement by protestors was an adherence to color blindness and a stanch denial of the reality the economically and racially marginalized navigate—as if racial inequalities do not exist because one has the privilege not believe it to be so.

The protestors, like LaBelle, acted as if the Department of Justice findings were something they could argue with or reject because of their adherence to unscientific, and frankly, intellectually lazy, opinions. The belief that everyone lives with the same choices and opportunities, sadly, blocks these pro-police protestors (for the most part[9]) from seeing the opportunities strategic policing reform can bring to the region and to the public safety they claimed concern for. To the extent that people are able to acknowledge race, rationalizations were crafted to justify the actions of police. For example, in the same report by journalist Camille Phillips (2015a), another local resident (Joe Weissman) stated, "You know when you look at the numbers, there's a lot more African Americans in that area. So to me mathematically it's just more likely they're going to get pulled over" (Phillips, 2015a).

As in several of the rationalizations made by lay people, law enforcement, and commentators, on the surface, this kind of argument makes good sense. More people of one race, more arrests of that same race. However, for those with critical minds, who are willing to challenge their assumptions and test the limits of easy answers, a question concerning how these arrests match up across communities is needed. For example, do we see similar arrest rates in vicinities that are white or racially diverse? If not, then we must dig deeper (if we seek an accurate and scientifically sound answer—not just one that carefully hides our privilege so we do not have to acknowledge it). For a quick answer to Weissman's statement, to check on its validity, one simply need visit the library or the internet, as the state of Missouri keeps vehicle stop information available to the public, and a search of these records proves that people of color, including blacks, are disproportionately stopped and searched.[10] Said another way, compared to their population size, they are stopped more—a clear disparity (Lippman, 2014). What is it about Ferguson, specifically the sections of the city that are predominately black, which attracts higher arrest rates?

The answer to this requires careful wording for those who follow the point of view of LaBelle or Weissman—for it can easily come down to a conversation about who does the most crime. Again, common sense might say "if the police are making the arrests, then black folks must be doing more crime," but this simply is not true (see Lippman, 2014 for an example). Police operate at the intersections of race, class, gender, and dis/ability. All are components of how we create criminals, or people stigmatized as "bad," "up to no good," and in need of observation. Black people are not inherently criminal, nor are poor people of any race. What is inherent is that these populations have more difficulty avoiding the hyper-vigilant eye of the law and, once picked up, have a more difficult job navigating the criminal justice system. This is not news. Michelle Alexander's *The New Jim Crow* (2010) not only makes this argument, but also provides historical evidence as to why we have the criminal justice system we have today.

In short, there is no room for lazy assumptions when it comes to policing in the era of Black Lives Matters. Every aspect of institutions, including law enforcement, is worthy of analysis and challenge. And if the answers one comes up with are along the lines of "that is how it has always been" or "those people are criminals" or "police have a hard enough job without all of this . . . ," then you are the reason why we, as a society, still have to have conversations about racial inequality. History shows us that the ways we have acted as a society have historically been to the advantage of those who are white—especially if they are white, have some wealth, and are male. Without conscious and purposeful revisions, like those proposed by former Attorney General Eric H. Holder, the Department of Justice, and Ferguson Commission, society and its institutions run the high risk of repeating patterns of oppression (like stereotyping and carte blanche acceptance of certain groups of people) with ease—it is, after all, the way it has always been. The leaders of this era must act with clarity, innovation, and courage to challenge hegemonic inequalities. Leaders in this era must be dealers in hope.

SOLUTIONS

Leaders who deal in hope pay attention to the past, as to not reproduce those same issues in the present. History has provided us with several examples from which to learn, metabolize, and grow. Other cities have been subject to riots following violence or shootings of unarmed black people. Before Ferguson, there was Cincinnati (2001). Before Cincinnati, there was Los Angeles (1992 and 1965) and Detroit (1967). Michael Brown Jr. joined a long list of black bodies who have been the casualties of unchecked bias and violent policing tactics. Like Brown, the deaths of Timothy Thomas, Rodney King, and Marquette Frye led communities members to publicly call policing agencies to accountability. Historians and cultural critics can certainly add to this list too (for example, see the work of Lupo, 2010). Said another way, the violent death of blacks at the hands of police is not new. In each instance, society had the opportunity to learn a lesson and adjust practices and policies. "Pattern or practice" lawsuits[11] have provided a successful avenue to reform in the aftermath of race-related policing turmoil by calling attention to the everyday practices of law enforcement (Freivogel, 2014).

Settlements in these cases have revolutionized policing and acted as the beginning in mending bridges between mistrustful communities and the police. For example, settlements have required officers to wear video cameras and required departments to provide new training on use of force. With brave leadership, these settlements have also led to the establishment of citizen review boards, tracking of officers with troubled civilian relationships, and the naming (and subsequent release of those names) of police involved in shootings (Freivogel, 2014).

Outside of lawsuits by victims and settlements by policing municipalities, funding (by the federal government) has also been an effective tool in changing local departments. Departments with non-innovative leaders fail to make changes, as warranted by the Department of Justice's Community Oriented Policing Services, and find themselves without the financial support (Freivogel, 2014).

Lastly, leaders find the impetus and strength to be innovative and brave through their relationships with the communities they serve. This is true in all careers and policing is no exception. Interim Ferguson Police Chief Andre Anderson engaged in one such forum—seeking to construct a community policing plan (Phillips, 2015b). As a precursor to the planning, the Interim Chief had officers walk the areas they serve and talk to residents, and is attempting to change the ideology from one of officers as "warriors" to one of officers as "guardians" (Phillips, 2015b; also addressed in Gilbert, 2017—as a take-away from President Obama's Task Force on 21st Century Policing).

Officers need to be leaders who "practice patience" (Derrick Collins as quoted by Gilbert, 2017)—meaning that they should expend more time on people, slowing down to be strategic, and avoiding the use of force because they have the leadership skills necessary to steer the interaction in a non-violent way. Starting a conversation is a governance skill learned in de-escalation training along with active listening. This is a departure from "ask, tell, make" models, but a departure that is life saving and life changing (Gilbert, 2017).

CONCLUSION

"What we want to do is bring the nobility of policing back" (Interim Ferguson Police Chief Andre Anderson, as quoted by Camille Phillips, 2015b). To do this, we need to (as a society) hold police uniformly to the standard of acting as community-based leaders.[12] The leaders of this era are called to act with more skill and tact than brute force. While there are cases in which force, including lethal force, will still be necessary, the argument here, by the Department of Justice and by the Ferguson Commission, is that less force and less punitive policing is needed when officers and the agencies they serve at the leisure of, do the hard work of becoming part of the neighborhoods they claim to serve.

As addressed at the very beginning of the chapter, policing is a calling and should be reserved for those who are qualified to not only do the job, but rise to the occasion and learn—as the circumstances in which the job is done changes. In this new era of accountability, black, brown, and white bodies are calling for an end of policing as usual. The republic is calling for police to surpass the stereotype some have long held of them. Yes, they are brave. Yes, their job is hard. But in reaching to new levels of nobility and regaining the trust of a country that has been brought to its knees by the on-camera shootings and deaths of black and brown people, policing must include the development of organic leadership skills. They must be a part of the communities they police. They must know the lay of the land and the culture of the space. They must be leaders who inspire trust and collaborations. They must bring hope, as our relations with the profession and the people have all but been destroyed.

This is not only the mandate of critiques of Ferguson. It is the promise of what rebirth can bring when we accept the challenge, learn from our trials, and grow.

NOTES

1. The companion website can be found by visiting http://forwardthroughferguson .org/.

2. Institutions often skirt progress by engaging in these kinds of campaigns. On the surface, they look good. They have a diverse workforce by numbers, for example. This is what, then, Missouri Attorney General Chris Koster planned for, as "minority officers" made up only 7 percent of law enforcement in Ferguson (Mannies, 2014). Minority is, of course, a ubiquitous term—it could mean black, but it could also mean white females. Regardless, numbers and phenotypes conceal underlying issues of equity, racism, and anti-racism work. This kind of culture is easy to detect by those trained to see inequity. These cultures are harder to change, however, as leaders seek efficiency rather than justice.

3. For example, curators from the Saint Louis Public Radio group put together the following listing of articles related to policing and courts in the region: http://apps .stlpublicradio.org/ferguson-project/topic.html#police.

4. Consider Grinberg's (2015) coverage of the Twitter response to Sandra Bland's death in her article, "Twitter responds to jail deaths with 'if I die in police custody.'"

5. The double consciousness is a concept from the indisputably prophetic Dr. W. E. B. Du Bois (2004). In short, it is about the burden one carries when he or she understands how prejudice and discrimination color all of the efforts. Hard as one might try, it is nearly impossible to escape the consequences of one's phenotypes. This creates a veil or barrier when in spaces that are not inclusive or are operating within the simulation of colorblindness.

6. Consider the difference empathy and bias reduction made in the policing practices of (former) Officer Darren Wilson's former colleague, field-training Officer Mike McCarthy: http://www.newyorker.com/magazine/2015/08/10/the-cop.

7. Though the gear police had, as seen in images from the demonstrations following Brown's death, appeared to be from the US military, Admiral John Kirby has stated that the military did not provide the tools and that Ferguson only received unarmored Humvees, a generator, and a trailer (Howard, 2014a). U.S. Senator Claire McCaskill led the community-based call to investigate and provide oversight to the Department of Defense 1033 program, which provides materials to local policing agencies (Howard, 2014b). She was supported by President Barack Obama and US Senator Rand Paul (Howard, 2014b).

8. According to the report, consistent and cost-effective training can happen at one facility and use a common curriculum and number of training hours (Ferguson Commission, 28–29). Within such training, education on officer well-being needs incorporation too (Ferguson Commission, 28).

9. Within Camille Phillip's report, pro-police protestor Becky Hutt did not co-sign fully with the pro-police/bad protestors in Ferguson dichotomy. According to Phillips, Hutt "could see why people were protesting 'a little bit'" (Phillips, 2015a).

10. For the statute on racial profiling and traffic stops, see http://www.moga .mo.gov/mostatutes/stathtml/59000006501.html. For Missouri Attorny General Josh Hawley's report for 2013, see https://ago.mo.gov/home/vehicle-stops-report/2013 -executive-summary.

11. A pattern or practice lawsuit alleges that a police department has a pattern of unconstitutional policing practices (Freivogel, 2014). In Cincinnati, there was a pattern of unconstitutional police use of force.

12. Community-based does not mean that the officer must live in the neighbor-hood or even city they service. The point made by Jill Gronewald, a Ferguson officer, is important: the safety of the officer and his or her family is important and living in the same space in which you have made arrests can put family members in harm's way (Lecci, 2015). Just the same, officers who strike a balance—treating the place they work as if it were where they lived—is what is called for.

REFERENCES

Alexander, M. (2010). *The new Jim Crow: Mass incarceration in the age of color-blindness*. New York, NY: The New Press.

Blow, C. M. (2014, September 7). "Crime, bias, and statistics." *New York Times.* Retrieved from https://www.nytimes.com/2014/09/08/opinion/charles-blow-crime-bias-and-statistics.html?_r=0

Butler, P. (2017, June). "When black America was pro-police." *The Atlantic.* Retrieved from https://www.theatlantic.com/magazine/archive/2017/06/when-black-america-was-pro-police/524481/

Davidson, J. (2016, August 16). "Implicit bias training seeks to counter hidden prejudice in law enforcement." Retrieved from https://www.washingtonpost.com/news/powerpost/wp/2016/08/16/implicit-bias-training-seeks-to-counter-hidden-prejudice-in-law-enforcement/?utm_term=.9bf1813722ec

Davies, D. (2012, January 16). "Legal scholar: Jim Crow still exists in America." *National Public Radio.* Retrieved from http://www.npr.org/2012/01/16/145175694/legal-scholar-jim-crow-still-exists-in-america

Dawsey, D. (1990, July 8). "25 years after the Watts riots: McCone commission's recommendations have gone unheeded." *Los Angeles Times.* Retrieved from http://articles.latimes.com/1990-07-08/local/me-455_1_watts-riots

Du Bois, W. E. B. (2004). *The souls of black folk: 100th anniversary edition.* Boulder, CO: Paradigm Publishers.

Freivogel, W. H. (2014, December 8). "Police use of force: how did we get here and where can we go?" Retrieved from http://news.stlpublicradio.org/post/police-use-force-how-did-we-get-here-and-where-can-we-go#stream/0

Gilbert, C. (2017, May 5). "Most states neglect ordering police to learn de-escalation tactics to avoid shootings." Retrieved from http://www.apmreports.org/story/2017/05/05/police-de-escalation-training

Graham, L. (2016, March 10). "The Kerner Commission and why its recommendations were ignored." *Michigan Radio.* Retrieved from http://michiganradio.org/post/kerner-commission-and-why-its-recommendations-were-ignored

Griffin, M. (2015, December 1). "New training standards for Missouri law officers include de-escalation techniques." Retrieved from http://news.stlpublicradio.org/post/new-training-standards-missouri-law-officers-include-de-escalation-techniques#stream/0

Grinberg, E. (2015, July 20). "Twitter responds to jail deaths with 'if I die in police custody.'" Retrieved from http://www.cnn.com/2015/07/18/us/feat-sandra-bland-if-i-die-in-police-custody/

Howard, J. (2014a. August 22). "Pentagon says Ferguson did not get all that military gear from its program." Retrieved from http://news.stlpublicradio.org/post/pentagon-says-ferguson-did-not-get-all-military-gear-its-program#stream/0

Howard, J. (2014b, September 8). "Militarization of local police departments goes before Senate Homeland Security Committee." Retrieved from http://news.stlpublicradio.org/post/militarization-local-police-departments-goes-senate-homeland-security-committee#stream/0

Joseph, G. (2017, May 12). "Where ICE already has direct lines to law-enforcement databases with immigrant data." *National Public Radio*. Retrieved from http://www.npr.org/sections/codeswitch/2017/05/12/479070535/where-ice-already-has-direct-lines-to-law-enforcement-databases-with-immigrant-d

Lecci, S. (2015, August 8). "Ferguson police officer joins force days after Brown's death, aims to build community ties." Retrieved from http://news.stlpublicradio.org/post/ferguson-police-officer-joins-force-days-after-browns-death-aims-build-community-ties#stream/0

Lippman, R. (2014, December 2). "Despite state law, police departments in Missouri still struggle with bias in policing." Retrieved from http://news.stlpublicradio.org/post/despite-state-law-police-departments-missouri-still-struggle-bias-policing#stream/0

Lippman, R. (2015, August 6). "Training for police officers in Missouri to get an upgrade." Retrieved from http://news.stlpublicradio.org/post/training-police-officers-missouri-get-upgrade#stream/0

Los Angeles Times. (1991, July 10). "The Christopher Commission on Tuesday issued a 228-page report on the activities of the Los Angeles Police Department." *Los Angeles Times*. Retrieved from http://articles.latimes.com/1991–07–10/news/mn-1962_1_lapd-officers-excessive-force-officers-laurence-m-powell

Lupo, L. (2010). *Flack-catchers: One hundred years of riot commission politics in America.* Lanham, MD: Lexington Books.

Mannies, J. (2014, August 25). "Koster to hold workshops to encourage more minorities in law enforcement." Retrieved from http://news.stlpublicradio.org/post/koster-hold-workshops-encourage-more-minorities-law-enforcement#stream/0

Nunberg, G. (2016, July 28). "Is Trump's call for 'law and order' a coded racial message?" *National Public Radio*. Retrieved from http://www.npr.org/2016/07/28/487560886/is-trumps-call-for-law-and-order-a-coded-racial-message

Office of Missouri Governor. (November 18, 2014). "Gov. Nixon announces members of the Ferguson Commission." Retrieved from https://governor.mo.gov/news/archive/gov-nixon-announces-members-ferguson-commission

Phillips, C. (2015a, March 28). "Police supporters rally in St. Louis, call for fewer restrictions on law enforcement." Retrieved from http://news.stlpublicradio.org/post/police-supporters-rally-st-louis-call-fewer-restrictions-law-enforcement#stream/0

Phillips, C. (2015b, November 7). "Ferguson police turn to residents for input on community policing." Retrieved from http://news.stlpublicradio.org/post/ferguson-police-turn-residents-input-community-policing#stream/0

Phillips, C., Kellogg, S., and Rosenbaum, J. (2015, August 7). "St. Louis County NAACP calls for free legal aid for children, more training for police." Retrieved from http://news.stlpublicradio.org/post/st-louis-county-naacp-calls-free-legal-aid -children-more-training-police#stream/0

The President's Task Force on 21st Century Policing. (2015, May). Retrieved from https://cops.usdoj.gov/pdf/taskforce/TaskForce_FinalReport.pdf

Rosenbaum, J. (2016, April 29). "On the trail: After the Ferguson commission, a new group steps forward." Retrieved from http://news.stlpublicradio.org/post/trail -after-ferguson-commission-new-group-steps-forward

Samuelsohn, D. (2016 June 26). "The lonely lives of latinos for Trump." *Politico.* Retrieved from http://www.politico.com/story/2016/06/donald-trump-hispanic -voters-224789

Tonry, M. (2011). *Punishing race: A continuing American dilemma.* New York, NY: Oxford University Press.

Chapter Ten

Unfriending the Policing Culture

The Reawakened Black Consciousness

Tony Gaskew

On May 5, 2016, I participated with twelve other educators from around the nation in a roundtable discussion at the White House on criminal justice reform. During my thirty-year journey in the smoke and mirrors of the criminal justice system, which includes working as a police-detective at the Melbourne Police Department,[1] assigned as a member of the Department of Justice's Organized Crime Drug Enforcement Task Force,[2] and as a tenured associate professor of criminal justice and founding director of a nationally recognized prison education program at the University of Pittsburgh (Bradford), there is very little that I have not seen, heard, or done in the business of crime and justice. I have relied upon the powerful metaphysics of my blackness to navigate through the truths of thousands of arrests, convictions, and prison sentences, including death penalty cases, as a mitigator of justice (Gaskew, 2014; Gaskew, 2016). I brought W.E.B. Du Bois to every arrest, James Baldwin to every court proceeding, and Ralph Ellison to every sentencing. There was never a moment throughout my career as a black American criminal justice professional immersed within the policing culture that Kwame Ture, Jamil Al-Amin, and Malcolm X were not with me, injecting their wisdom in regards to building a *resistance consciousness*.[3]

This roundtable discussion and all the subsequent meetings at the White House was no different. Regardless of the political agenda, because there is always a political agenda, the larger narrative always came back to an applied concept that I have researched, published on, and, more importantly, "collectively lived" as part of my black American experience: the systemic humiliation of black spaces within the constructs of crime and justice. The synergy of direct and structural violence aimed at black American diaspora by the criminal justice system is much more complex and destructive than it sounds. Over the past 400 years, the criminal justice system, specifically the policing culture, has been used to create a fictional narrative of the black American experience under a multilayered set of systemic humiliations (Gaskew, 2014; Gaskew, 2016).

Systemic humiliations, such as the disproportionate amount of arrests and use of force by the police, prosecutions and draconian sentencing guidelines by the courts, and the use of arbitrary discipline and solitary confinement, all directed at blackness, are a static set of institutionally owned and constructed rules, customs, and beliefs designed to create and sustain a culture that inherits the crippling effects of shame, self-segregation, and transgenerational learned helplessness (Gaskew, 2014; Gaskew, 2016). Systemic humiliations attempt to intentionally strip away any level of dignity and respect and sets into motion a climate void of the universal tenets of connectivity, compassion, mercy, and humility. Its recipients have always been America's indigenous populations, and none greater than its native sons, black Americans. By way of the policing culture, systemic humiliations have been applied to generations through the likes of the Black Codes, Jim Crow, and mass incarceration[4] (Bell, 1992) with the sole intent to destroy a culture of blackness in America. However, speaking the language of a social scientist, systemic humiliations are not the root *cause* of this failed attempt at cultural genocide but the insidious *side effect* of an invisible history of micro- and macro-aggressions against blackness. Born from the womb of our nation's *original sin* of chattel enslavement and the black American Holocaust, the mental illness of *white supremacy* is the fundamental "cause" in this social experiment of human suffering and continues to sit at the core of how black spaces are "effected" through institutionally controlled and constructed forms of criminal justice oppression, marginalization, and humiliation (Gaskew, 2014; Gaskew, 2016). The policing culture, by way of the original stop-and-frisk enforcers—slave patrols—was nourished and grew inside the womb of white supremacy. The four centuries–old illusion of white superiority and black inferiority has saturated the poisons of greed, anger, and ignorance (Williams, 2000) into the hearts, minds, and souls of tens of millions of people willing to embrace its ugly distortion of self-preservation without moral accountability (Thompson & Stevens, 2015; Thompson, Boyd, & Colon, 2016).

Using the fundamental tragedy of Freddie Gray and the City of Baltimore[5] as a perfect example, given the disproportionate use of direct and structural violence inflicted on black bodies under the constructs of crime and justice, there is very little doubt the policing culture has weaponized the psychosis of white supremacy. Today, despite making up less than 5 percent of the adult population, black men occupy nearly 40 percent of our nation's prison cells (The Sentencing Project, 2015). Black American spaces are more likely to be stopped, more likely to be arrested, and more likely to be incarcerated. As a result, today a police officer can walk into any maternity ward in America, and with an almost statistical certainty, place handcuffs on 1 out of every 3 nameless newborn black American infants.[6] You see, crime is a constructed humiliation designed to place a psychological veil over the true richness, beauty, and essence of blackness in America.

The systemic humiliations masking the black American experience constructed through the eyes of the policing culture are metaphysical in nature, scope, and understanding; thus, it's only logical that a black ontological lens be used to unmask true solutions. In the brief space of this chapter, using a critical autoethnographic methodology, I will attempt to synergize the thousands of interviews and group discussions I've had as an active participant observer during my thirty-year study of crime and justice, and examine how a reawakened black consciousness can challenge, destabilize, and reframe the existing policing cultural narrative. A reawakening that will apply the essence of black fearlessness to completely restructure the fictional narrative the policing culture has created of black lives.

THE REAWAKENING OF BLACK CONSCIOUSNESS: BLACK CULTURAL PRIVILEGE

James Baldwin (1965) believed that black Americans are the conscience of America and to be black and conscious in America, is to be in a constant state of rage. You see, a strong and vibrant black consciousness has always been the moral compass of saving America from itself. Black consciousness is at the forefront of mitigating the uncontrolled desires of greed, anger, and ignorance. Black consciousness is the physical, psychological, and spiritual heartbeat of redemption, forgiveness, and healing. Black consciousness is the voice for the voiceless. Black consciousness serves as the vanguard dark matter for social movements around the world searching for answers to human decolonization. Whether it was the Student Nonviolent Coordinating Committee, the Black Panther Party, the US Organization, the Black Women's United Front, the Republic of New Afrika, the Revolutionary Action Movement, the National Welfare Rights Organization, the Nation of Islam, the Organization of Afro-American Unity, the African Liberation Support Committee, or the Black Lives Matter movement, black bodies have always led the fight for revolution, decolonization, and liberation. As a black American man born in inner-city Chicago the early 1960s, I saw first-hand in my neighborhood "the call to service" and the incredible life force of black consciousness with the awakening of the Black Power Movements, giving birth to a generation of revolutionaries who immersed themselves in the collective goals echoed by Karenga[7] (2010): to solve pressing problems within the black American community and to continue the revolutionary struggle being waged to end white supremacy, racism, and oppression against black spaces. I am very proud to say that I was one of them. Today, black consciousness needs a reawakening. A reawakening I describe as *Black Cultural Privilege* (BCP), in *Rethinking Prison Reentry: Transforming Humiliation into Humility*. BCP being the physical, mental, and spiritual awareness that connects the rich diverse history of an African past with the ever-evolving journey into the legacy of the collective lived black American experience. It's an unconscious bond that exists among a people whose roots share an indestructible cultural DNA that has only been strengthened by 400 years of direct and structural violence, enslavement, the Black Codes, and Jim Crow. BCP defines the essence of blackness in America (Gaskew, 2014; Gaskew, 2016).

Without a doubt, we, as an entire universe of living beings, are one. Everything in it, around it, and shaped by it is alive, always in motion, and connected to everything else. We know this for a fact because our common senses are designed for the sole purpose of this synergy. When the sun shines, the wind blows, or the rain falls, it brings with it the same window of life to all living beings. Nothing in the universe is spared. However, the human connection to this vast universe is only between 6,000 and 150,000 years old, depending on which story you enjoy, science or faith. Regardless of the version, the human connection with the universe began in the rich cultural soil of Africa, the original Garden of Eden, and through the DNA of its black African people, the original Adam and Eve. Black bodies were the first human students of the universe and black Americans are their living testament. Black bodies were the first human voices, created the first human languages, and the first human civilizations. Black bodies were the first human beings to be taught the gifts of truth, humility, and forgiveness; that we all share the same duty of preserving life; that we are all connected under the universal principle that if one living being suffers, all living beings suffer; they were the first to absorb the life lessons of compassion, mercy, pride, empathy, righteousness, courage, unity, compromise, and love; the first to apply the gift of the *fourth eye*. Black bodies were the first scholars of metaphysics, the ethnosphere, spirituality, enlightenment, faith, and karma (Karenga, 2010; Williams, 2000); the first to apply the philosophical concepts of awareness, morality, and wisdom (Williams, 2000); the first to be taught about the poisons of greed, anger, and ignorance (Karenga, 2010, 46); the first to use the family building blocks of teachers, teachings, and communities (33–35); the first to understand the universal rule of cause and effect, that pain and happiness, along with life and death, are all part of the interconnected cycle of life. Black bodies were the first to apply the principles of fearlessness (166) as a life road map; the first to recognize the duty of not contributing to evil, doing good, and doing good for others (91). The universe taught the world's first human beings, black people, *the art of life* (7).

Just to be clear, this reawakening is not just another layer of Afrocentricity (Asante, 2003). Black Americans are no longer negotiating from a position of social, political, or economic weakness. Those days are over. We have the resources to frame and define the constructs of crime and justice. Kwame Ture (1967) once noted that "confusion is the greatest enemy of the revolution" (viii). There is no longer any confusion in our revolution. We know exactly what to do. We now simply have to do it. This reawakening is the natural evolution of the black American consciousness. It's a metaphysical force that filters, deconstructs, and eliminates the by-products of shame, self-segregation, and transgenerational learned helplessness (Gaskew, 2014) inherited by 400 years of white supremacy. It empowers black spaces in the ideological war against white superiority and black inferiority. It produces a cultural fearlessness that challenges the legitimacy of any construct in America that attempts to criminalize blackness. It confronts the systemic actors of direct and structural violence, that use the mask of law and order to conspire against the black American diaspora. It compels truth and demands accountability, holding institutional stakeholders responsible for maintaining justice to standards established and owned by black American voices. As the founders of humanity, black people must take responsibility for their own destiny. Black Americans must make peace with their own historical legacy. Black Americans must take ownership of either transforming or disposing of the current criminal justice system and policing culture. Black Americans must wake up each morning and take full responsibility for the changes that we want to make in *our* lives and in *our* world (Williams, 2000, 178). The reawakening of a 21st century black American consciousness will end the life cycle of white supremacy and place the moral compass back into the hands of the universes first human beings. At the core of BCP sits a set of *cultural demands* that will challenge, destabilize, and reframe the existing policing cultural narrative: *truth, accountability, empowerment,* and *healing.*

CULTURAL TRUTH

This first hurdle black Americans must overcome is mastering truths about the criminal justice system and the policing culture. As a people, we need to stop lying to ourselves. We don't have either a good or bad relationship with the justice system. We simply don't have a relationship. A relationship, at the core, is a recognition of truth, a connective sense of humanity, and a keen understanding that no single being is larger than the sum of the universe. The policing culture recognizes none of these tenets. The criminal justice system is not part of the organic connective bond that living beings have within the universe. The criminal justice system does not recognize the cultural legacy of the first humans on the planet. The actors whose livelihood depends on the criminal justice system do not recognize their duty to not spread evil, to do good, and to do good for others. Its inner core is based on the foundational poisons of greed, anger, and ignorance, all directed at the dehumanization of the black experience in America. Thus, as black Americans we must first decide whether creating a relationship with the criminal justice system and its gatekeepers, the policing culture, is even worth the effort. Is the system even worth reforming or saving? The construct which started off as slave patrols, conducting stop and frisks on black bodies for over three centuries, transcending into Jim Crow and legalized oppression, has never morphed into anything other than a weaponized tool of white superiority and black inferiority. I ask again, is reforming the criminal justice system and its policing culture even worth the cosmic energy of the founders of humanity?

Additionally, there are two cultural truths about the criminal justice system that black America should consider before moving forward. First, white supremacy will always be embedded within the policing culture and the criminal justice system. The City of Baltimore had a black American police chief and nearly 45 percent of the agency's police officers are black Americans; and the city has a black American district attorney, yet the policing culture was one of the most brutal in the nation toward its own black American communities.[8] Regardless of the sincerity of any reform efforts, the social institutions of policing, courts, and corrections were made by white Americans, are controlled by white Americans, only to serve and benefit white Americans and to dehumanize black Americans. The criminal justice system in America is the *Great White Shark* (Gaskew, 2014), a corporately constructed 24 hours a day, 7 days a week eating machine and multi-trillion-dollar-a-year business (Gaskew, 2016) with the sole purpose of morally destroying black bodies, black culture, and black potential (Karenga, 2010). What did you think the War on Drugs and the disproportionate drug sentencing guidelines were really about? Every single presidency from Nixon, to Reagan, to Clinton, to Obama and to Trump, have all cashed in on the economic colonization of black bodies. Today, nearly 30 percent of all black American male bodies are convicted felons, creating a multi-generation trillion-dollar business model we know as *enslavement*. It will never willingly surrender its cultural influence to inflict systemic humiliations against black spaces. Its power must be taken, and its culture humbled.

Second, only a complete state of black American hopelessness in the justice apparatus will usher in the opportunity for systemic transcendence. There is much more pain and suffering that needs to be absorbed. Please keep in mind, a nation that was founded on the universal evils of greed, anger, and ignorance (Williams, 2000) has a created a very high threshold for violence, which karmically does not bode well for the policing culture. Over the last four centuries, the mental illness of white supremacy has very effectively enslaved a segment of the black American population, convincing them that their black lives, the lives of their black families, and the lives of their black communities are worthless and inferior, while at the same time, convincing them that white lives, the lives of white families, and the lives of white communities are valuable and superior. Black inferiority and white superiority has resulted in the killings of black bodies at the hands of other black bodies as well as the attempted extermination of black culture and black potential through the holocaust of mass incarceration. For the most part, the policing actors who maintain its culture from the original sins of this nation, the colonization and criminalization of black bodies, have escaped the cosmic wrath of their actions. However, those days are coming to an end. The metaphysics of violence has shifted. Black voices, whether they are framed by scholarship or clergy, that white fragility historically counted on to pacify young black rage against state-sponsored violence, are now silent. You see, over the past several hundred years, the policing culture has demanded two basic needs from black America: *respect* and *fear*. Black America never respected the policing culture and never will. When newly elected President Barak Obama used his platform to articulate to the nation that "Cambridge Police acted stupidly" while openly criticizing the arrest of Harvard University's Dr. Henry Louis Gates Jr., he gave voice to invisible histories of millions of black Americans who have been oppressed, marginalized, and brutalized by the policing culture over the past 400 years. Subsequently, every time President Obama spoke to the nation during his presidency, after every suspicious police encounter that destroyed the life of an unarmed black body, whether that was Tamir Rice, Eric Gardner, Walter Scott, or defending the Black Lives Matter (BLM) movement, his tone and tenure reflected what his cultural DNA could not deny: a lack of respect for the policing culture. It is impossible to respect anyone or anything that does not understand the oneness of humanity. However, some black American communities provided the policing culture the *fear* they demanded. There are generations of black American bodies who have been corporately conditioned not to make eye contact with the policing culture; to treat them as overseers on a plantation; to run and hide at the very mention of the police, for little or no justification. In fact, an argument can be made that the transgenerational trauma of *police fear* is regenerated every time black parents have the legendary "talk" with black sons or black daughters on how to survive a police encounter.

The universal dilemma facing the policing culture today is that slowly but surely, black souls are being *woken*. The illusion of justice is being exposed and the primary tool of fear used to enslave black people is quickly losing its effectiveness—too many unlawful stops, arrests, and shootings—too many excuses, lies, and cover-ups—too much greed, anger, and ignorance—too much death and indifference—too much evil. Black America has reawakened to the reality that there is nothing else the criminal justice system can inflict on their souls that has not already been tried to void their entire human condition: oppression, marginalization, alienation, subjugation, enslavement, incarceration, and even extermination. Economic, employment, medical, housing, and educational sanctions. Basic human rights denied. All modes of evil tried and failed. Now, fearlessness is beginning to take hold among black spaces. The same black spaces who once saw no value or worth in their own black lives are beginning to see no value or worth in police lives. The same black spaces who once saw themselves as active peacemakers are now sitting back and waiting for the universe to correct itself. Violence begets violence, and the policing culture will no longer be bystanders to karma. The policing culture will never be safe as long as black America is not safe.

CULTURAL ACCOUNTABILITY

As Fanon (1967) suggested regarding the process of decolonization, "to tell the truth, the proof of success lies in a whole social structure being changed from the bottom up" (35). If black America decides it is worth their human investment to decolonize the criminal justice system and the policing culture, then their full and unwavering cultural commitment is required. There will no longer be a moral middle-ground on issues of black humanity. It's either all or nothing, and black America must be prepared to hold the criminal justice system fully accountable. Black America must be willing to *unfriend* the gatekeepers of the criminal justice system, the police. The unfriending process involves cultural tough love. No different than managing the lifestyle changes of someone who is suffering from an addiction, black America must stop enabling the policing culture—that is, eliminating all *black funding*, *black patronage*, and *black empathy* for the policing culture.

First, black America must withdraw all economic support for the policing culture, which includes opposing any and all efforts that increase the monetary coffers of policing. New pay raises, new equipment, or new training should never receive black support; oppose the hiring of any new officers or police staff; and vote anyone out of office that supports any of these efforts.

In any case of alleged police misconduct, black America must levy federal civil litigation against the city, the agency, and the officers involved. Black America must file official complaints on every police contact. This includes any police encounter, whether a traffic stop, a pedestrian stop, and any level of verbal or physical force used by the police. Black America must make every single black American contact with the police cost the justice system. Second, black America must entirely withdraw their community support for the policing culture. Do not participate in police–community relations meetings, volunteer police academies, or the police athletic league; oppose any effort to establish community-oriented policing in black neighborhoods; and do not support the use of school resource officers, in any educational setting that serves black students. As well, black America must actively withdraw any future employment participation within the policing career field. Although black Americans serving as police officers nationwide have always been sparse (Bureau of Justice Statistics, 2014), the policing culture does not deserve the human potential and moral sacrifice of one more young, dignified, and talented black American body among its rank and file. Black American police will no longer be caught in the crossfire between *black and blue*.

Third and finally, black America must abandon all of its emotional support for the policing culture. The biggest advantage of being from a family of black American police officers with over 70 years of combined participant observation experience is that you are completely immersed into the emotional makeup of the policing culture. Without a doubt, the absolute worst and most seductive vice the policing culture has ever inherited from black communities across the nation is their emotional permission of *perceived entitlement*. Since the twilight years of the Black Power Movement, black inferiority and white superiority in policing has successfully framed a narrative of *good* and *bad* black America. The rules are simple. If you unquestionably believe the American system of justice is fair, equitable, and color blind, openly support the policing culture, and, the most important, publicly criticize and degrade black spaces that do not, you are a good black American. If not, you are a bad black American. As noted in *Rethinking Prison Reentry* (Gaskew, 2016), there is a segment of black America that is very comfortable with this narrative because it allows them a psycho-social window to escape the weight of 400 years of dehumanization. Keep in mind, David Clarke, the black American sheriff of Milwaukee County, Wisconsin, who maligns the Black Lives Matter (BLM) movement, often referring to BLM as a terrorist movement, a hate group, *Black Lies Matter,* and its supporters as *subhuman creeps*, has been reelected overwhelmingly four times under a Democrat ticket, in a county racial demographic that is roughly 30 percent black.[9] Thus, good black Americans have given the policing culture emotional carte blanche to police bad black Americans—that is, the emotional permission to basically do whatever the policing

culture wants, whenever the policing culture wants, and to whomever the policing culture wants, as long as they don't *incarcerate* good black Americans;
the emotional permission to do no wrong, and to never admit guilt, fault, or
weakness about anything, anywhere, or anytime, as long as they don't *humiliate* good black Americans; and the emotional permission to embrace a pseudo-
warrior mentality, where the policing culture is given hero-like status, have
funeral processions reserved for mythical royalty, and openly rewarded for
acts of direct and structural violence, as long as they don't *terrorize* good black
Americans and; the emotional permission that has allowed police chiefs from
Baltimore, Chicago, and New York to look right into the eyes of good black
Americans and successfully frame the narrative that black-on-black crime is
the fault of bad black Americans. In 2017, Chicago Police Superintend Garry
McCarthy told the entire nation that his former agency was in a serious "crisis"
following the video-taped shooting death of 17-year-old Laquan McDonald
by one of his police officers, while at the exact same time, suggesting the
record-setting homicide rate in the city is because of the Black Lives Matter
movement.[10] Perhaps even more telling, the emotional permission to unlaw-
fully stop, search, arrest, and kill black bodies and to know with a degree of
absolute certainty that they will never be held accountable by so-called good
black Americans. Thus, the manufactured narrative of two opposing black
Americas must be exposed, confronted, and fused, and the emotional support
for policing must be culturally rescinded by all of black America.

Black America must allow the policing culture to fail; to take back the gift
of black forgiveness; to withdraw black empathy, mercy and compassion;
to remove black trust, dignity, and any sense of love. No more black truth,
righteousness, or wisdom. Black America must stop apologizing for and
protecting the policing culture from black America; to let white supremacy,
permeate and suffocate the policing culture; to admit that the policing culture
has spread evil; to allow the universal poisons of greed, anger, and ignorance
to completely consume the policing culture; to welcome the onset of fear and
mortality within the policing culture; to concede that pain and suffering are
universal truths that the policing culture must also face. Black America must
get out of the way of karma. Police cultural fragility is the best kept secret in
the business of crime and justice.

CULTURAL EMPOWERMENT

The black American experience must define and frame the policing culture.
Black community controlled policing, from bottom to top, must project is
own sense of black connective humanity into the policing role, purpose, and
culture (Coordinating Committee of the Black Liberation Army, 1976). Black

voices must approve the hiring of every single new police officer across the nation. No pay raises, promotions, or union perks will go unchecked without black control. The process of all citizen-initiated complaints regarding police misconduct toward black bodies, and all subsequent internal investigations, will be controlled by black people. Every black space will require every single police officer in the nation to retake their oaths and rededicate their allegiance to serve and protect under the tenets of dignity, mercy, and compassion. The purpose of policing will no longer be to serve the best interests of their fellow officers, their agency, or the corporate greed of the criminal justice system. Black spaces will shift the narrative of the policing culture. First, there are no *good* or *bad* cops. Over my thirty years as an insider of the policing culture, I've discovered there are simply *righteous, rotten, or riddled* people, all who happen to have badges and guns. Those who are righteous, the mitigators of justice (Gaskew, 2014), simply try *to do the right thing.* Those who are rotten, the corruptors of justice, simply try *to do evil.* And those who are riddled, the cowards of justice, simply try *to do nothing.* Second, the overwhelming majority of police officers today and the true enemy of black America live comfortably within the riddled spectrum of the policing culture. These are the police officers, both black and white, that witness the daily racial humiliations projected on black bodies under the rule of law and use the power of their silence to protect the policing culture who engage in systemic dehumanization of blackness from truth and accountability. Their cowardice must be exposed and punished. And third, more black bodies must be willing to sacrifice and share their black essence by serving as mitigators of justice. A reawakened black consciousness will usher in an ultra-professional policing culture, which includes a synergized black American police officer. More black American police officers, serving in the role of mitigators, will actively *police* the officers who are seduced by the cultural offerings of greed (money, power, and sex), anger (punishing blackness), or ignorance (assimilating to white supremacy). The blue wall of silence will come to an end, and the policing culture as we know it will either shift toward the essence of blackness or become extinct. However, a reawakening of black consciousness without a sense of *healing* only sows the seeds of shame, self-subjugation, and transgenerational learned helplessness. That realm of metaphysical violence will no longer be accepted. This process also requires the policing culture to publicly confess and to publicly accept culpability for its *crimes against black humanity.*

CULTURAL HEALING

First, truth and accountability panels must be held across the nation, where police officers, police agencies, and the policing culture publicly admit the damage they have intentionally inflicted upon black bodies. These actors of direct and structural violence must admit their crimes against black humanity, and accept full accountability for their actions. Without exception, every policing agency in America must submit to actively participating in this process of systemic healing. Second, every single black body that has ever been shamed, self-segregated, or transgenerationally traumatized by the policing culture will be made whole again by investment in his or her human potential. Every single black body that has been jailed or imprisoned will be compensated. Every single black body that has come under the control of community corrections will be compensated. Every single black child whose parent has been subjected to the corrupters or cowards of justice will be compensated. Every single police officer in America will understand that when he or she makes a decision to enslave a black body under the tenets of white superiority and black inferiority, a compensatory price will be paid. Third and finally, the policing culture will be the source of the compensation. Every single dollar obtained through civil asset forfeiture, court fines, and associated fees nationwide will be used to make black bodies whole again. According to the National Institute for Justice (2015) since 2001, nearly $30 billion has been seized through civil asset forfeiture and sits in the *drug war chest* of the policing culture. This number grows exponentially each year by $4 billion. Unfortunately, there is a dearth of research on the exact dollar amount collected by each of our 35,000 municipalities regarding the criminal court costs associated with the enslavement of black bodies. But, if a town the size of Ferguson, Missouri, with a population of roughly 22,000, can issue nearly 33,000 warrants and collect $2.6 million in revenue during a single year (US Department of Justice, 2014), can you just imagine the hundreds of billions of dollars being generated annually by the policing culture from black bodies? Can you imagine the trillions of dollars that the policing culture has pilfered by dehumanizing black bodies, black culture, and black potential since the inception of slave patrols? The time has come for black America to demand payment on a 400-year-old debt.

FINAL THOUGHTS

When black America finally decides to choose the proverbial *red pill*,[11] game over. The only plausible way that fewer than one million full- and part-time sworn members of the policing culture, given its level of fragility, and its appetite for the universal poisons of greed, anger, and ignorance, can systemically humiliate 43 million black bodies is because black lives choose the proverbial *blue pill*.[12] The entire criminal justice system is just a magic trick, designed to hypnotize black spaces into believing in the *illusion of justice*. All of its historic authority and entitlement rests on the assumption that black America will continue to fear, pray, and forgive. Black Cultural Privilege calls on the essence of blackness to reawaken its universal power of fearlessness; to challenge the policing culture, exposing its weakness and fragility; to destabilize the policing culture, demanding truth, accountability, empowerment, and healing; and to reframe the policing culture, forcing either its humility or humiliation. The only question remaining is when.

NOTES

1. I retired from MPD in 2004, in order to complete my doctoral research.
2. OCDETF: https://www.justice.gov/criminal/organized-crime-drug-enforce ment-task-forces.
3. From *Stokely Speaks: From Black Power to Pan Africanism.*
4. Policies and laws specifically designed to criminalize the black American experience (post enslavement), which drove America's prison population to dramatic and unmatched historic increases with Black people as the majority of those being incarcerated.
5. Department of Justice (DOJ) Executive Summary on the Baltimore Police Department: https://www.justice.gov/opa/file/883381/download.
6. Based upon a Bureau of Justice Statistics Special Report that stated about 1 in 3 Black American males are expected to go to prison during their lifetime. See http://www.bjs.gov/content/pub/pdf/piusp01.pdf.
7. Dr. Maulana Karenga is professor and chair of African Studies at California State University at Long Beach. Dr. Karenga has played a cultural vanguard role in shaping the Black Power Movement since the 1960s. See http://www.maulanak arenga.org/
8. Department of Justice consent decree with the City of Baltimore: https://www. justice.gov/opa/file/883376/download.
9. Politifact—Pro-Sheriff David Clarke group says Clarke called Black Lives Matter hate group, terrorist movement: http://www.politifact.com/wisconsin/state ments/2017/apr/17/sheriff-david-clarke-us-senate/pro-sheriff-david-clarke-group -says-clarke-called-/.
10. Ex-Chicago top cop blames Black Lives Matter for skyrocketing murder rates: http://www.nydailynews.com/news/national/ex-chicago-top-blames-black-lives-mat ter-surge-murders-article- 1.2932236
11. The *red pill* and its opposite, the *blue pill*, are eastern philosophical symbols that were culturally popularized in the movie *The Matrix*. They represent the choice between embracing the sometimes-painful truth of reality (red pill) and the blissful ignorance of illusion (blue pill). See *Influence of Buddhism on Popular Culture* and *Wake Up! Gnosticism and Buddhism in The Matrix.*
12. Ibid.

REFERENCES

Asante, M. (2003). *Afrocentricity: The Theory of Social Change.* Souk Village, IL: African American Images.

Baldwin. J. (1965, August 20). *Negro Leaders on Violence, Time,* 86, 17–21.

Bell, D. (1992). *Faces at the Bottom of the Well.* New York, NY: Basic Books.

Bureau of Justice Statistics. (2015). *Employment and Expenditure.* Retrieved from http://www.bjs.gov/

Coordinating Committee of the Black Liberation Army. (1976). *Message to the Black Movement: A Political Statement from the Black Underground.* Author.

Du Bois, W.E.B. (1994). *The Souls of Black Folk.* Mineola, NY: Dover Publications.

Fanon, F. (1967). *The Wretched of the Earth.* London: Penguin.

Flannery-Dailey, Frances and Wagner, Rachel L. (2016) "Wake up! Gnosticism and Buddhism in The Matrix," Journal of Religion & Film, 5 (4), 1–30.

Gaskew, T. (2014). *The Policing of the Black American Male: Transforming Humiliation into Humility in Pursuit of Truth and Reconciliation.* In I. Michelle Scott, *Crimes Against Humanity in the Land of the Free: Can a Truth and Reconciliation Process Heal Racial Conflict in America?* Santa Barbara, CA: ABC-CLIO Publishing.

Gaskew, T. (2016). *Rethinking Prison Reentry: Transforming Humiliation into Humility.* Lanham, MD: Lexington Books.

Karenga, M. (2010). *Introduction to Black Studies.* Los Angeles, CA: University of Sankore Press.

The National Institute for Justice. (2015). *Policing for Profit.* Retrieved from http://ij.org/report/policing-for-profit/executive-summary/

The Sentencing Project. (2015). *Black Lives Matter: Eliminating Racial Inequity in the Criminal Justice System.* Retrieved from http://sentencingproject.org/wp-content/uploads/2015/11/Black-Lives-Matter.pdf

The United States Department of Justice. (2014). *Investigation of the Ferguson Police Department.* Retrieved from https://www.justice.gov/sites/default/files/opa/press-eleases/attachments/2015/03/04/ferguson_police_department_report.pdf

Thompson, S. & Stevens, C. (2015). *The United States of America vs. The United States of America* [Lecture Notes]. Retrieved from https://courseweb.pitt.edu/webapps/blackboard/content/listContentEditable.jsp?content_id=_202494731&course_id=_320452_1&mode=reset

Thompson, S., Boyd, A., & Colon, C. (2016). *Just Mercy: A Transformative Criminal Justice Journey to Expose and Uproot White Supremacy* [Lecture Notes]. Retrieved from https://courseweb.pitt.edu/webapps/blackboard/content/list Content Editable.jsp?content_id=_21479986_1&course_id=_352616_1 &mode=reset

Ture, K. (1967). *Black Power: The Politics of Liberation.* New York, NY: Vintage Books.

Ture, K. (1971). *Stokely Speaks: From Black Power to Pan-Africanism.* New York, NY: Random House.

Williams, A. (2000). *Being Black: Zen and the Art of Living with Fearlessness and Grace.* New York, NY: Penguin Compass Press.

Index

community trust; *see* public trust, 28, 176, 179

consent decrees, 28, 30

contraband, 40

controlling images, 122, 131–32, 141

Cooper v. Sheehan, 49

convict leasing system, 14–15, 22

Conyers, John; *see* End Racial Profiling Act, 46

Corrections Corporations of America (CCA), 99; *see* detention or detention system, for profit facilities and the GEO group

coyote, 123, 128

Crawford III, John, 27

criminalization, 16, 58, 75–76, 79, 81, 132, 140, 150, 155, 195

crimmigration, 77–79, 81

criminal profiling or offender profiling, 19, 21, 38–40, 47, 56, 58, 64, 79, 83, 85, 140–41, 156–57, 176

cross-burnings, 54

Crowley, James, 19, 157

Crutcher, Terence, 24–25, 147, 160

Cruz, Ted, 121

Cullors, Patrisse, 65, 147

cultural competence, 158, 164, 179

Cuomo, Andrew, 42

Customs and Border Protection (CBP), 102, 112, 123, 126

D., Chuck; *see* Chuck D., 26

Dallas, Texas, 20, 66

dashboard cameras, 26, 28, 53, 62, 64–65, 145

Davis, Jordan, 28

deadly force, use of, 24–25, 27, 37, 41–44, 63, 160, 179, 180

debt peonage, 14

de-escalation tactics, 158, 173, 176, 179–80, 184

Deferred Action for Childhood Arrivals (DACA), 7, 27, 97–100, 102–105; rights and legal counsel, 104–110

Democratic National Committee (DNC), 89

Department of Defense, (1033 Program), 23, 178

Department of Homeland Security (DHS), 79, 80, 83, 86, 100, 101, 112, 132; *see* Appropriations Act

Department of Justice or Justice Department, 22, 25, 28–30, 142, 156, 165, 167, 175, 180–81, 183, 189, 200

Department of Justice's Organized Crime Drug Enforcement Task Force, 189

Deportation, 27, 30, 76, 78–79, 80–81, 83–84, 87, 90, 97, 99, 101–102, 127, 132

"Deporter in Chief," 123; *see* Obama, Barack Hussein

detention or detention system, 27, 76, 79, 81, 83–84, 86–90, 101–102, 105, 108–110; *see* for profit facilities

Detroit, 15, 23, 174, 183

Diagnostic and Statistical Manual of Mental Disorders, Fourth Edition, Text Revision (DSM-IV-TR), 58

Diallo, Amadou, 18–19, 53, 157

Diaz, Junot, 91

discrimination, 40, 58, 60, 76, 78, 142, 144, 176

District of Columbia Public Defender Service, 39

diversity, 25, 129, 175

diversity training, 29, 179

Dorobek, Joseph S., 163; *see* "To Protect and to Serve"

double marginalization, 162

driving while black (DWB), 22, 39

Drug Abuse Act, 1986, 17

Drug Enforcement Administration (DEA), 16, 87

drug offenses, 55

Du Bois, W. E. B., 139, 143, 150, 189

DuBose, Sam, 22

due process, 84, 101, 103, 105

About the Contributors

Hector Y. Adames received his doctorate in Clinical Psychology from the APA-accredited program at Wright State University in Ohio and completed his APA pre-doctoral internship at the Boston University School of Medicine's Center for Multicultural Training in Psychology (CMTP). By training, he is a neuropsychologist and currently an Associate Professor at The Chicago School of Professional Psychology. He is the editor of *Latina/o Psychology Today* (LPT) and the co-author of a textbook focusing on skin-color and physiognomy among US Latino/as titled, *Cultural Foundations and Interventions in Latino/a Mental Health: History, Theory and within Group Differences* by Routledge Press. His research focuses on how socio-race, skin-color, colorism, and ethnic and racial group membership influence wellness. He has earned a number of awards including the 2014 Distinguished Professional Early Career Award from the National Latina/o Psychological Association (NLPA).

Marlon L. Bailey currently holds a Master of Science in Social Work and is a doctoral graduate student in the Counseling Psychology program at the University of Texas at Austin. He is very proud of his contribution to *Law Enforcement in the Age of Black Lives Matter: Policing Black and Brown Bodies*. He is published in the *Journal of Counseling Psychology* and his research interests include imposter phenomenon, activism, social psychology, and violence.

Derrick R. Brooms is faculty in Sociology and Africana Studies at the University of Cincinnati and serves as a youth worker as well. He specializes in the sociology of African Americans, particularly black males, with research and activism that focus on educational equity, race and racism, diversity and inequality, and identity. He is author of *Being Black, Being Male on Campus: Understanding and Confronting Black Male Collegiate Experiences* (SUNY, 2017) and is co-editor of *Living Racism: Through the Barrel of the Book* (Lexington Press, 2017).

Nayeli Y. Chavez-Dueñas received her doctorate in Clinical Psychology from the APA-accredited program at Southern Illinois University at Carbondale. She is an Associate Professor at The Chicago School of Professional Psychology where she serves as the faculty coordinator for the concentration in Latina/o Mental Health in the Counseling Psychology Department. She is the associate editor of *Latina/o Psychology Today* (LPT); and the co-author of a textbook that focuses on skin-color and within group differences among Latino/as in the US titled, *Cultural Foundations and Interventions in Latino/a Mental Health: History, Theory and within Group Differences* by Routledge Press. Her research focuses on colorism, skin-color differences, parenting styles, immigration, unaccompanied minors, multiculturalism, and race relations. She has earned a number of awards including the 2012 Distinguished Teaching Award for Excellence in Multicultural Pedagogy by TCSPP.

Kevin Cokley is a Professor of Educational Psychology and African and African Diaspora Studies at the University of Texas at Austin. He is a UT System Distinguished Teaching Professor and Director of the Institute for Urban Policy Research & Analysis. Dr. Cokley's research and teaching can be broadly categorized in the area of African American psychology. He is the past Editor-in-Chief of the *Journal of Black Psychology*, and was elected to Fellow status in the American Psychological Association for his contributions to ethnic minority psychology and counseling psychology. He has written several op-eds in major media outlets including the *St. Louis Post Dispatch*, *Dallas Morning News*, *San Antonio Express*, *The American Prospect*, *The Huffington Post, The Conversation, The Grio*, and *The Hill* on topics such as blacks' rational mistrust of police, the aftermath of Ferguson, and police and race relations.

Ramya Garba is a first-year Ph.D. student in Educational Psychology at the University of Texas at Austin. She also serves as a student researcher under the mentorship of Dr. Kevin Cokley. Her research interests and endeavors broadly center around the academic and psychosocial concerns of underrepresented minorities in the academy, as well as the role of implicit bias in clinical decision making and health disparities. Prior to embarking on her doctoral work, she served as Assistant Director of Academic Support and Counseling at the Albert Einstein College of Medicine in New York City.

Tony Gaskew is Associate Professor of Criminal Justice, Director of Criminal Justice, and Founding Director of the *Prison Education Program* at the University of Pittsburgh (Bradford). He is a Fulbright Hays Scholar and a University of Pittsburgh Faculty Diversity Fellow. He is a national reviewer for the Fulbright Specialist Program, Peace and Conflict Resolution Section. He is the book series editor of *Critical Perspectives on Race, Crime, and Justice* (Lexington) and also serves on the editorial board for the *Journal of Prison Education and Reentry*. He is the author of over thirty publications focusing on race, crime, and justice including his latest book, *Rethinking Prison Reentry: Transforming Humiliation into Humility*. Dr. Gaskew is a former police-detective at MPD, where he was assigned as a member of the Department of Justices, Organized Crime Drug Enforcement Task Force (OCDETF).

Warren K. Graham is the Director of Field Education for Hunter College's BSW Program, and Assistant Director of Field Education in the MSW Program. Warren has taught on both the graduate and undergraduate levels at Touro College, Fordham University, and Hunter College, and has been active in NASW, having been elected as Delegate to the National Assembly, Division Director, and selected as Advocacy and Governmental Relations Committee member. Warren has authored *Specialized Opportunities for Social Workers in the Courts* (NASW, 2010), co-authored *The Death of Black Males: The Unmasking of Cultural Competence and Oppressive Practices in a Micro-Aggressive Environment* (Routledge, 2016), and "Evidence Based Practices for the Criminal Justice System" (in-press). Warren is also a Board member of DC based non-profit, Darnice's Place, and on the Board of Advisors for the Center for Children, Families, and the Law at Hofstra University.

Dee Hill-Zuganelli is Assistant Professor of Child and Family Studies at Berea College. He is the lead author of the forthcoming article, "Arizona Uncertainty: Arbitrary Barriers in Accessing Institutional Need-Based Aid" (*Journal of Student Financial Aid*). He completed his dissertation, *Chicano Studies: Proliferation of the Disclipline and the Formal Institutionalization of Community Engagement, 1965 to Present*, in 2016 at the University of Arizona. His research focuses on enhancing campus support and community engagement with Latina/o and underrepresented minorities through formal ethnic studies programs.

Ashley N. Hurst is a doctoral student in the Counseling Psychology program at the University of Texas at Austin. They earned her master's degree in Counselor Education at UT Austin where they decided to further pursue research. They are interested in exploring how the mental health and academic performance of students of color are affected by manifestations of oppression within the academic domain. Their latest publication is called the "Impostor Feelings as a Moderator of the Relationship between Perceived Discrimination and Mental Health among Ethnic Minority College Students" (*Journal of Counseling Psychology*, 2017). They are also an Assistant Instructor in the Educational Psychology Department for a course called "Strategic Learning for the 21st Century."

Shakira A. Kennedy is an Assistant Professor and Coordinator of At-Risk Populations Research and Grant Initiatives for Touro College Graduate School of Social Work. Dr. Kennedy has over 13 years of practice experience working with children, families, and single adults diagnosed with mental illness and or HIV/AIDS along with extensive management experience. Her research focuses on addressing the needs of vulnerable populations and examining organizational culture and climate within various work settings. She has co-authored *The Death of Black Males: The Unmasking of Cultural Competence and Oppressive Practices in a Micro-Aggressive Environment* (Routledge, 2016). Dr. Kennedy continues her connection to the community by being an active member of Westchester Black Women's Political Caucus and an active journal reviewer for SAGE Open publications and a consulting editor for the journal *Children & Schools*.

Nolan T. Krueger is a Counseling Psychology doctoral student in Dr. Kevin Cokley's Multicultural Lab at the University of Texas at Austin. His current work explores social justice and activism among black college students. He presented "Racial Identity, Race-Related Stress, and Social Justice Beliefs and Values as Predictors of African American Activism: A Replication and Extension" (Krueger, N., Bailey, M., Garba, R., Hurst, A., Stone, S., Cokley, K.) at the 2017 Black Graduate Conference in Psychology. His research also examines psychosocial barriers to higher education and coping mechanisms for students of color as well as multiracial ethnic identity development.

Dwayne A. Mack is Professor of History and Carter G. Woodson Chair of African American History at Berea College. His research focuses on the black West; the civil rights movement; policing in America; and equity, inclusion, and diversity in academia. He is the co-editor of *Violence Against Black Bodies: An Intersectional Analysis of How Black Lives Continue to Matter* (Routledge 2017) and *Freedom's Racial Frontier: African Americans in the Twentieth-Century West* (University of Oklahoma Press, 2017), lead editor of *Beginning a Career in Academia: A Guide for Graduate Students of Color*

(Routledge, 2015), *Mentoring Faculty of Color: Essays on Professional Advancement in Colleges and Universities* (McFarland Publishers, 2013), and author of *Black Spokane:The Civil Rights Struggle in the Inland Northwest* (University of Oklahoma Press, 2014). Mack has also published scholarly articles and book chapters.

Felicia W. Mack is part-time faculty at Eastern Kentucky University in Richmond, Kentucky. She also is a Visiting Lecturer at Berea College in Berea, Kentucky, and Contributing Faculty in the College of General Studies at Walden University. Her research interests include documenting race and gender in online learning. She is a regular contributor to blackpast.org., where she documents the black experience and the founding of historical black churches in America.

Rebecca G. Martínez is an Assistant Professor in the Department of Women's and Gender Studies at the University of Missouri. She is a medical anthropologist whose research encompasses issues of race, ethnicity, class, and gender as related to cancer and reproductive health. She has a forthcoming book with Stanford University Press entitled: *Marked Women: The Cultural Politics of Cervical Cancer in Venezuela.*

Folusho Otuyelu is Assistant Professor of Clinical Social Work-Children and Adolescents and MSW Liaison-Child Welfare for Touro College's Graduate School of Social Work. She has been practicing in the field of social work for over 20 years working with prominent non-profit organizations. Her clinical practice focus is on the effects of trauma on children and adolescents. She is a contributing editor for *Children and Schools* (NASW Press).

Wornie Reed obtained his Ph.D. in Sociology at Boston University. Currently, he is Professor of Sociology and Africana Studies and Director of the Race and Social Policy Research Center at Virginia Tech University. Previously, he developed and directed social science research centers at three universities, including the William Monroe Trotter Institute at UMass/Boston. Among his scholarly accomplishments, Reed directed the project, "Assessment of the Status of African Americans," which involved sixty-one scholars and resulted in the production of a four-volume work published by Auburn House Publishers. He is past president of the National Congress of Black Faculty (1990–1993) and the Association of Black Sociologists (2000–2001).

F. Tyler Sergent is Assistant Professor of History and General Studies at Berea College. He is a medieval historian and activist for racial justice on and off the college campus. He is first editor and author of *Unity of Spirit: Studies on William of Saint-Thierry* (Cistercian Publications, 2015) and editor and author of the forthcoming *A Companion to William of Saint-Thierry* (Brill, 2018).

Sandra E. Weissinger is Assistant Professor of Sociology at Southern Illinois Edwardsville. *Violence Against Black Bodies* (2017) is her most recent co-edited work. Additional recent scholarship includes "Gender Matters. So Do Race and Class: Experiences on the Wal-Mart Shop Floor" in *Race, Class & Gender: An Anthology* (Cengage, 2016), "If at First You Don't Succeed: Motivation for Finding the Best Institutional Fit" in *Beginning a Career in Academia: A Guide for Graduate Students of Color* (Routledge, 2015), and "Everyday Justice: Tactics for Navigating Micro, Macro and Structural Discriminations from the Intersection of Jim Crow and Hurricane Katrina" in *Research Justice: Methodologies for Social Change* (Policy Press/University of Chicago, 2015).